CO

To Caroline, for her encouragement, love and (above all) patience.

Research & Text: William Fricker

Photography: William Fricker (Unless captioned with ss)

First published in the United Kingdom in 2006 by Goldeneye, Unit 10 Chivenor Business Park, Chivenor, Barnstaple, North Devon EX31 4AY

www.goldeneyemaps.com

Editor in Cornwall: Liz Luck

Cartographic Consultants: Cox Cartographic Ltd

Maps taken from Goldeneye's Digital Database

Special thanks to the attractions in the guide and the National Trust Photographic Library at Lanhydrock for supplying photographs.

Photo Credits

ab	Andrew Besley,
ac	Al Churcher
bc	Bob Croxford
jh	Jon Hicks
wh	W. Hocking
nt	National Trust's Regional Library, Lanhydrock
ds	David Skehan
ejs	E J Spear.

Abbreviations in Text

C14	14th century
Mar-Oct	1 March to 31 October
NT	National Trust property
EH	English Heritage property
BHs	Bank Holidays
W/E	Weekend
East	Easter
E/C	Early Closing
TIC	Tourist Information Centre
M	Monday
Tu	Tuesday
W	Wednesday
Th	Thursday
F	Friday
Sa	Saturday
Su	Sunday
*	Description in text

English Heritage opening times

Good F or 1 Apr (whichever is earlier) to 30 Sept, daily 10-6 (from 9 in July/Aug). 1 Oct to Maundy Th or 31 Mar (whichever is earlier), Tu-Su 10-4, closed 24-26 Dec & 1 Jan.

Beach & Surfing Abbreviations

HT	High Tide
HZ	Hazardous/Dangerous
Ls	Lefts (left turns)
LG	Lifeguard
LT	Low Tide
N	North
P	Parking
Rs	Rights (right turns)
S	South
S-B	Surfboard
SW	Southwest
WC	Toilets

With special thanks to the guys at Atlantic Surfboards and Surf South West for checking our surfing details.

St Michael's Mount rr/nt

A CIP catalogue record for this book is available from the British Library

ISBN 1-85965 163 1

Printed in England

Correct information: The contents of this publication were believed to be correct and accurate at the time of printing. However, Goldeneye accepts no responsibility for any errors, omissions or changes in the details given, or for the consequences arising thereto, from the use of this book. However, the publishers would greatly appreciate your time in notifying us of any changes or new attractions (or places to eat, drink and stay) that you consider merit inclusion in the next edition. Your comments are most welcome for we value the views and suggestion of our readers. Please write to; The Editor, Goldeneye, 10 Chivenor Business Park, Barnstaple EX31 4AY, Great Britain.

Cornwall is a county of great diversity, of strange customs and superstitions, of romantic legends and Arthurian myths. A county with its own language, culture and outlook.

Remote, and cut off from the rest of Britain by the River Tamar, the Cornish have developed a proud individuality and resilient independence. The close proximity to the Gulf Stream provides a warm and equable climate. The magnificent coastline, relentlessly shaped by the elements, with its contorted rocks, precipitous cliffs, deep estuaries, smugglers coves, golden beaches and picturesque harbours, is unmatched elsewhere in England.

The landscape is haunted by countless landmarks of early man (and relics from the industrial past); Long Barrows (burial chambers), Quoits/Dolmens (stones from Megalithic-Neolithic tombs), Fogues (underground storage chambers), Hill Forts and Promontory Forts (strategic settlements or animal enclosures) and Stone Circles (ancient boundary/grave marks, or places of ritual). Only a small selection are described in this book – but many others are indicated on the maps. To put them into an historic context; the Neolithic gave place to the Bronze Age around 2000 BC, the Iron Age lasted from about 500 BC up to Roman times, the first 4 centuries AD.

The Cornish skyline has been shaped by the silhouettes of chimneys and engine houses, and by ramshackle desolate buildings beside the road; the remains of a once prosperous tin and copper mining industry. Many examples are to be found in the Camborne - Redruth area, and on the Penwith Peninsula. Some engine houses have been restored by the National Trust. They stand in spectacular positions and are well worth a visit. The better known are:- Wheal Coates Engine House, Nr St Agnes and Wheal Prosper Copper Mine, Nr Porthleven.

In areas of past mining activity it is vitally important to keep to the evident pathways. Walkers and their dogs have been known to disappear down hidden shafts!

With few exceptions, Cornwall has been noted for the setting of architecture rather than architecture itself. However, there are fine examples of medieval fortresses and elegant country houses surrounded by spacious gardens. And beyond the written page, and the ubiquitous beach is a Cornwall often neglected; a land of ancient sites, hidden creeks and isolated villages.

Botallack Engine House

LOCATOR MAP | How the maps relate to each other

- THE SOUTH EAST
- THE EAST
- THE NORTH COAST
- THE SOUTH COAST
- THE SOUTH WEST

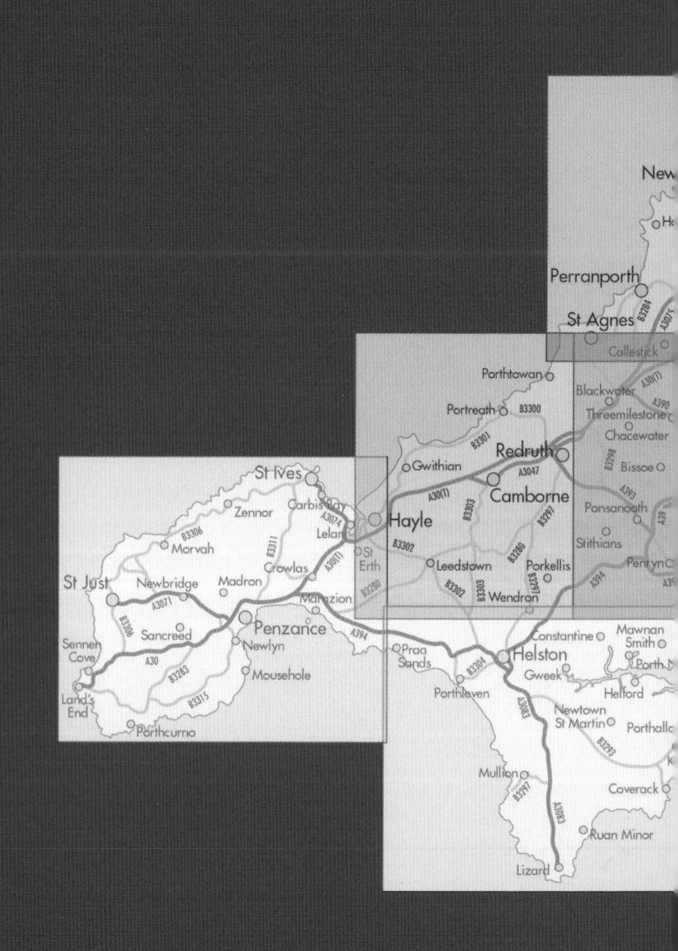

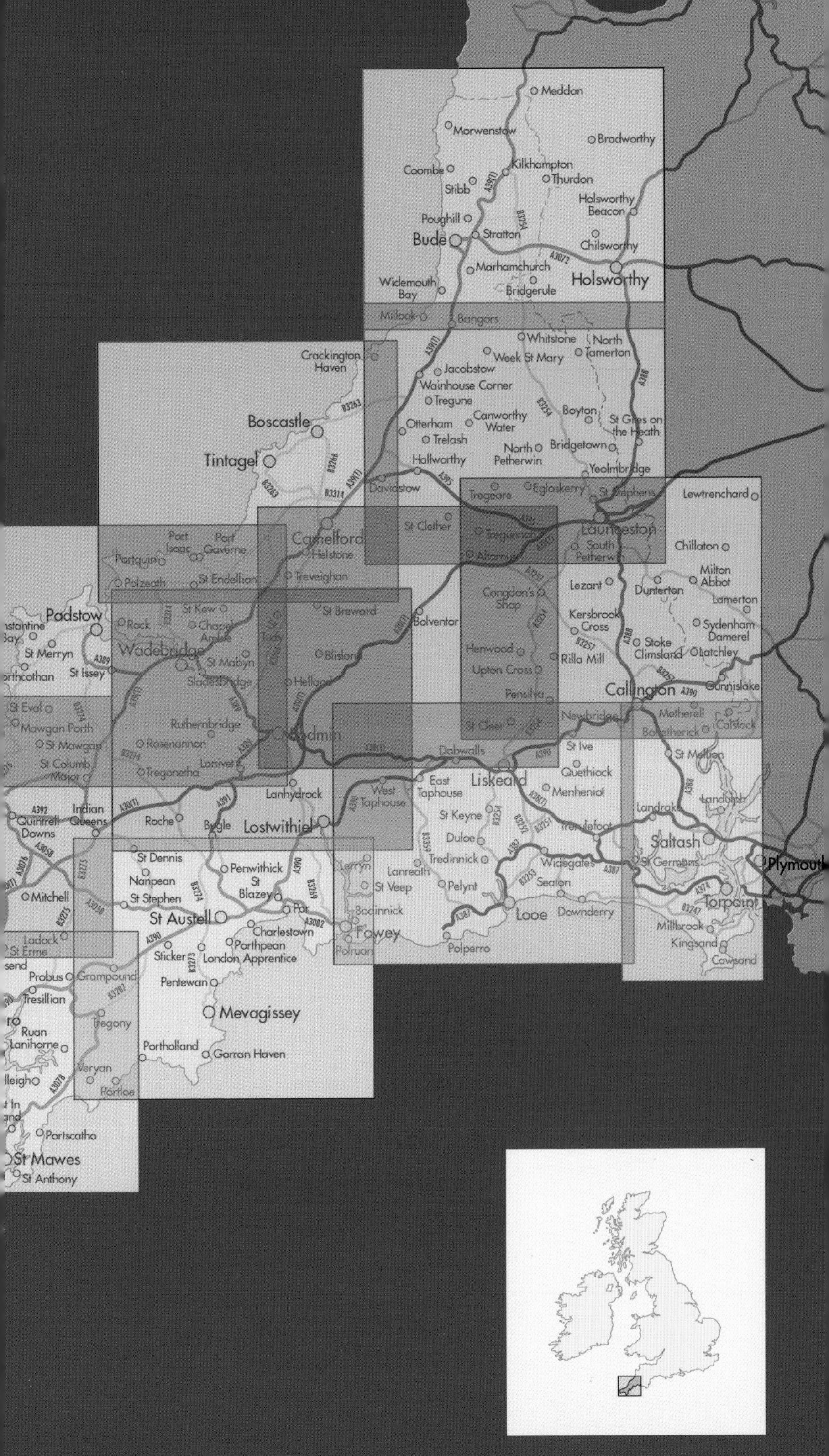

Meddon
Morwenstow
Bradworthy
Coombe
Kilkhampton
Stibb
Thurdon
Holsworthy Beacon
Poughill
Bude
Stratton
Chilsworthy
Marhamchurch
Holsworthy
Widemouth Bay
Bridgerule
Millook
Bangors
Whitstone
North Tamerton
Crackington Haven
Week St Mary
Jacobstow
Wainhouse Corner
Tregune
Boscastle
Otterham
Canworthy Water
Boyton
St Giles on the Heath
Trelash
North Petherwin
Bridgetown
Tintagel
Hallworthy
Yeolmbridge
Davidstow
Tregeare
Egloskerry
St Stephens
Lewtrenchard
St Clether
Camelford
Helstone
Tregunnon
Launceston
South Petherwin
Chillaton
Port Isaac
Port Gaverne
Altarnun
Milton Abbot
Portquin
Treveighan
Lezant
Dunterton
Polzeath
St Endellion
Congdon's Shop
Lamerton
St Kew
St Breward
Kersbrook Cross
Sydenham Damerel
Padstow
Rock
Chapel Amble
St Tudy
Bolventor
Stoke Climsland
Latchley
Constantine Bay
St Merryn
Wadebridge
St Mabyn
Blisland
Henwood
Rilla Mill
Porthcothan
St Issey
Sladesbridge
Helland
Upton Cross
Callington
Gunnislake
Pensilva
St Eval
Mawgan Porth
Rutherbridge
St Cleer
Newbridge
Metherell
Botetherick
Calstock
St Mawgan
Rosenannon
Bodmin
Dobwalls
St Ive
St Mellion
St Columb Major
Lanivet
Tregonetha
Liskeard
Quethiock
Lanhydrock
East Taphouse
Menheniot
Landulph
West Taphouse
St Keyne
Landrake
Quintrell Downs
Indian Queens
Roche
Bugle
Lostwithiel
Trerulefoot
Saltash
Duloe
St Dennis
Tredinnick
Widegates
St Germans
Plymouth
Penwithick
Lerryn
Lanreath
Nanpean
St Blazey
St Veep
Pelynt
Seaton
Mitchell
St Stephen
Par
Torpoint
Bodinnick
Looe
Downderry
St Austell
Charlestown
Fowey
Ladock
Porthpean
Millbrook
St Erme
Sticker
London Apprentice
Polruan
Polperro
Kingsand
Probus
Grampound
Cawsand
Tresillian
Pentewan
Tregony
Mevagissey
Ruan Lanihorne
Portholland
Gorran Haven
Veryan
Portloe
Portscatho
St Mawes
St Anthony
A39(T)
B3254
A3072
A388
B3263
B3266
B3314
A395
A30(T)
B3257
B3314
B3274
A389
A391
A390
A38(T)
B3254
B3252
B3251
B3359
A387
B3253
A374
B3247
A392
A3058
A3076
B3275
B3269
A3082
B3273
B3287
A3078

centurion
s mary sister of lazarus
jesus christ
s mary virgin
saint paul
saint matthew
saint mark
saint stephen
saint luke
saint john
TO THE GLORY OF GOD
THIS WINDOW IS
DEDICATED BY THE
DONOR ALFRED BURTON
IN THE YEAR 1896

For Peace & Tranquility, Picturesque Harbours, Shark Fishing and Sub-Tropical Gardens...

Enter Cornwall over the River Tamar on the A38 and admire Brunel's last great masterpiece of engineering, the Royal Albert Bridge. Looking south, down river you may be able to spy the Rame Peninsula, the "Forgotten Corner". Here you will find the former smuggler's villages of Kingsand and Cawsand. Narrow streets snake between colour washed cottages, pubs and gift shops. There are fine views over Plymouth Sound, and if feeling energetic tackle the coastal path through Mount Edgcumbe, or walk south to Rame Head with more stunning views. All about you is peace and calm, an oasis of tranquillity, the antidote to a stressful life.

Travelling west you must visit St Germanus at St Germans with its stained glass window designed by Burne-Jones and made up by the William Morris Co.

Further west the picturesque fishing harbours of Looe, Polperro and Polruan, each with its own special characteristics. In Looe you can feed on fresh fish and lobster straight of the boats, in Polperro stay behind when the crowds have dispersed to listen to the Fisherman's choirs practice. If Polruan is your destination and you can manage the steep descent to the quay the Lugger Inn will reward you with a fine pint of ale.

But, if you choose to cross the Tamar further upstream via the A390 be prepared to tackle the beautiful, densely wooded lanes through St Dominick, Calstock to Cotehele Quay with fine views over the Tamar.

St Germanus Church, St Germans

Brunel's Royal Albert Bridge, Saltash

How to identify our Map symbols

- Abbey/Cathedral
- Battle Site
- Bed & Breakfast Accomodation
- Café
- Castle
- Church/Chapel of Interest
- Cinema
- Craft Interest
- Cross
- Cycleway
- Fun Park/Leisure Park
- Hill Fort/Ancient Settlement
- Historic Building
- Hotel
- Industrial Interest
- Karting
- Lighthouse
- Mining Interest/Engine Houses
- Misc/Natural Attraction
- Museum/Art Gallery
- Pottery
- Pub/Inn
- Railway Interest
- Restaurant
- Standing Stone/Barrow
- Theatre/Concert Hall
- Tourist Information (Summer)
- Tumulus/Tumuli
- Viewpoint
- Windmill/Wind Farm
- Airfield
- Aquarium
- Boat Trips
- Camping Site (Tents)
- Caravan Site
- Ferry (Pedestrians)
- Ferry (Vehicles)
- Fishing Trips
- 9/18 Hole Golf Course
- Harbour
- Inshore Rescue Boat
- Leisure/Sports Centre
- Lifeboat
- Parking
- Picnic Site
- Tents & Caravans
- Sailing
- Surfing
- Tourist Information (All Year)
- Windsurfing
- Youth Hostel
- Agricultural Interest
- Arboretum
- Bird Reserve
- Garden of Interest
- Vineyard
- Walks/Nature Trails
- Wildlife Park
- Zoo
- National Trust Car Park

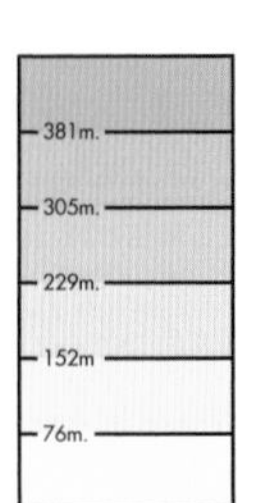

A Road

B Road

Minor Road

Other Road or Track
(not necessarily with public or vehicular access)

Railway

Cycleway

Open Space owned by the National Trust

Built-up Area

Scale 1:100,000

0 1 (miles) 2

0 1 2 (km)

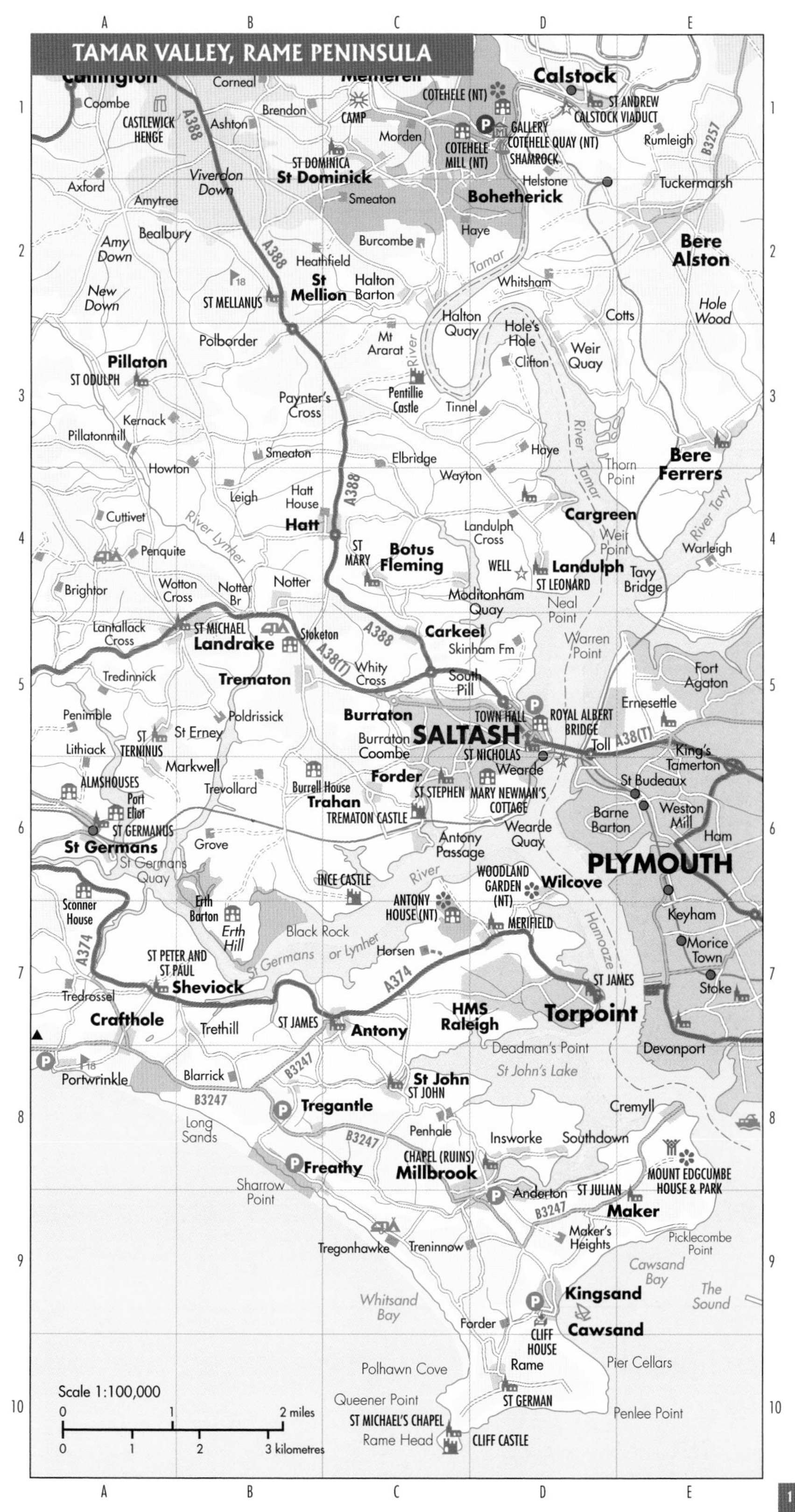
TAMAR VALLEY, RAME PENINSULA
Calstock
ST ANDREW
CALSTOCK VIADUCT
COTEHELE (NT)
GALLERY
COTEHELE QUAY (NT)
SHAMROCK
COTEHELE MILL (NT)
CAMP
Morden
Rumleigh
B3257
Tuckermarsh
Helstone
Bohetherick
Haye
Coombe
CASTLEWICK HENGE
Corneal
Brendon
Ashton
A388
ST DOMINICA
St Dominick
Smeaton
Viverdon Down
Axford
Amytree
Bealbury
Amy Down
New Down
Burcombe
Heathfield
St Mellion
ST MELLANUS
Halton Barton
Tamar
Whitsham
Bere Alston
Hole Wood
Cotts
Halton Quay
Hole's Hole
Clifton
Weir Quay
Mt Ararat
River
Polborder
Pillaton
ST ODULPH
Pentillie Castle
Tinnel
Paynter's Cross
Kernack
Pillatonmill
Smeaton
Howton
Elbridge
Haye
Wayton
River Tamar
Thorn Point
Bere Ferrers
Leigh
Hatt House
Hatt
Cuttivet
River Lynher
Penquite
Cargreen
Weir Point
River Tavy
Warleigh
Landulph Cross
ST MARY
Botus Fleming
WELL
Landulph
ST LEONARD
Tavy Bridge
Brightor
Wotton Cross
Notter Br
Notter
Moditonham Quay
Neal Point
Lantallack Cross
ST MICHAEL
Landrake
Stoketon
A38(T)
Carkeel
Skinham Fm
Warren Point
Fort Agaton
Tredinnick
Trematon
Whity Cross
South Pill
Penimble
Poldrissick
Burraton
TOWN HALL
ROYAL ALBERT BRIDGE
Ernesettle
ST TERNINUS
St Erney
SALTASH
Burraton Coombe
ST NICHOLAS
Toll
King's Tamerton
Lithiack
Markwell
Wearde
ALMSHOUSES
Port Eliot
Trevollard
Burrell House
Trahan
Forder
ST STEPHEN
MARY NEWMAN'S COTTAGE
St Budeaux
Weston Mill
Barne Barton
ST GERMANUS
St Germans
TREMATON CASTLE
Grove
St Germans Quay
Antony Passage
Wearde Quay
Ham
PLYMOUTH
INCE CASTLE
WOODLAND GARDEN (NT)
Wilcove
Sconner House
Erth Barton
Erth Hill
ANTONY HOUSE (NT)
MERIFIELD
Keyham
Black Rock
Morice Town
Hamoaze
A374
St Germans or Lynher
Horsen
ST PETER AND ST PAUL
Sheviock
ST JAMES
Stoke
Tredrossel
Crafthole
Trethill
ST JAMES
Antony
HMS Raleigh
Torpoint
Devonport
Deadman's Point
St John's Lake
Portwrinkle
Blarrick
B3247
St John
ST JOHN
Cremyll
Tregantle
Long Sands
Penhale
Insworke
Southdown
CHAPEL (RUINS)
Millbrook
Freathy
MOUNT EDGCUMBE HOUSE & PARK
Sharrow Point
Anderton
ST JULIAN
Maker
Maker's Heights
Picklecombe Point
Tregonhawke
Treninnow
Cawsand Bay
The Sound
Whitsand Bay
Kingsand
Forder
CLIFF HOUSE
Cawsand
Rame
Pier Cellars
Polhawn Cove
ST GERMAN
Scale 1:100,000
0
1
2 miles
0
1
2
3 kilometres
Queener Point
Penlee Point
ST MICHAEL'S CHAPEL
Rame Head
CLIFF CASTLE
A B C D E
1 2 3 4 5 6 7 8 9 10

Trevor Price, Cotehele Gallery ss

CALSTOCK.

Attractive old river port on the Tamar. Steep wooded riverbank and the abundance of fruit growing provide a splendour in spring, 12 arch viaduct. Numerous disused mining chimneys and engine houses haunt the landscape. (D1)

Calstock Viaduct.
12 arch viaduct built to carry railway wagons from local mines to Calstock Quay. Whereby the wagons were raised and lowered in a lift. (D1)

CAWSAND & KINGSAND

Twin villages with narrow streets and colourful houses. Former C18 smuggling centre and historic anchorage for Plymouth. Walks along coast to Cremyll Ferry. Inns. (D9)

Cliff House Kingsand,
Delightful Grade 11 listed house. Three bedrooms with bath. First floor Living Room overlooking Plymouth Sound and coastal path. Wholefood cuisine from local produce.
T 01752 823110. (D9)

SALTASH.

Attractive river port with steep streets running down to Tamar estuary. C18 Guildhall. Royal Albert Bridge. May Fair - 1st week. Regatta - June 3rd week. (D5)

Mary Newman's Cottage,
48 Culver St. C15 Cottage of Mary Newman, first wife of Sir Francis drake. Furniture supplied by the Victoria and Albert Museum.
Open May-Sept Th 12-4 and BHM's 11-4. (D6)

Royal Albert Bridge.
An iron single-track railway bridge built by I.K. Brunel in 1859, his last great feat of engineering. (D5)

ST GERMANS

Cornwall's cathedral city until 1043. Attractive village with almshouses and magnificent church. Port Eliot, ancient seat of the Eliot family. (A6)

St Germanus. Founded as an Augustinian priory, and later a cathedral in the Anglo-Saxon period. Only the S.aisle and nave remain. Magnificent Norman doorway and E. window glass by E. Burne-Jones. (A6)

Special Places to Visit...

Antony Woodland Gardens.
Privately owned by the Carew Pole Garden trust has 100 acres of woodland, 300 types of camellias bordering the River Lynher.
Open Tu W Th & W/Es Mar-Oct 11-5.30. (D6)

Antony House & Gardens (NT).
Built for Sir William Carew from 1711-1721 and considered the most distinguished example of early C18 architecture in Cornwall. Colonnades, panelled rooms and family portraits. Open 4 Apr-31 Oct Tu, W, Th & BH M's 1.30-5.30 (also Su June-Aug). (C7)

Cotehele Gallery (National Trust Cotehele).
Showcasing professional artists and makers from the South West in seven exhibitions annually. Open daily Feb to Christmas - Summer 11.30-5, Winter 11.30-4.30.
www.nationaltrust.org.uk. (D1)

Cotehele House (NT). ✓
Medieval house of grey granite (built 1485-1627) in romantic position overlooking the River Tamar and Devon beyond. For centuries,

The Library, Antony House nt

Cotehele ab/nt

the Edgcumbe family home containing original furniture, C17 tapestries, armour and needlework. The gardens lie on several levels. Medieval dovecote. Ancient clock in chapel. Refreshment and shop. Open daily except F (house closed), 18 Mar-31 Oct 11-5 (4.30 in Oct). Gardens open all year 10.30-dusk. (D1)

Cotehele Quay (NT). Picturesque C18 and C19 buildings beside the River Tamar. A small outstation of the National Maritime Museum and berth for the restored Tamar sailing barge. 'Shamrock'. Museum, Art and craft gallery and tea room. Open daily Apr-Oct. (D1)

Mount Edgcumbe House & Park. Sensitively restored Tudor mansion in beautiful landscaped parkland. Formal English, French and Italian Gardens. National Camellia Collection. Park and gardens open daily all year. House and Earl's Garden open Apr-Sept W-Su & BH's 11-4.30. (E8)

Churches of Interest...

Calstock Church. Grand position above Tamar Valley C17 monuments. (D1)

Landulph Church. Woodland setting on R. Tamar. Rood screen. (D4)

Rame Church. C11-15. Rough stone with spire. No electricity; hand-pumped organ. Nearby, simple chapel on Rame Head built by monks who directed ships with fire beacons into Plymouth Sound. (D10)

Cliff House, Kingsand ss

Coastal Path

Portwrinkle to Cremyll Ferry: Approx. 16 miles. The path hugs the cliff edge and you can now walk through the M.O.D. ranges at Tregantle, except during firing when you will be rerouted inland. Around the great sweep of Whitsand Bay to Rame Head with views of Plymouth Sound beyond. Along to the twin villages of Kingsand and Cawsand, passing Mount Edgcumbe, and to Cremyll Ferry which has carried passengers across the Tamar since the C13.

Beaches

Whitsand Bay. 4 miles of sand - glorious on a sunny day. But BEWARE this bay has a history of fatal bathing accidents, and is also a graveyard of many ships. The strong currents make bathing very HZ and is not recommended for the casual swimmer. Difficult access. Surfing - Warm up with the 10 minute walk to Tregantle. Good breaks at HT. Rips are powerful. Popular location for Plymouth surfers. (C9)

Tregantle Longsands. Access near M.O.D. range. Prohibited when red flag flys. P/WC. (B8)

Freathy / Tregonhawke. Smoothe white sands, strong currents, surfing. P/LG. (C9)

Cawsand / Kingsand. Easy access to shelving, pebbled beach - sand at LT. Good bathing, well protected from Sou'westerlies. Glorious views of ships sailing up to Plymouth Sound. P/WC/cafe. (D9)

Salmon fishing, Cotehele Quay nt

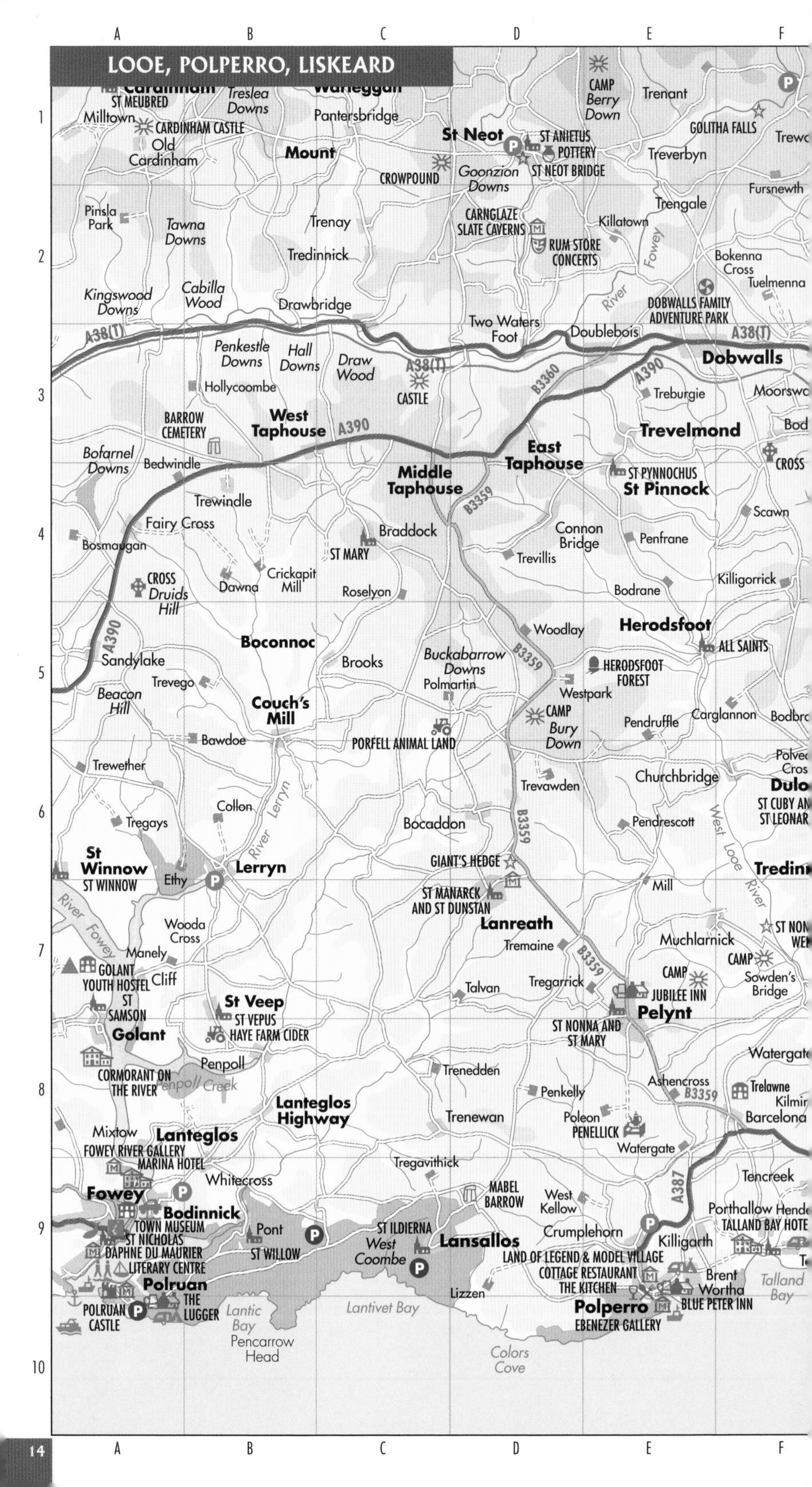

St Neot
ST ANIETUS
POTTERY
ST NEOT BRIDGE
CAMP Berry Down
Trenant
GOLITHA FALLS
Treverbyn
Fursnewth
Trengale
Killatown
CARNGLAZE SLATE CAVERNS
RUM STORE CONCERTS
Goonzion Downs
CROWPOUND
Mount
Pantersbridge
ST MEUBRED
Milltown
CARDINHAM CASTLE
Old Cardinham
Treslea Downs
Pinsla Park
Tawna Downs
Trenay
Tredinnick
Kingswood Downs
Cabilla Wood
Drawbridge
Bokenna Cross
Tuelmenna
DOBWALLS FAMILY ADVENTURE PARK
River Fowey
Two Waters Foot
Doublebois
A38(T)
Dobwalls
Penkestle Downs
Hall Downs
Draw Wood
CASTLE
Hollycoombe
B3360
A390
Treburgie
BARROW CEMETERY
West Taphouse
Trevelmond
East Taphouse
Bofarnel Downs
Bedwindle
Middle Taphouse
ST PYNNOCHUS
St Pinnock
CROSS
Trewindle
B3359
Scawn
Fairy Cross
Braddock
Connon Bridge
Penfrane
Bosmaugan
ST MARY
Trevillis
CROSS
Druids Hill
Dawna
Crickapit Mill
Roselyon
Bodrane
Killigorrick
Woodlay
Herodsfoot
ALL SAINTS
Boconnoc
Buckabarrow Downs
HERODSFOOT FOREST
Sandylake
Brooks
Polmartin
Westpark
Trevego
Beacon Hill
Couch's Mill
CAMP Bury Down
Pendruffle
Carglannon
Bawdoe
PORFELL ANIMAL LAND
Trewether
Trevawden
Churchbridge
Collon
River Lerryn
Bocaddon
Tregays
Pendrescott
West Looe River
St Winnow
ST WINNOW
Ethy
Lerryn
GIANT'S HEDGE
ST MANARCK AND ST DUNSTAN
Mill
River Fowey
Wooda Cross
Lanreath
Tremaine
Muchlarnick
Manely
GOLANT YOUTH HOSTEL
Cliff
CAMP
Sowden's Bridge
ST SAMSON
St Veep
ST VEPUS
Talvan
Tregarrick
JUBILEE INN
Golant
HAYE FARM CIDER
ST NONNA AND ST MARY
Pelynt
Penpoll
Penpoll Creek
CORMORANT ON THE RIVER
Trenedden
Ashencross
B3359
Trelawne
Penkelly
Lanteglos Highway
Trenewan
Poleon
PENELLICK
Barcelona
Mixtow
Lanteglos
FOWEY RIVER GALLERY
MARINA HOTEL
Watergate
Tregavithick
Whitecross
MABEL BARROW
West Kellow
A387
Tencreek
Fowey
Bodinnick
TOWN MUSEUM
ST NICHOLAS
DAPHNE DU MAURIER LITERARY CENTRE
Pont
ST WILLOW
ST ILDIERNA
West Coombe
Lansallos
Crumplehorn
Killigarth
Porthallow
LAND OF LEGEND & MODEL VILLAGE
COTTAGE RESTAURANT
THE KITCHEN
Brent
Wortha
Polruan
THE LUGGER
POLRUAN CASTLE
Lantic Bay
Pencarrow Head
Lantivet Bay
Lizzen
Polperro
BLUE PETER INN
EBENEZER GALLERY
Talland Bay
Colors Cove

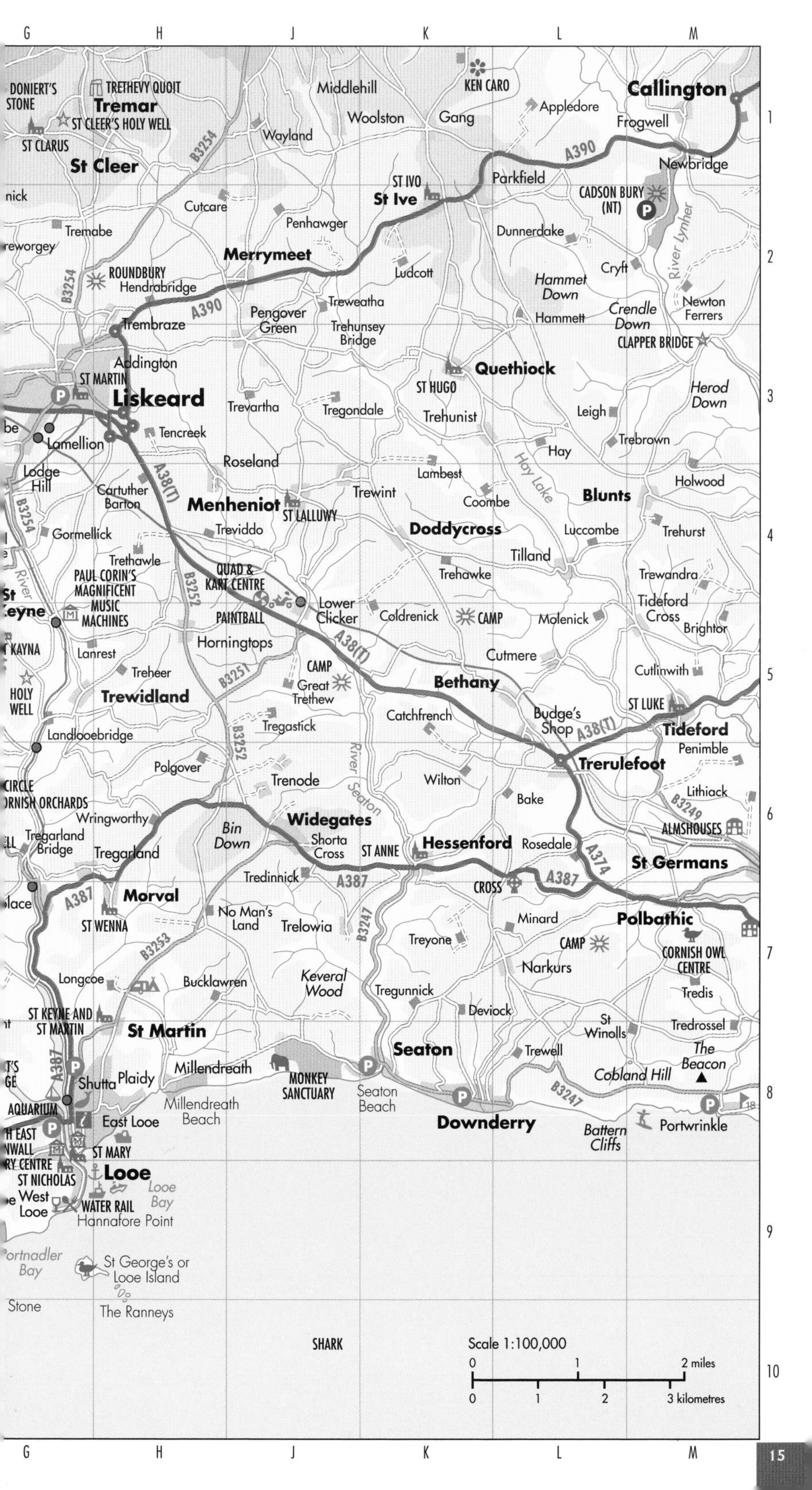

G
H
J
K
L
M
DONIERT'S STONE
TRETHEVY QUOIT
Tremar
ST CLEER'S HOLY WELL
ST CLARUS
St Cleer
Middlehill
KEN CARO
Woolston
Gang
Wayland
Appledore
Callington
Frogwell
A390
Newbridge
B3254
Parkfield
ST IVO
St Ive
CADSON BURY (NT)
Cutcare
Tremabe
Penhawger
Dunnerdake
Merrymeet
River Lynher
Cryft
ROUNDBURY
Hendrabridge
Ludcott
Hammet Down
Treweatha
Newton Ferrers
Pengover Green
Trehunsey Bridge
Hammett
Crendle Down
Trembraze
CLAPPER BRIDGE
Addington
ST MARTIN
Liskeard
Quethiock
ST HUGO
Herod Down
Trevartha
Tregondale
Trehunist
Leigh
Lamellion
Tencreek
Hay
Trebrown
Hay Lake
Roseland
Lambest
Holwood
Lodge Hill
A38(T)
Cartuther Barton
Trewint
Coombe
Blunts
Menheniot
ST LALLUWY
B3254
Treviddo
Doddycross
Luccombe
Trehurst
Gormellick
Tilland
Trethawle
Trehawke
Trewandra
PAUL CORIN'S MAGNIFICENT MUSIC MACHINES
QUAD & KART CENTRE
B3252
River
Lower Clicker
Coldrenick
CAMP
Tideford Cross
PAINTBALL
Molenick
Brighton
St Keyne
Horningtops
A38(T)
Cutmere
Lanrest
CAMP
Cutlinwith
Treheer
Great Trethew
Bethany
B3251
ST LUKE
HOLY WELL
Trewidland
Catchfrench
Budge's Shop
Tideford
Tregastick
Landlooebridge
Penimble
River Seaton
Trerulefoot
Polgover
Wilton
Trenode
Lithiack
B3252
Bake
B3249
Wringworthy
Widegates
ALMSHOUSES
Tregarland Bridge
Bin Down
Shorta Cross
ST ANNE
Hessenford
Rosedale
A374
Tregarland
St Germans
Tredinnick
A387
A387
CROSS
A387
Morval
No Man's Land
Minard
Polbathic
ST WENNA
Trelowia
B3247
Treyone
CAMP
B3253
CORNISH OWL CENTRE
Keveral Wood
Narkurs
Longcoe
Bucklawren
Tregunnick
Tredis
Deviock
ST KEYNE AND ST MARTIN
St Winolls
St Martin
Tredrossel
A387
Trewell
Seaton
The Beacon
Millendreath
Shutta
Plaidy
Cobland Hill
MONKEY SANCTUARY
Seaton Beach
B3247
AQUARIUM
Millendreath Beach
East Looe
Downderry
Battern Cliffs
Portwrinkle
ST MARY
Looe
ST NICHOLAS
West Looe
Looe Bay
WATER RAIL
Hannafore Point
Portnadler Bay
St George's or Looe Island
Stone
The Ranneys
SHARK
Scale 1:100,000
0
1
2 miles
0
1
2
3 kilometres
1
2
3
4
5
6
7
8
9
10

Polperro

POLPERRO

Exquisitely picturesque in a dramatically steep, narrow valley ending in small harbour; a timeless ambience pervades the narrow streets, pastel-shaded cottages and busy fishing harbour. Land of Legend & Model village and tea/gift shops. Fishing trips and Regatta - mid July. Park at top of village. (E10)

Ebenezer Gallery, The Coombes. East Cornwall Society of Artists members exhibit here plus two floors of paintings and ceramics. Open May-Oct. (E9)

Land Of Legend And Model Village. Replica of Polperro built locally with animated display of Cornwall's history and legends. Open daily East-Oct 10.30-6 (9 high season). (E9)

Where to Eat, Drink & Be Merry...

Cottage Restaurant. Cosy and snug white-washed cottage, locally caught fish in a picture-perfect village. Wow. No dogs. T 01503 272217. (E9)

The Kitchen, The Coombes. Park at top of village and walk down to this fisherman's cottage for spicy Goan and Thai cuisine. Dinner 7-9.30. T 01503 272780. (E9)

LISKEARD.

Once an important Stannary Town surrounded by prosperous copper mines. Today, a busy market town for the agricultural community. Attractive Georgian and Victorian cottages. Impressive large C15 Church, carnival - June (3rd week). Fat stock show - Nov (2nd week). (H3)

Monkey Sanctuary ss

LOOE. ✓

A typically active Cornish fishing village with busy quay, tidal harbour and a web of narrow streets. Today, a centre for deep sea and shark fishing. Walk the Looe Valley Line, a number of waymarked trails lead off along 8 miles of railway from Looe to Liskeard - leaflets available. Fish Market on East Looe Quay, Sub-Aqua club, boat trips, Aquarium*. (H9)

Marine Aquarium, The Quay Head. Displays of local marine fish caught within 1 mile of Banjo Pier. Open Spring BH-Sept 10-6 (-9 July & Aug). (H8)

Monkey Sanctuary. Unique environmental charity caring for South American Primates. Refreshments. Open East-Sept Su-Th 11-4.30. T 01503 262532. (J8)

South East Cornwall Discovery Centre. The gateway to exploring the beauty, culture and wildlife of SE Cornwall. Open Mar-Dec; East, then May-Sept daily 10-6. Other times M-F 10-4, Su 11-3. (G8)

Where to Eat, Drink & Be Merry...and Sleep...

Water Rail, Lower Market St. Retro-style dining rooms offering sea food with rich sauces. Try the Specials. T 01503 262314. (H9)

Talland Bay Hotel. Small, family-friendly hotel set in 2 acres of sub-tropical gardens. Bright, contemoprary decor. Heated outdoor pool. Cottage lets. T 01503 272667. (F9)

POLRUAN.

Attractive village with busy boatyard. The main street plunges almost vertically to the small quay. Cars not encouraged. Pedestrian ferry to Fowey.

The Lugger. Famous Inn noted for its high quality pub grub and fine ales. Worth the ferry trip. (A10)

Special Family Places to Visit

Cornish Owl Centre. One of the largest collections, from all corners of the world. Open daily 10-6. T 01503 230079. (M7)

Dobwalls Adventure Park. Forest Railroad; steam-diesel locos. Wildlife art gallery. Large indoor & outdoor adventure play areas. Open most days East-Oct 10.30-5, winter W/Es & school hols 10.30-4. (Limited facilities). T 01579 320325. (F2)

Paul Corins Magnificent Music Machines. The Marquis of Campden's 1912 Aeolian Pipe Organ, orchestrions and the Mighty Wurlitzer Theatre Organ. Open daily Good F-Oct 10.30-5. (H5)

Porfell Animal Land. Designed for all ages to enjoy domestic and exotic wild animals, play area and walks in lovely countryside. Open daily Apr-Oct 10-6. (D5)

Quad & Kart Centre. Zip karts, quads, scorpions, kiddies electric cars in disused quarry. Open daily East-Oct 10-5.30. Paintball parties open daily, all year. T 01579 340678. (J4)

Ancient Cornwall

Barrow Cemetery. Linear cemetery of 8 bowl barrows. (B3)

Special Places to Visit

Herodsfoot Forest. Deer park, walks and cabins for self catering holidays. (E5)

Cornish Orchards. Handcrafted apple juices, ciders and honeys from West Country orchards. Farm shop open Good F-Oct from 10. ((G6)

Looe

Carnglaze Slate Caverns. Famous subterranean lake with crystal clear blue-green water in huge underground chamber. Open all year M-Sa 10-5. (D2)

Haye Farm Cider, St Veep. Real, traditional, local farm scrumpy – cider matured in wooden barrels. Open daily. T 01208 872250. (B8)

Ken-Caro Gardens. 5 acre connoisseurs garden full of unusual plants and shrubs, making it a garden of interest all year. Panoramic views. Open Feb 26 - Sept 29 Su-F 10-5.30. T 01579 362446. (L1)

The Rum Store, Carnglaze Caverns. Classical and pop concerts put on in underground 400 seat auditorium. Superb acoustics. T 01579 320251. (D2)

St Neot Pottery, The Old Chapel. Pots made on premises from earthenware clay and decorated by hand. Open M-Sa. T 01579 320216. (D1)

Churches of Interest

Lanreath Church. Norman cruciform, medieval screens and monuments. (D7)

Liskeard Church. Perpendicular, second largest in county. 13 consecretion crosses - a unique feature. (H3)

St Martin-By-Looe Church. Norman origins with C15 additions and ceiled wagon roof. (H7)

St Winnow Church. Overlooks the River Fowey, C15-C16 glass, bench ends. (A6)

Lanteglos-By-Fowey. C13 font. C16 bench ends. (B8)

Coastal Footpath

Polruan to Portwrinkle: Approx. 26 miles. First, six miles of magnificent lonely cliff-top walking to Polperro. Inland grazed fields and gentler contours, but the coast path is steep and hard-going. Polperro* must be explored, then along a well maintained path following the cliff edge to Looe. Soon to leave Cornwall's rugged coastline; Battern Cliffs (450ft), the highest cliffs in South Cornwall, remind one of the dramas left behind to the little harbour of Portwrinkle.

Beaches & Surfing

Lantic Bay. 10 mins walk from NT P. Follow path across fields, and down a steep 400ft climb to a lovely beach at LT. (D10)

Lantivet Bay. 15 mins walk from Lansallos, secluded beach with pebbles and shingle. (C9)

Talland Bay. Access via a steep narrow lane, shingle, rocks and sand at LT flanked by cliffs. P/WC/cafe. (F9)

Portnadler Bay. Follow coastpath for 1 1/4 mile from West Looe to a quiet sandy beach with rock pools. (G9)

West Looe - Hannifore. Rock pools and pebbles, sandy patches at LT. WC/cafe/kiosk. (H9)

East Looe - Banjo Pier. Suntrap behind pier, sands and pebbles, good bathing. (H8)

East Looe - Plaidy Beach. Access by foot from Banjo Pier. Rock pools and shale. WC/cafe. (H8)

Mildendreath Beach. Sands with patches of rock, bathing pool for children. P/WC/Café. (H8)

Seaton. Fine bathing, safe beach with pebbles and grey sand. P/W. Surfing - Sheltered position. (K8)

Downderry. Grey sands and rocks, palm trees. P/WC/Inn. (L8)

Portwrinkle. Surfing - Good following big swells. At HT rocks are invisible so take care with your fins. (M8)

The Rum Store, Carnglaze Caverns ss

For Ancient Sites, Castles, Country Lanes, Stone Circles, Steam Railways and Wilderness...

Between the County Town of Bodmin and the walled town of Launceston lies the mysterious Bodmin Moor. A compact area of open moorland and a mere ten miles by ten in size. And yet, it appears far more expansive given its wildness and isolation. But, beware of sudden mists and descending clouds for they foster disorientation and loss of place amidst bog and Tor.

All about you is ancient history; Early Man settled here to escape the wild beasts of forest and plain. Stone Age Man left Stone Circles and burial chambers. The Moor's appearance of bareness was hastened by the clearance of granite boulders for building stonewalls, farms and villages. In the centre, isolated and bruised by the elements, stands Jamaica Inn, the legendary smuggler's haunt, widely known through Daphne Du Maurier's novel. Imagine arriving on foot, or cart, lonely, tired and drenched to be greeted by rough-tongued smugglers and highwayman.

Not to be overlooked is the fertile countryside on the eastern side of the Moor drained by the rivers Tamar and Lynher. A blissful, pastoral landscape reminiscent of old England; small farmsteads and hamlets with beautiful churches; Linkinhorne, South Hill and Lezant, and often to be found, surprisingly good inns, for example the Springer Spaniel at Treburley. These villages are linked by narrow lanes and steep hedgerows.

Launceston is dominated by its Norman castle and is the only walled town in Cornwall. It is a town of hills that calls for exploration. The exterior walls of the church of St Mary Magdalene are quite exceptional with images of foliage and shields carved out of the granite.

The Long Gallery, Lanhydrock nt

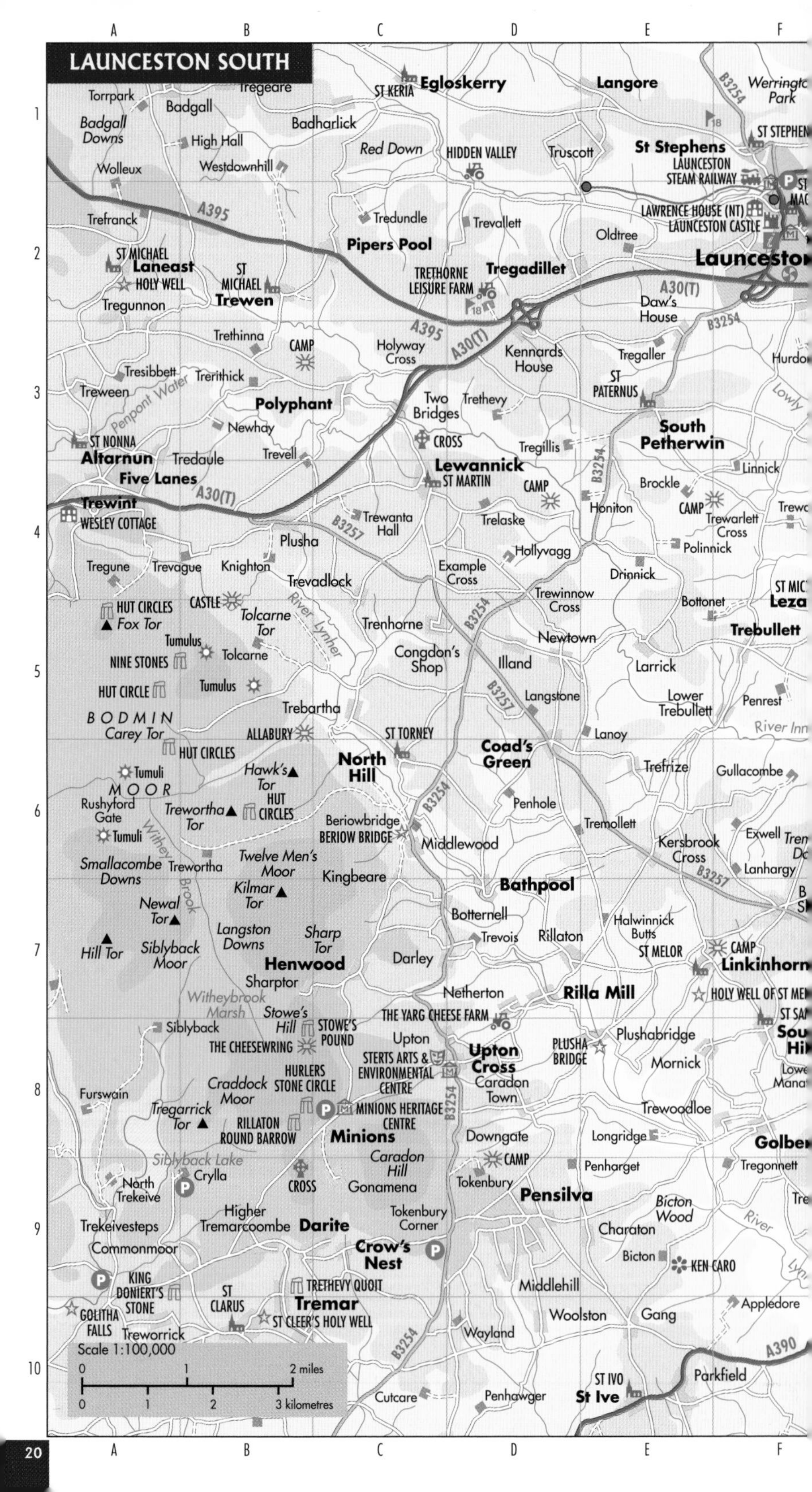
LAUNCESTON SOUTH
Egloskerry
ST KERIA
Langore
Werrington Park
Torrpark
Badgall
Tregeare
Badgall Downs
Badharlick
High Hall
Red Down
HIDDEN VALLEY
Truscott
St Stephens
LAUNCESTON STEAM RAILWAY
Wolleux
Westdownhill
A395
Trefranck
Tredundle
Trevallett
LAWRENCE HOUSE (NT)
LAUNCESTON CASTLE
Oldtree
Pipers Pool
Launceston
ST MICHAEL
Laneast
HOLY WELL
Tregunnon
ST MICHAEL
Trewen
TRETHORNE LEISURE FARM
Tregadillet
A30(T)
Daw's House
B3254
Trethinna
CAMP
Holyway Cross
Kennards House
Tregaller
Tresibbett
Trerithick
Penpont Water
Treween
Polyphant
Two Bridges
Trethevy
ST PATERNUS
Newhay
CROSS
South Petherwin
ST NONNA
Altarnun
Tredaule
Trevell
Tregillis
Lewannick
ST MARTIN
Linnick
Brockle
Five Lanes
CAMP
Honiton
CAMP
Trewarlett Cross
Trewint
WESLEY COTTAGE
Trewanta Hall
Trelaske
B3257
Plusha
Hollyvagg
Polinnick
Tregune
Trevague
Knighton
Example Cross
Drinnick
Trevadlock
HUT CIRCLES
Fox Tor
CASTLE
Tolcarne Tor
River Lynher
Trenhorne
Trewinnow Cross
Bottonet
Trebullett
Tumulus
Tolcarne
NINE STONES
Congdon's Shop
Newtown
Illand
Larrick
HUT CIRCLE
Tumulus
Langstone
Lower Trebullett
Penrest
BODMIN
Carey Tor
Trebartha
ALLABURY
ST TORNEY
Lanoy
River Inny
HUT CIRCLES
Coad's Green
Tumuli
MOOR
Hawk's Tor
North Hill
Trefrize
Gullacombe
Rushyford Gate
Treworthа Tor
HUT CIRCLES
Penhole
Tumuli
Witheybrook
Beriowbridge
BERIOW BRIDGE
Middlewood
Tremollett
Exwell
Kersbrook Cross
Smallacombe Downs
Treworthа
Twelve Men's Moor
Kingbeare
Lanhargy
Kilmar Tor
Bathpool
Newal Tor
Botternell
Halwinnick Butts
Hill Tor
Siblyback Moor
Langston Downs
Sharp Tor
Trevois
Rillaton
ST MELOR
CAMP
Linkinhorne
Henwood
Darley
Sharptor
Netherton
Rilla Mill
HOLY WELL OF ST MELOR
Witheybrook Marsh
Stowe's Hill
STOWE'S POUND
THE YARG CHEESE FARM
Siblyback
THE CHEESEWRING
Upton
Upton Cross
PLUSHA BRIDGE
Plushabridge
Mornick
STERTS ARTS & ENVIRONMENTAL CENTRE
HURLERS STONE CIRCLE
Caradon Town
Craddock Moor
Furswain
Tregarrick Tor
RILLATON ROUND BARROW
MINIONS HERITAGE CENTRE
Trewoodloe
Minions
Downgate
Longridge
Caradon Hill
CAMP
Siblyback Lake
Crylla
Penharget
Tregonnett
North Trekeive
CROSS
Gonamena
Tokenbury
Pensilva
Bicton Wood
Higher Tremarcoombe
Tokenbury Corner
Trekeivesteps
Darite
Charaton
River Lynher
Commonmoor
Crow's Nest
Bicton
KEN CARO
KING DONIERT'S STONE
TRETHEVY QUOIT
Middlehill
ST CLARUS
Tremar
Appledore
GOLITHA FALLS
ST CLEER'S HOLY WELL
Woolston
Gang
Treworrick
Wayland
A390
Scale 1:100,000
0 1 2 miles
0 1 2 3 kilometres
Parkfield
ST IVO
St Ive
Cutcare
Penhawger
A B C D E F
1 2 3 4 5 6 7 8 9 10

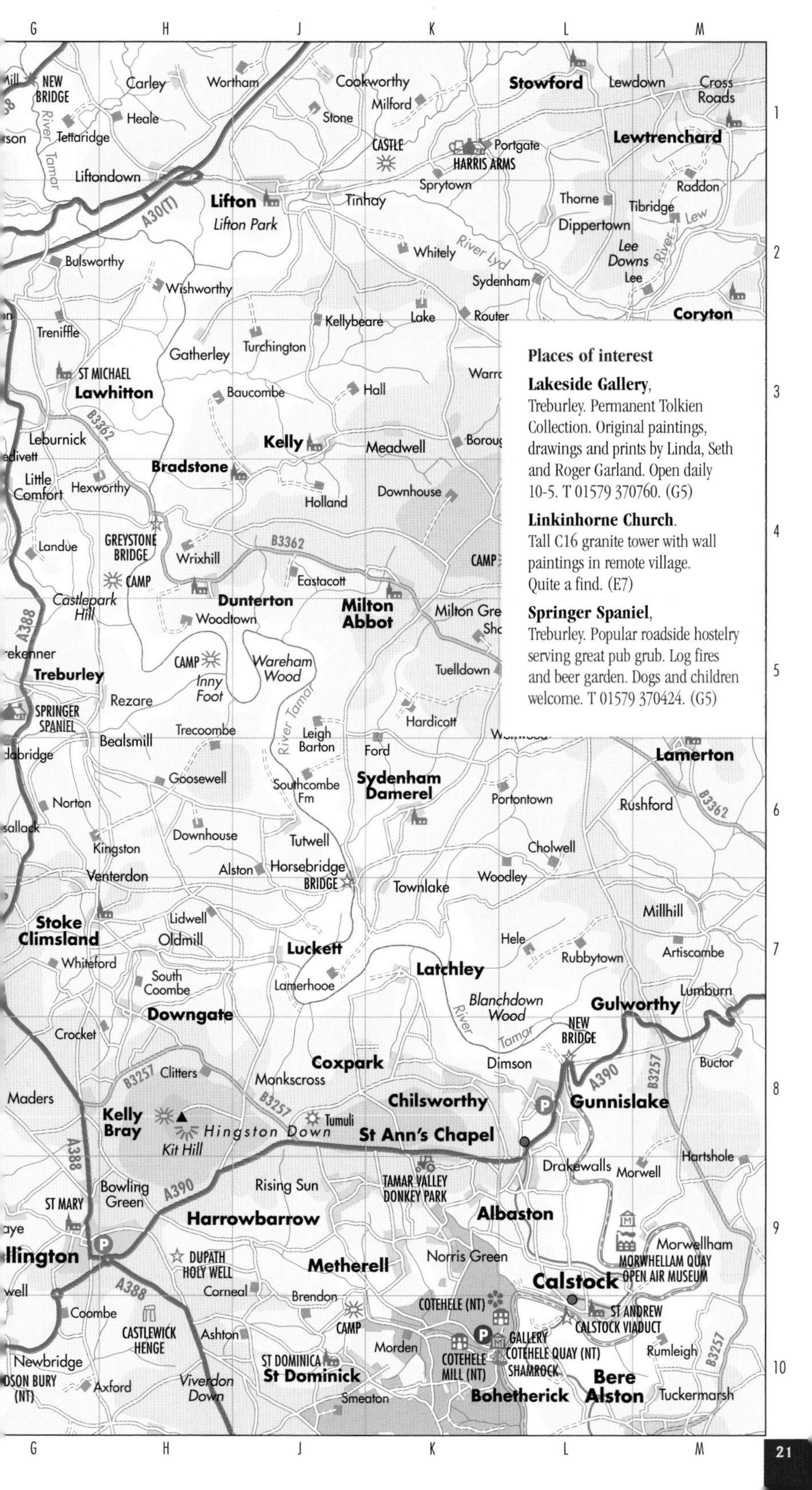

Places of interest

Lakeside Gallery, Treburley. Permanent Tolkien Collection. Original paintings, drawings and prints by Linda, Seth and Roger Garland. Open daily 10-5. T 01579 370760. (G5)

Linkinhorne Church. Tall C16 granite tower with wall paintings in remote village. Quite a find. (E7)

Springer Spaniel, Treburley. Popular roadside hostelry serving great pub grub. Log fires and beer garden. Dogs and children welcome. T 01579 370424. (G5)

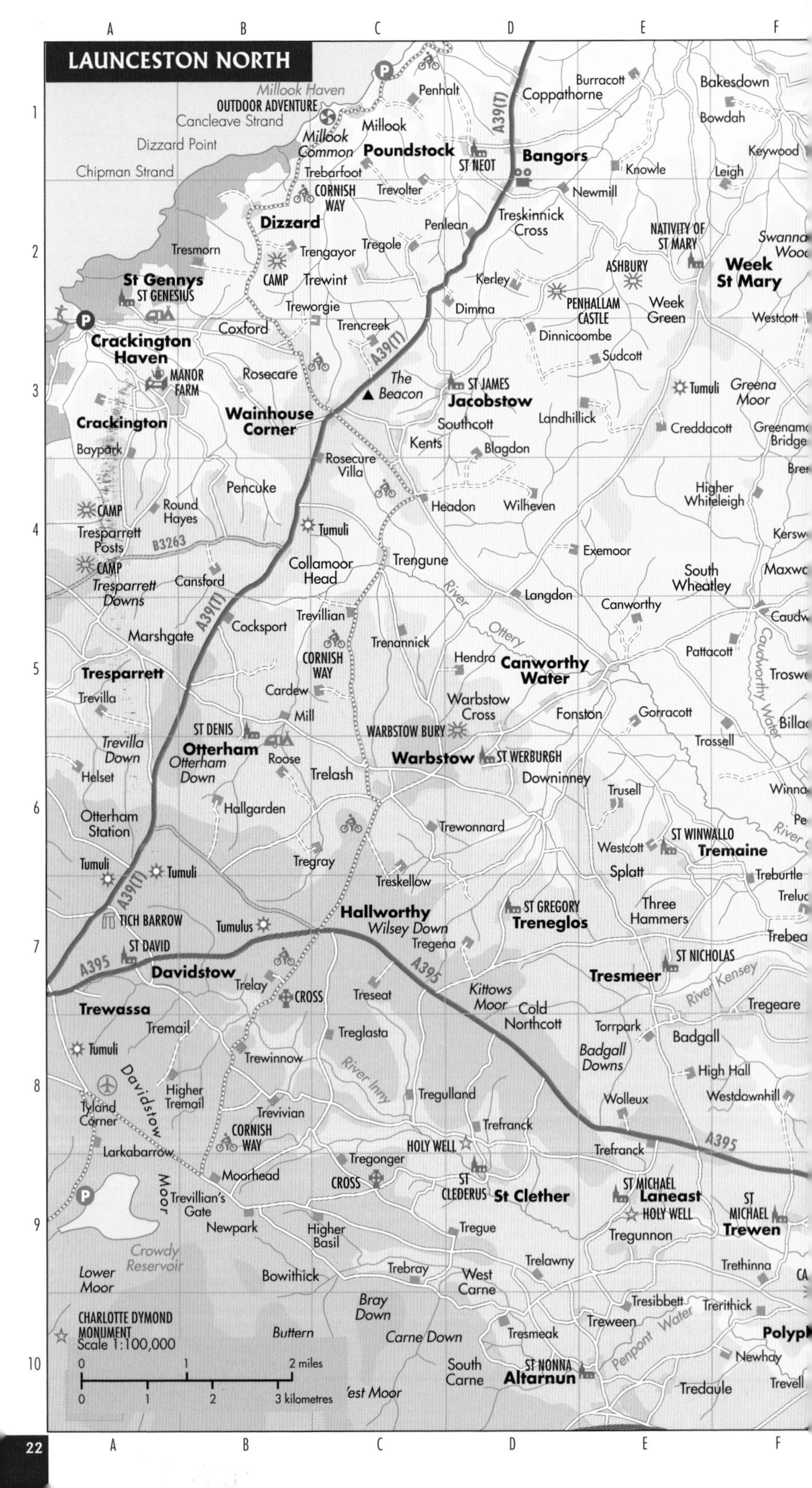
LAUNCESTON NORTH
A
B
C
D
E
F
1
2
3
4
5
6
7
8
9
10
Millook Haven
OUTDOOR ADVENTURE
Cancleave Strand
Dizzard Point
Chipman Strand
Millook Common
Penhalt
Millook
Poundstock
ST NEOT
A39(T)
Coppathorne
Burracott
Bangors
Knowle
Newmill
Bakesdown
Bowdah
Keywood
Leigh
Trebarfoot
CORNISH WAY
Trevolter
Dizzard
Penlean
Treskinnick Cross
NATIVITY OF ST MARY
Tresmorn
Trengayor
Tregole
ASHBURY
Week St Mary
St Gennys
ST GENESIUS
CAMP
Trewint
Kerley
PENHALLAM CASTLE
Week Green
Dimma
Westcott
Treworgie
Crackington Haven
Coxford
Trencreek
Dinnicoombe
Sudcott
Rosecare
The Beacon
ST JAMES
Jacobstow
Tumuli
Greena Moor
MANOR FARM
Crackington
Wainhouse Corner
Southcott
Landhillick
Creddacott
Baypark
Kents
Blagdon
Rosecure Villa
Pencuke
Headon
Wilheven
Higher Whiteleigh
Round Hayes
Tresparrett Posts
B3263
Collamoor Head
Trengune
Exemoor
South Wheatley
Tresparrett Downs
Cansford
River Ottery
Langdon
Canworthy
Trevillian
Cocksport
Marshgate
Trenannick
Hendra
Canworthy Water
Pattacott
Caudworthy Water
Tresparrett
Cardew
Warbstow Cross
Fonston
Gorracott
Trevilla
Mill
ST DENIS
WARBSTOW BURY
Trevilla Down
Otterham
Otterham Down
Roose
Warbstow
ST WERBURGH
Trossell
Helset
Trelash
Downinney
Trusell
Otterham Station
Hallgarden
Trewonnard
ST WINWALLO
Westcott
Tremaine
Tregray
Splatt
Treburtle
Tumuli
Treskellow
ST GREGORY
Treneglos
Three Hammers
TICH BARROW
Tumulus
Hallworthy
Wilsey Down
Tregena
ST DAVID
A395
Davidstow
Trelay
ST NICHOLAS
Tresmeer
River Kensey
Trewassa
CROSS
Treseat
Kittows Moor
Cold Northcott
Tregeare
Tremail
Treglasta
Torrpark
Badgall
Badgall Downs
Trewinnow
River Inny
High Hall
Davidstow
Higher Tremail
Tregulland
Wolleux
Westdownhill
Tyland Corner
Trevivian
Trefranck
Larkabarrow
HOLY WELL
Tregonger
ST CLEDERUS
St Clether
ST MICHAEL
Laneast
Moor
Moorhead
Trevillian's Gate
Newpark
Higher Basil
Tregue
Tregunnon
ST MICHAEL
Trewen
Crowdy Reservoir
Trelawny
Trethinna
Lower Moor
Bowithick
Trebray
West Carne
Tresibbett
Trerithick
Bray Down
CHARLOTTE DYMOND MONUMENT
Buttern
Carne Down
Tresmeak
Treween
Penpont Water
Newhay
Scale 1:100,000
0
1
2 miles
0
1
2
3 kilometres
West Moor
South Carne
ST NONNA
Altarnun
Tredaule
Trevell

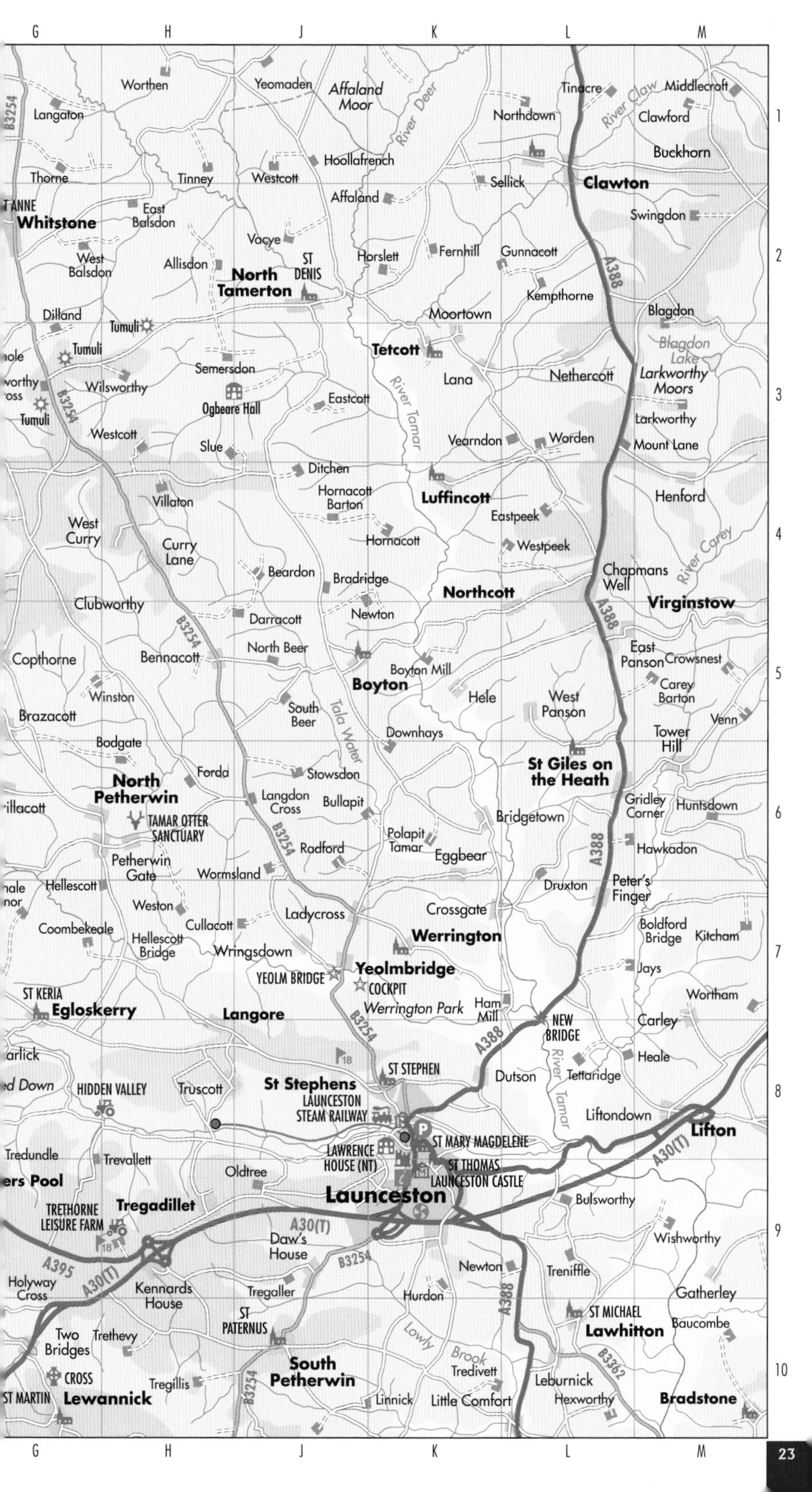

Worthen
Yeomaden
Affaland Moor
River Deer
Tinacre
Middlecroft
Langaton
Northdown
River Claw
Clawford
Hoollafrench
Buckhorn
Thorne
Tinney
Westcott
Sellick
Clawton
Affaland
Swingdon
Whitstone
East Balsdon
Vacye
West Balsdon
Allisdon
North Tamerton
ST DENIS
Horslett
Fernhill
Gunnacott
Kempthorne
Dilland
Tumuli
Moortown
Blagdon
Tetcott
Blagdon Lake
Semersdon
Lana
Nethercott
Larkworthy Moors
Wilsworthy
Ogbeare Hall
Eastcott
River Tamar
Larkworthy
Westcott
Slue
Vearndon
Worden
Mount Lane
Ditchen
Hornacott Barton
Luffincott
Villaton
Henford
Eastpeek
West Curry
Curry Lane
Hornacott
Westpeek
River Carey
Beardon
Bradridge
Chapmans Well
Clubworthy
Northcott
Virginstow
Newton
Darracott
North Beer
Copthorne
Bennacott
Boyton Mill
East Panson
Crowsnest
Winston
Boyton
Hele
West Panson
Carey Barton
Brazacott
South Beer
Tala Water
Venn
Downhays
Tower Hill
Bodgate
North Petherwin
Forda
Stowsdon
St Giles on the Heath
Langdon Cross
Bullapit
Gridley Corner
Huntsdown
Bridgetown
TAMAR OTTER SANCTUARY
Polapit Tamar
Radford
Eggbear
Hawkadon
Petherwin Gate
Wormsland
Hellescott
Druxton
Peter's Finger
Weston
Ladycross
Crossgate
Coombekeale
Cullacott
Boldford Bridge
Kitcham
Hellescott Bridge
Werrington
Wringsdown
Yeolmbridge
Jays
YEOLM BRIDGE
COCKPIT
ST KERIA
Wortham
Egloskerry
Langore
Werrington Park
Ham Mill
NEW BRIDGE
Carley
River Tamar
Heale
ST STEPHEN
Dutson
Tettaridge
HIDDEN VALLEY
Truscott
St Stephens
LAUNCESTON STEAM RAILWAY
Liftondown
Lifton
Tredundle
ST MARY MAGDELENE
Trevallett
LAWRENCE HOUSE (NT)
Oldtree
ST THOMAS
LAUNCESTON CASTLE
Launceston
Bulsworthy
Tregadillet
TRETHORNE LEISURE FARM
A30(T)
Wishworthy
Daw's House
Holyway Cross
Kennards House
Newton
Treniffle
Tregaller
Hurdon
Gatherley
ST PATERNUS
ST MICHAEL
Lawhitton
Baucombe
Two Bridges
Trethevy
Lowly Brook
South Petherwin
Tredivett
CROSS
Tregillis
Leburnick
ST MARTIN
Lewannick
Linnick
Little Comfort
Hexworthy
Bradstone
B3254
A388
A395
B3362
G H J K L M
1 2 3 4 5 6 7 8 9 10

Launceston Castle

LAUNCESTON

A town of hills dominated by the commanding position of the Castle*, and the only walled town in Cornwall. Splendid collection of Georgian houses in Castle Street. Lawrence House (NT)* and the Eagle Hotel. St Mary Magdalene*. C16 packhorse bridge. Agricultural show - Aug (2/3 weeks).
E/C Th. (K9)

St Mary Magdalene.
Noted for the famous exterior; panels of foliage and shields carved in granite cover most of the walls. C14 tower and a rare painted pulpit. (K8)

Launceston Castle (EH).
Norman castle built in c.1070 in timber. It was the main seat of Robert de Mortain, brother of William the Conqueror. Rebuilt C12-13. Good example of a motte and bailey structure. Open as English Heritage times. (K9)

Launceston Steam Railway.
Two-foot gauge steam railway using Victorian Locomotives along a beautiful country line. After 2 1/2 miles, Newmills Station, access to farm park. Transport and Industrial Museum with working exhibits. Cafe, shop and bookshop. Open East week, Spring BH & Oct 1/2 term, July-Sept Su-F, also June Su-W, 10.30-4.30. (K8)

Lawrence House Museum (NT)
property used as a local history museum. Many objects of interest including the Feudal dues.
Open Apr-Oct M-F 10.30-12.30, 2.30-4.30. (K8)

Special Paces to Visit Outside Launceston...

Hidden Valley.
Adventure park and garden railway centre. Treasure hunts based around a shipwreck. Play area. Farm animals. Cafe. Open daily mid-Apr to Sept Su-F 10.30-5.30. (G8)

Laneast Church.
C13 with fine C16 pulpit and wagon roofing. (E9)

St Mary Magdalene, Launceston

Lakeside Gallery, Treburley ss

Tamar Otter Sanctuary
20 acres of mature woodland where three species of deer roam free. British and Asian Otters in large semi-natural enclosures. The only place in West Country breeding British Otters for release into the wild. Waterfowl, nature trail and picnic area. Teas and gifts. Open daily Apr-Oct 10.30-6. T 01986 893470. (H6)

Trethorne Leisure Farm.
Undercover family entertainment; milk a cow, bottle feed lambs, see chicks hatch. Ten pin bowling (open 10am-11pm), gladiator duels, dropslide, astraslide, restaurant, bar and shop. Open all year M-Sa 10-6. (G9)

Tamar Otter Sanctuary ss

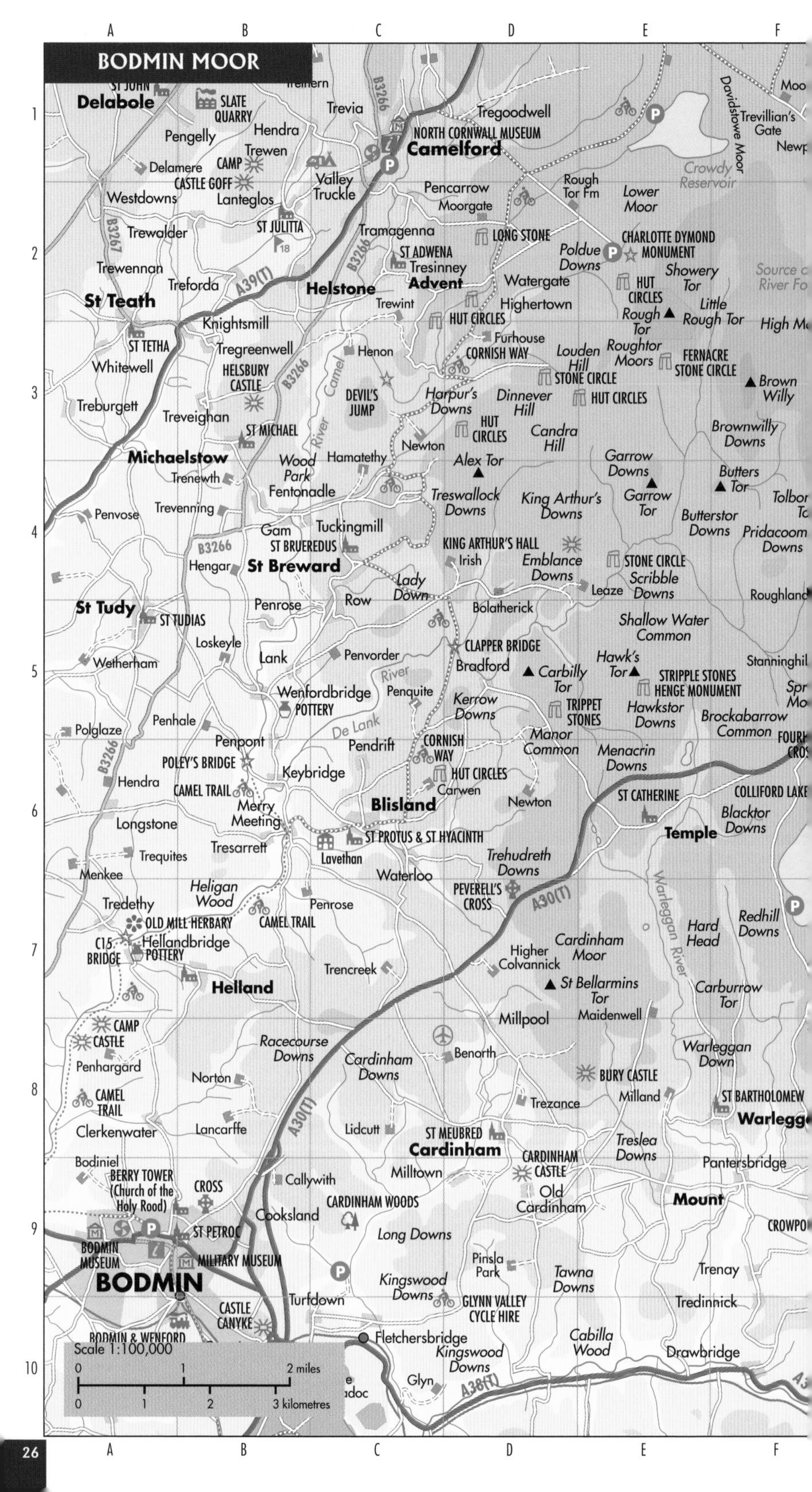

BODMIN MOOR
A
B
C
D
E
F
Delabole
ST JOHN
SLATE QUARRY
Treligga
Trevia
B3266
Tregoodwell
Pengelly
Hendra
NORTH CORNWALL MUSEUM
Camelford
Trewen
CAMP
Delamere
CASTLE GOFF
Valley Truckle
Westdowns
Lanteglos
Pencarrow
Moorgate
Rough Tor Fm
Lower Moor
Crowdy Reservoir
Davidstowe Moor
Trevillian's Gate
B3267
Trewalder
ST JULITTA
Tramagenna
LONG STONE
CHARLOTTE DYMOND MONUMENT
Poldue Downs
Trewennan
B3266
ST ADWENA
Tresinney
Advent
Showery Tor
Treforda
A39(T)
Helstone
Watergate
HUT CIRCLES
Rough Tor
Little Rough Tor
St Teath
Trewint
Highertown
High Moor
Knightsmill
HUT CIRCLES
Furhouse
ST TETHA
Tregreenwell
Henon
CORNISH WAY
Louden Hill
Roughtor Moors
FERNACRE STONE CIRCLE
Whitewell
HELSBURY CASTLE
B3266
Camel
STONE CIRCLE
Brown Willy
Treburgett
DEVIL'S JUMP
Harpur's Downs
Dinnever Hill
HUT CIRCLES
Treveighan
River
HUT CIRCLES
Candra Hill
Brownwilly Downs
ST MICHAEL
Newton
Michaelstow
Wood Park
Hamatethy
Alex Tor
Garrow Downs
Butters Tor
Trenewth
Fentonadle
Treswallock Downs
King Arthur's Downs
Garrow Tor
Penvose
Trevenning
Butterstor Downs
Pridacoom Downs
Gam
Tuckingmill
B3266
ST BREUREDUS
KING ARTHUR'S HALL
Irish
Emblance Downs
STONE CIRCLE
Hengar
St Breward
Lady Down
Scribble Downs
Leaze
Roughland
St Tudy
Penrose
Row
ST TUDIAS
Bolatherick
Shallow Water Common
Loskeyle
CLAPPER BRIDGE
Lank
Penvorder
Bradford
Hawk's Tor
Wetherham
River
Carbilly Tor
STRIPPLE STONES HENGE MONUMENT
Wenfordbridge
Penquite
POTTERY
Kerrow Downs
TRIPPET STONES
Hawkstor Downs
Polglaze
Penhale
De Lank
Brockabarrow Common
Manor Common
B3266
Penpont
Pendrift
CORNISH WAY
Menacrin Downs
POLEY'S BRIDGE
Hendra
Keybridge
HUT CIRCLES
CAMEL TRAIL
Carwen
ST CATHERINE
COLLIFORD LAKE
Merry Meeting
Blisland
Newton
Blacktor Downs
Longstone
Temple
ST PROTUS & ST HYACINTH
Tresarrett
Lavethan
Trequites
Trehudreth Downs
Menkee
Waterloo
Heligan Wood
PEVERELL'S CROSS
A30(T)
Warleggan River
Tredethy
Penrose
OLD MILL HERBARY
CAMEL TRAIL
Redhill Downs
Hard Head
C15 BRIDGE
Hellandbridge
POTTERY
Cardinham Moor
Higher Colvannick
Trencreek
Helland
St Bellarmins Tor
Carburrow Tor
Maidenwell
Millpool
CAMP
CASTLE
Racecourse Downs
Benorth
Warleggan Down
Penhargard
Cardinham Downs
Norton
BURY CASTLE
CAMEL TRAIL
Milland
Trezance
ST BARTHOLOMEW
Clerkenwater
Lancarffe
A30(T)
Lidcutt
ST MEUBRED
Cardinham
Treslea Downs
Bodiniel
CARDINHAM CASTLE
Pantersbridge
BERRY TOWER (Church of the Holy Rood)
CROSS
Callywith
Milltown
Old Cardinham
Mount
CARDINHAM WOODS
Cooksland
BODMIN MUSEUM
ST PETROC
Long Downs
CROWPOUND
MILITARY MUSEUM
Pinsla Park
BODMIN
Tawna Downs
Trenay
Kingswood Downs
Turfdown
GLYNN VALLEY CYCLE HIRE
Tredinnick
CASTLE CANYKE
BODMIN & WENFORD
Fletchersbridge
Cabilla Wood
Drawbridge
Scale 1:100,000
0
1
2 miles
0
1
2
3 kilometres
Kingswood Downs
Glyn
A38(T)
1
2
3
4
5
6
7
8
9
10

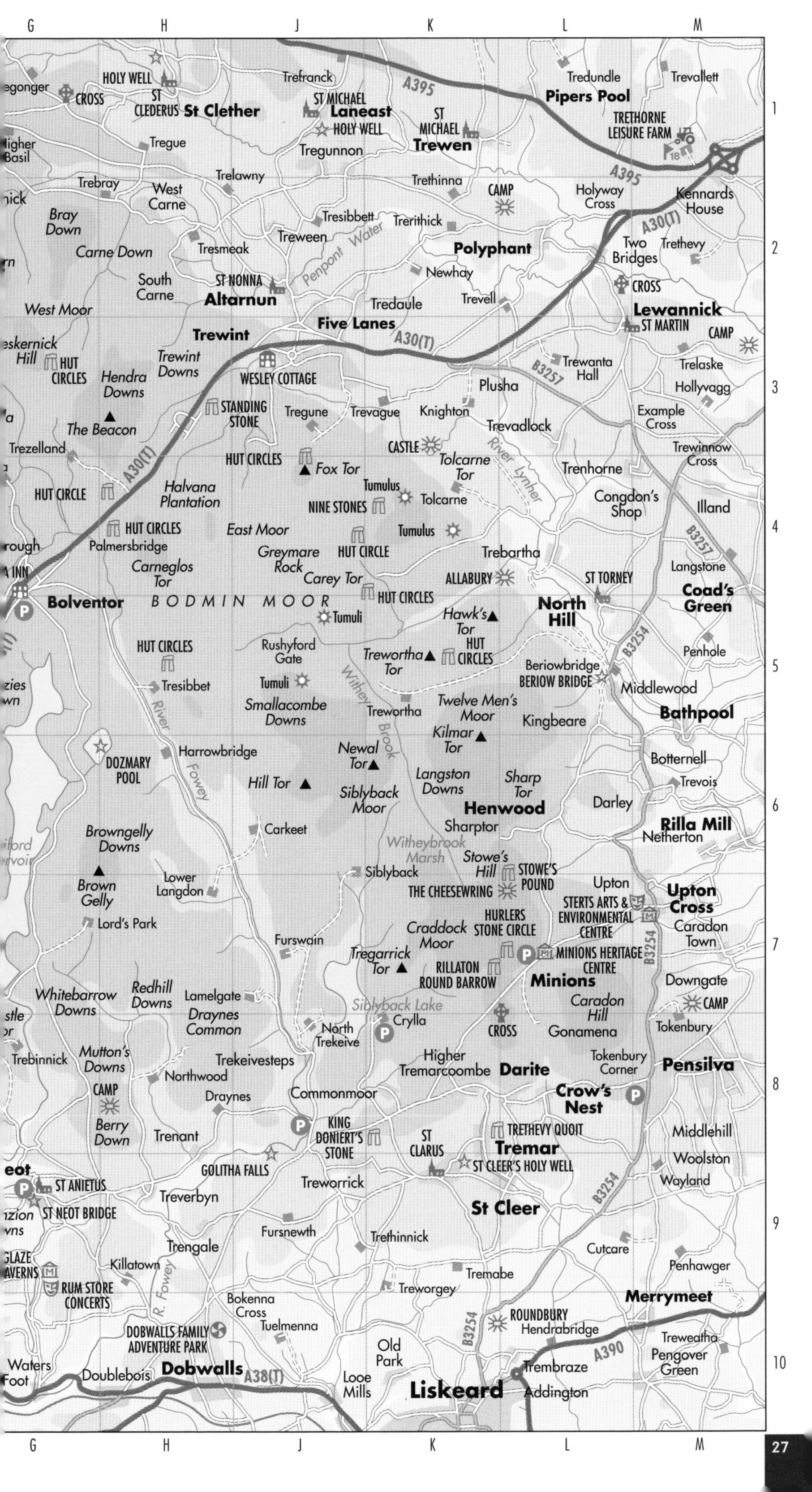

G
H
J
K
L
M
HOLY WELL
ST CLEDERUS
St Clether
CROSS
Trefranck
ST MICHAEL
Laneast
HOLY WELL
A395
ST MICHAEL
Trewen
Tredundle
Trevallett
Pipers Pool
TRETHORNE LEISURE FARM
Tregue
Tregunnon
Trelawny
Trebray
West Carne
Bray Down
Carne Down
Trethinna
CAMP
Holyway Cross
Kennards House
A30(T)
Tresibbett
Trerithick
Treween
Penpont Water
Tresmeak
Polyphant
Two Bridges
Trethevy
Newhay
South Carne
ST NONNA
Altarnun
CROSS
West Moor
Tredaule
Trevell
Five Lanes
Lewannick
ST MARTIN
CAMP
Trewint
Trewint Downs
HUT CIRCLES
Hendra Downs
WESLEY COTTAGE
Trewanta Hall
B3257
Trelaske
Plusha
Hollyvagg
STANDING STONE
Tregune
Trevague
Knighton
Example Cross
The Beacon
Trevadlock
Trezelland
CASTLE
Tolcarne Tor
River Lynher
Trewinnow Cross
HUT CIRCLES
Fox Tor
Trenhorne
HUT CIRCLE
Halvana Plantation
Tumulus
NINE STONES
Tolcarne
Congdon's Shop
Illand
HUT CIRCLES
East Moor
Tumulus
Palmersbridge
Greymare Rock
HUT CIRCLE
Trebartha
Carneglos Tor
Carey Tor
ALLABURY
ST TORNEY
Langstone
Bolventor
BODMIN MOOR
HUT CIRCLES
Coad's Green
Tumuli
Hawk's Tor
North Hill
HUT CIRCLES
Rushyford Gate
Trewortha Tor
HUT CIRCLES
B3254
Penhole
Beriowbridge
BERIOW BRIDGE
Tumuli
Tresibbet
Middlewood
Smallacombe Downs
Withey Brook
Trewortha
Twelve Men's Moor
Bathpool
Kingbeare
River Fowey
Kilmar Tor
DOZMARY POOL
Harrowbridge
Newal Tor
Botternell
Langston Downs
Sharp Tor
Trevois
Hill Tor
Siblyback Moor
Henwood
Darley
Rilla Mill
Netherton
Sharptor
Carkeet
Browngelly Downs
Witheybrook Marsh
Stowe's Hill
STOWE'S POUND
Upton
Brown Gelly
Lower Langdon
Siblyback
THE CHEESEWRING
STERTS ARTS & ENVIRONMENTAL CENTRE
Upton Cross
Lord's Park
HURLERS STONE CIRCLE
Caradon Town
Craddock Moor
Furswain
Tregarrick Tor
MINIONS HERITAGE CENTRE
RILLATON ROUND BARROW
Minions
Downgate
Whitebarrow Downs
Redhill Downs
Lamelgate
Caradon Hill
CAMP
Draynes Common
Siblyback Lake
Crylla
North Trekeive
CROSS
Gonamena
Tokenbury
Trebinnick
Mutton's Downs
Trekeivesteps
Higher Tremarcoombe
Darite
Tokenbury Corner
Pensilva
Northwood
CAMP
Draynes
Commonmoor
Crow's Nest
Berry Down
Trenant
KING DONIERT'S STONE
ST CLARUS
TRETHEVY QUOIT
Tremar
Middlehill
GOLITHA FALLS
ST CLEER'S HOLY WELL
Woolston
ST ANIETUS
Treworrick
Wayland
Treverbyn
ST NEOT BRIDGE
St Cleer
Fursnewth
Trengale
Trethinnick
Cutcare
Killatown
Tremabe
Penhawger
RUM STORE CONCERTS
R. Fowey
Treworgey
Merrymeet
Bokenna Cross
ROUNDBURY
Hendrabridge
Tuelmenna
DOBWALLS FAMILY ADVENTURE PARK
B3254
Treweatha
Old Park
A390
Pengover Green
Waters Foot
Doublebois
Dobwalls
A38(T)
Looe Mills
Trembraze
Liskeard
Addington
1
2
3
4
5
6
7
8
9
10

Minions, Bodmin Moor

BODMIN MOOR.

A wild and remote landscape, of sudden mists and mysterious legend. A vegetation of boggy moorland, open heathland, granite tors and hidden valleys. The highest point is Brown Willy (1377ft). This remote wilderness, far from the dangerous beasts of the forest and plain, attracted prehistoric man. Hut circles, burial grounds and stone circles litter the landscape. An exhilarating place for pony trekking and walking, but beware of sudden mists. (H5)

Dozmary Pool.
Remote, uninspiring pool where 'Excalibur was thrown into these waters'. (H6)

Colliford Lake Park. Multiple attraction: alternative technology and education area. Nature conservation, indigenous species breeding and undercover play area, café and crafts (The Best of Bodmin Moor's Arts & Crafts), and gift shop. Open East-Sept 10.30-5, & winter W/Es 11-5. (F6)

ALTARNUM

A charming linear village with a superb C16 church, 'Cathedral of the Moors'. Packhorse bridge. (J2)

St Nonna. Superb C16 church; tall perpendicular tower rises to 109 ft. Norman font. C16 carved bench ends including man with bagpipes Known locally as 'The Cathedral of the Moors'. Overlooks an attractive linear village. (J2)

Wesley Cottage. John Wesley, the founder of Methodism, preached and rested during his preaching tours of Cornwall. Furnished in C18 style, collection of Wesleyana. Open daily 9-dusk. T 01566 86158. (J3)

Minions Heritage Centre, South Phoenix Mine. Explores the history of the local landscape. Open daily from 10-dusk. (L7)

Sterts Arts & Environment Centre. Lively programme of music, amphitheatre(canopied) and dance. Open daily (theatre June-Sept) except Su. (L7)

St Nonna ac

Churches of Interest

Cardinham Church.
C15 buttressed and pinnacled tower with celtic cross. (D8)

St Neot.
Imposing building in scenic valley famous for the 15 medieval stained glass windows. (G9)

Special Places to Visit

Golitha Falls. Trail starts at Redgate Bridge. Follows river bank and profusion of wild flowers to tranquil resting place. (J9)

Jamaica Inn. Former old coaching inn and inspiration for Daphne du Maurier's novel. Bars, restaurants, accommodation & gift shops. Attractions include Daphne Du Maurier Room, 'The Smugglers at Jamaica Inn'. Inn open daily, all year. (G4)

Wesley Cottage ss

Hurlers Stone Circle

St Neot

North Hill Church.
C15 granite tower and elaborate C17 monuments. Set in unspoilt village. (L5)

St Protus & St Hyacinth,
Blisland. Wonderfully restored church (a favourite of John Betjamin) in village with attractive village green and fine Inn. C15 granite tower and Norman font. C15 brasses. (C6)

Ancient Cornwall

Doniert's Stone. Possibly remains of Durngarth's grave d.875, King of Cornwall. Interlaced with Hibernia-Saxon inscription. (J8)

Fernacre Stone Circle.
64 stones, 150ft in diameter. Numerous hut circles. (E3)

Hurlers Stone Circle.
Three stone circles 110ft, 135ft and 105ft in diameter. According to legend - men turned to stone for playing the old cornish game of hurling on a Sunday. Similar game to Australian Rules. Access via 1/4 mile path from road. (L7)

King Arthur's Hall.
Neolithic enclosure 159ft x 60ft with large facing stones. (D4)

Rillaton Round Barrow.
A bronzdagger, and the Rillaton Cup were unearthed here in 1818. A gold cup, of ribbed and handled design (in British Museum) suggests it may have originated in Mycenae, Greece. (K7)

The Cheesewring.
Extraordinary formation of granite slabs weathered by wind and rain. Bronze Age cup (in British Museum) found in grave on Stowe's Hill. (K7)

Trethevy Quoit.
Impressive neolithic dolmen; 6 uprights support a massive capstone pierced by a circular hole. (L8)

Minions Heritage Centre

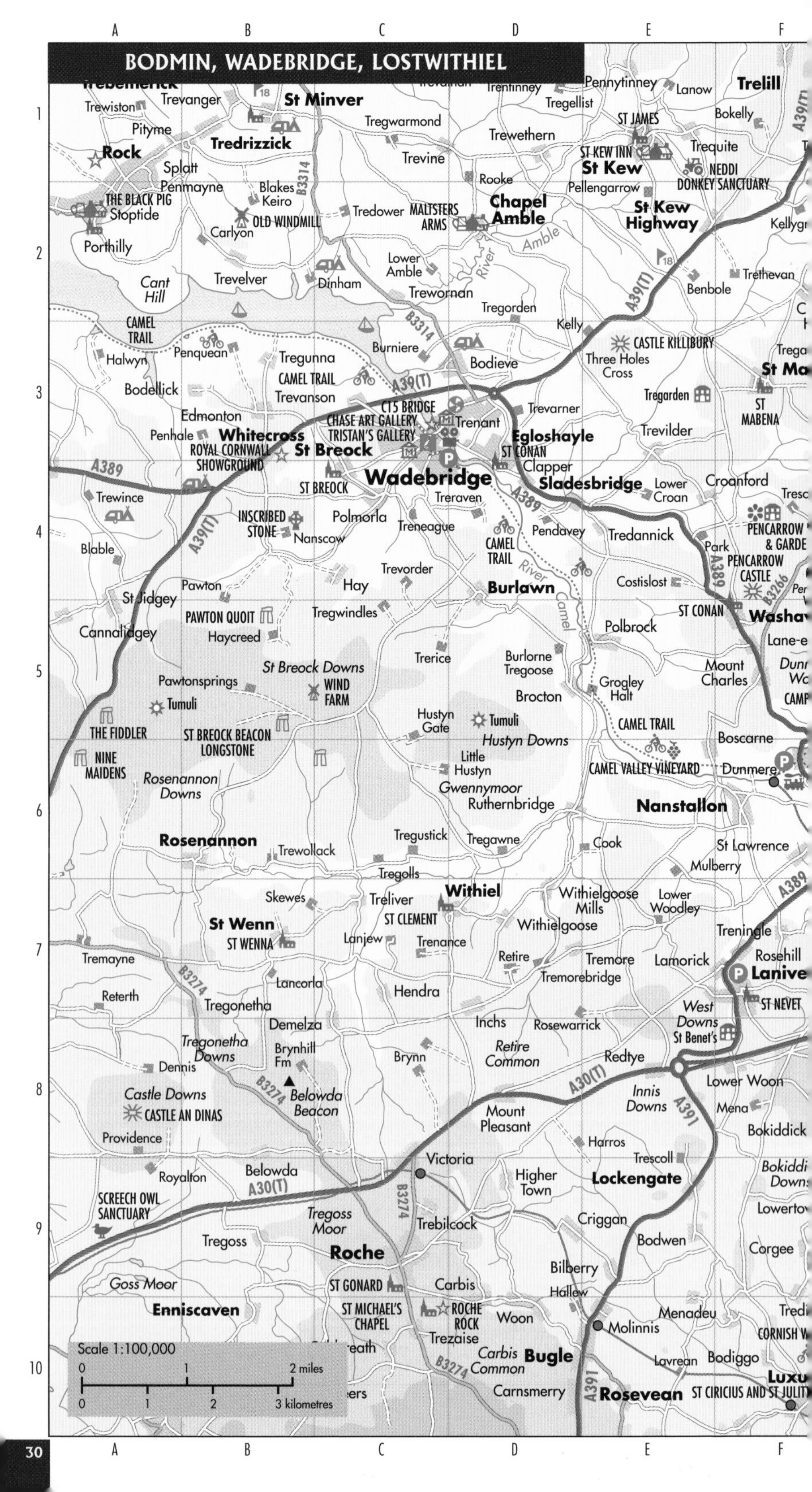

A B C D E F
St Minver
Rock
Tredrizzick
Trewiston
Trevanger
Pityme
Splatt
Penmayne
THE BLACK PIG
Stoptide
Porthilly
Blakes Keiro
Carlyon
OLD WINDMILL
Tregwarmond
Trevine
Tredower
MALTSTERS ARMS
Chapel Amble
Rooke
Trewethern
Trentinney
Tregellist
Pennytinney
Lanow
Trelill
ST JAMES
Bokelly
ST KEW INN
St Kew
Trequite
NEDDI DONKEY SANCTUARY
Pellengarrow
St Kew Highway
Kellygr
Trethevan
Benbole
Lower Amble
River Amble
Dinham
Trewornan
Tregorden
Cant Hill
Trevelver
CAMEL TRAIL
Halwyn
Penquean
Tregunna
Burniere
Bodieve
Kelly
CASTLE KILLIBURY
Three Holes Cross
St Ma
ST MABENA
Tregarden
Bodellick
CAMEL TRAIL
Trevanson
Edmonton
Penhale
Whitecross
ROYAL CORNWALL SHOWGROUND
St Breock
CT5 BRIDGE
CHASE ART GALLERY
TRISTAN'S GALLERY
Trenant
Trevarner
Egloshayle
ST CONAN
Clapper
Trevilder
Wadebridge
Sladesbridge
Lower Croan
Croanford
ST BREOCK
Trewince
Treraven
INSCRIBED STONE
Polmorla
Nanscow
Treneague
CAMEL TRAIL
Pendavey
Tredannick
PENCARROW & GARDE
Park
PENCARROW CASTLE
Blable
Pawton
Hay
Trevorder
Burlawn
River Camel
Costislost
St Jidgey
PAWTON QUOIT
Haycreed
Tregwindles
ST CONAN
Washa
Cannalidgey
Polbrock
Lane-e
Trerice
Burlorne Tregoose
Mount Charles
St Breock Downs
WIND FARM
Pawtonsprings
Tumuli
Grogley Halt
Brocton
THE FIDDLER
ST BREOCK BEACON LONGSTONE
Hustyn Gate
Tumuli
Hustyn Downs
CAMEL TRAIL
Boscarne
NINE MAIDENS
Rosenannon Downs
Little Hustyn
CAMEL VALLEY VINEYARD
Dunmere
Gwennymoor
Rutherbridge
Nanstallon
Rosenannon
Tregustick
Tregawne
Cook
St Lawrence
Trewollack
Mulberry
Tregolls
Skewes
Treliver
Withiel
Withielgoose Mills
Lower Woodley
ST CLEMENT
St Wenn
ST WENNA
Withielgoose
Treningle
Lanjew
Trenance
Retire
Tremore
Lamorick
Rosehill
Tremayne
Tremorebridge
Lanive
Lancorla
ST NEVET
Reterth
Hendra
Tregonetha
West Downs
Demelza
Inchs
Rosewarrick
St Benet's
Tregonetha Downs
Brynhill Fm
Retire Common
Redtye
Brynn
Dennis
Lower Woon
Belowda Beacon
Innis Downs
Castle Downs
Mount Pleasant
Mena
CASTLE AN DINAS
Bokiddick
Providence
Harros
Trescoll
Victoria
Higher Town
Lockengate
Bokiddi Down
Royalton
Belowda
SCREECH OWL SANCTUARY
Lowerto
Tregoss Moor
Trebilcock
Criggan
Tregoss
Bodwen
Corgee
Roche
Bilberry
Goss Moor
ST GONARD
Carbis
Hallew
Enniscaven
ST MICHAEL'S CHAPEL
ROCHE ROCK
Woon
Molinnis
Menadeu
Tredi
CORNISH W
Trezaise
Carbis Common
Bugle
Lavrean
Bodiggo
Luxu
Carnsmerry
Rosevean
ST CIRICIUS AND ST JULITT
A39(T)
A389
A30(T)
A391
B3314
B3274
B3266
Scale 1:100,000
0 1 2 miles
0 1 2 3 kilometres

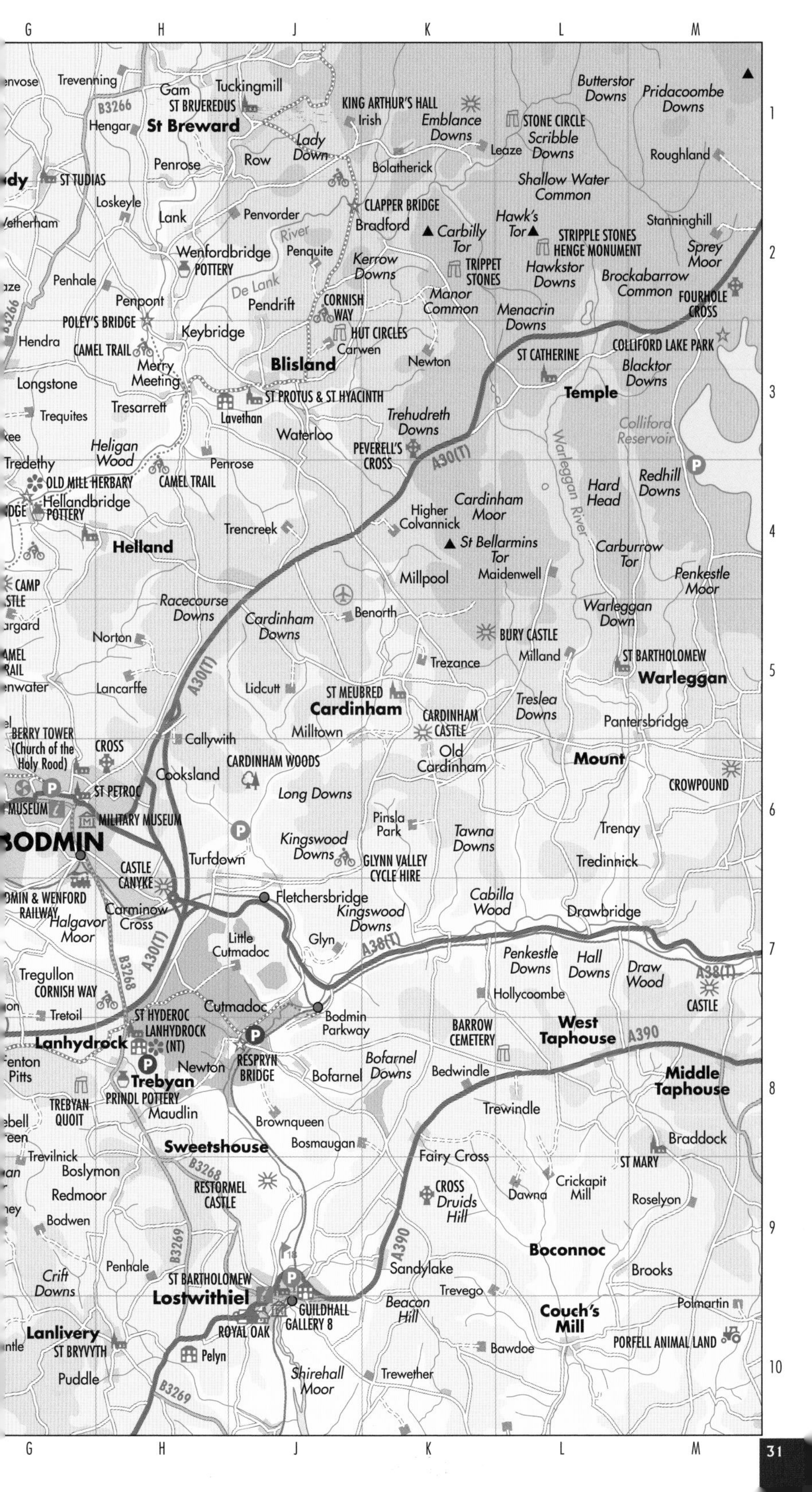
G
H
J
K
L
M
Trevenning
Gam
Tuckingmill
ST BRUEREDUS
KING ARTHUR'S HALL
Irish
Emblance Downs
STONE CIRCLE
Scribble Downs
Butterstor Downs
Pridacoombe Downs
B3266
Hengar
St Breward
Lady Down
Leaze
Roughland
Penrose
Row
Bolatherick
ST TUDIAS
Shallow Water Common
Loskeyle
Lank
Penvorder
CLAPPER BRIDGE
Bradford
Carbilly Tor
Hawk's Tor
STRIPPLE STONES HENGE MONUMENT
Stanninghill
River
Wenfordbridge
POTTERY
Penquite
Kerrow Downs
TRIPPET STONES
Hawkstor Downs
Brockabarrow Common
Sprey Moor
Penhale
De Lank
Pendrift
CORNISH WAY
Manor Common
Menacrin Downs
FOURHOLE CROSS
Penpont
POLEY'S BRIDGE
HUT CIRCLES
Hendra
Keybridge
Carwen
CAMEL TRAIL
Newton
ST CATHERINE
COLLIFORD LAKE PARK
Merry Meeting
Blisland
Blacktor Downs
Longstone
Temple
Tresarrett
ST PROTUS & ST HYACINTH
Lavethan
Trequites
Trehudreth Downs
Colliford Reservoir
Waterloo
Heligan Wood
PEVERELL'S CROSS
Warleggan River
Tredethy
Penrose
A30(T)
OLD MILL HERBARY
CAMEL TRAIL
Hard Head
Redhill Downs
Cardinham Moor
Hellandbridge
POTTERY
Higher Colvannick
Trencreek
Helland
St Bellarmins Tor
Carburrow Tor
Maidenwell
Millpool
Penkestle Moor
CAMP
Racecourse Downs
Warleggan Down
Benorth
Cardinham Downs
BURY CASTLE
Norton
Milland
ST BARTHOLOMEW
Trezance
Warleggan
Lancarffe
Lidcutt
ST MEUBRED
Cardinham
Treslea Downs
CARDINHAM CASTLE
Pantersbridge
BERRY TOWER (Church of the Holy Rood)
CROSS
Callywith
Milltown
Old Cardinham
Mount
CARDINHAM WOODS
Cooksland
CROWPOUND
ST PETROC
Long Downs
MUSEUM
MILITARY MUSEUM
Pinsla Park
Trenay
BODMIN
Kingswood Downs
Tawna Downs
Turfdown
GLYNN VALLEY CYCLE HIRE
Tredinnick
CASTLE CANYKE
Fletchersbridge
Cabilla Wood
RAILWAY
Carminow Cross
Kingswood Downs
Drawbridge
Halgavor Moor
Little Cutmadoc
Glyn
A38(T)
Penkestle Downs
Hall Downs
Draw Wood
B3268
Tregullon
CORNISH WAY
Hollycoombe
CASTLE
Cutmadoc
Tretoil
ST HYDEROC
LANHYDROCK (NT)
Bodmin Parkway
BARROW CEMETERY
West Taphouse
A390
Lanhydrock
Newton
RESPRYN BRIDGE
Bofarnel
Bofarnel Downs
Bedwindle
Middle Taphouse
Trebyan
PRINDL POTTERY
Pitts
TREBYAN QUOIT
Maudlin
Trewindle
Brownqueen
Braddock
Sweetshouse
Bosmaugan
Trevilnick
Fairy Cross
ST MARY
Boslymon
B3268
RESTORMEL CASTLE
CROSS
Druids Hill
Dawna
Crickapit Mill
Redmoor
Roselyon
Bodwen
B3269
A390
Penhale
Boconnoc
Sandylake
Crift Downs
ST BARTHOLOMEW
Brooks
Trevego
Lostwithiel
GUILDHALL GALLERY 8
Beacon Hill
Couch's Mill
Polmartin
Lanlivery
ROYAL OAK
ST BRYVYTH
PORFELL ANIMAL LAND
Pelyn
Bawdoe
Shirehall Moor
Trewether
Puddle
B3269
1
2
3
4
5
6
7
8
9
10

BODMIN

County town, and fine base for touring North Cornwall. C15 St Petroc is the largest Parish Church in the County. Historic prison, scene of public executions until 1862, and keeper of Crown Jewels in WW1. Good start-off point for the Camel Trail. Military Museum*, Lanhydrock*, Bodmin & Wenford Railway*, Indoor swimming pool. E/C W. (G6)

Poley Bridge, Camel Trail

Special Places to Visit....

Bodmin & Wenford Railway, Bodmin General Station. Standard gauge steam railway. Open East, Spring BHs and Su & W to end May, then daily June-Sept. Su Tu & W in Oct & Dec Specials. T 01208 73666 www.bodminandwenfordrailway.co.uk (G6)

Bodmin Museum, Mount Folly. Exhibits of local history, Victorian Kitchen. 'Echoes of Bodmin Moor!'. Open East-Sept 10.30-4.30, Oct 11-3. (G6)

Camel Trail. Eleven-mile trail from Bodmin to Padstow; suitable for jogging, walking, cycling and birdwatching. Cycle hire in Padstow and Wadebridge. (F5)

Gallery 8, Fore St. Original paintings and garden sculptures. Humorous etchings by Louise Vercoe. Open W-Sa 10.30-4.30, Su 11.30-4.30. (G6)

Military Museum, The Keep. Weapons, medals, uniforms, badges and military history based on the Duke of Cornwall's Light Infantry. Open M-F 10-5, Su in July/Aug 10-4. T 01208 72810. (H6)

Bodmin & Wenford Railway ss

The High Garden, Lanhydrock ejs/nt

Royal Oak, Duke St. C13 Inn with flagstone floor, cosy bar and full range of beers. Fine cuisine. B & B. T 01208 872552. (G6)

St Petroc, Bodmin. In C6 Cornwall's patron saint, St Petroc, founded a priory here. Later, in the C9 a monastery was established, and in the Middle Ages, the town became an important religious centre. The present large church was built mainly in the C15. Norman font and Wagon roof. (G6)

Just Outside Bodmin..

Camel Valley Vineyards. Award-winning wines from 8,000 vines growing on the south-facing valley. Tastings, shop and pre-booked tours at 2.30 and 5 pm W; 01208-77959. Open East-Sept M-F 2-5, some W/Es. (E5)

Screech Owl Sanctuary. Rescue and rehabilitation centre for sick and injured owls. Guided tours. Open daily Apr-Oct 10-6, winter 10-4. (A9)

LOSTWITHIEL

C13 capital of Cornwall set amidst the beautiful Fowey Valley with many beautiful buildings - C13 Duchy Palace on Quay Street, C13 parish church, C17 and C18 Georgian houses on Fore Street and C18 Guildhall. Important early C20 corrugated iron army drill hall. C13 bridge. Museum Restormel Castle. May Making ceremony, 'Beating the Bounds' - May (1st Monday) Carnival week - late July. E/C W. (J9)

Lostwithiel Church. Unusual octagonal spire and tower. Norman font. Clerestory windows. (J9)

Lanlivery Church. C15. Very tall impressive granite tower. (H10)

Restormel Castle (EH). A model of military architecture; classically symmetrical with circular moat, and strategically positioned allowing breathtaking views across the River Fowey. Built c.1100 with C13 additions. Owned by Simon de Montfort and Richard Earl of Cornwall. Open daily Apr-Oct 10-6 (5 in Oct). (J8)

Old Mill Herbary ss

Special Potteries to Visit...

Helland Bridge Pottery.
Riverside home and studio, of Paul and Rosie Jackson. A wide range of stunningly decorated hand-made pottery and garden sculpture. Fabulous water gardens. Open any time, but advised to 'phone first: T 01208 75240. (G4)

Prindl Pottery. Japanese inspired pots; some are of enormous size and originality, others are simply shaped in stoneware or porcelain. Open M-F, W/es by appoint. (H8)

Wenford Bridge Pottery.
Cardew family business since 1939; Hand-thrown decorated stoneware. Tuition on hand. Potter's Barn Restaurant & Coffee House. Open daily 10-5. T 01208 850471. (H2)

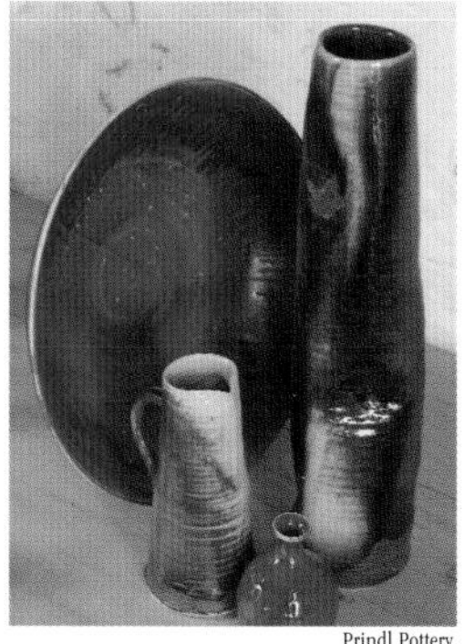

Prindl Pottery

Ancient Cornwall

Castle An Dinas. Four massive concentric rings; crowned by 'Roger's Tower', an C18 folly. Iron Age pottery found. (A8)

Houses & Gardens to Visit...

Lanhydrock House (NT).
Cornwall's grandest house. C17 but largely rebuilt after fire in 1881. Superb Victorian kitchens, magnificent plaster ceilings depicting scenes from the Old Testament, and a Long Gallery 116 feet long. C17 Gatehouse. Fine shrub and formal gardens. Woodland walks. Restaurants. Shop. Open daily 18 Mar-31 Oct except M when House only closed, but open BH Ms 11-5.30 (-5 in Oct), Gardens open all year 10-6. (H7)

Old Mill Herbary.
5 acre semi-wild garden by the River Camel. C14 Hellandbridge, mature woodland, island walks, 1.75 acre Arboretum, mill leat, bog garden, camomile lawn around unabashed fertility theme. Unique botanical & historical interest. A tranquil oasis. (now Site of Special Scientific Interest & Special Area of Conservation status). Open daily Apr-Sept except W, 10-5. T 01208 841206. (G3)

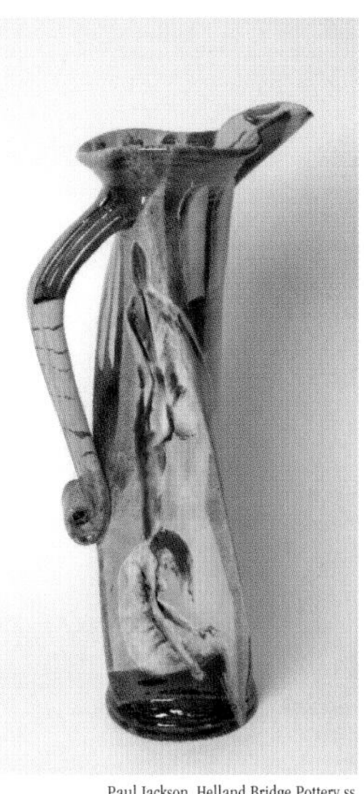

Paul Jackson, Helland Bridge Pottery ss

Pencarrow House.
Georgian house set in extensive grounds. Fine collection of pictures, furniture and porcelain. Cafe, craft centre, plant shop and children's play area. Open daily from Apr-Oct except F & Sa 1.30-5.30, BHM's and June-Aug from 11am. (F4)

Roche Rock.
C15 chapel/hermitage perched on top of rocks. (C9)

For Dramatic Scenery, Family Holidays, Gastronomic Delights and Surf Beaches...

The coastal footpath that runs along the North Coast must be one of the natural wonders of Britain. At times, wild and remote, and hard going in places, it affords spectacular views and rewards you with sheltered harbours where you can sample local fayre and fine ales. When the Equinoxes arrive you can, in places, walk the golden sands and admire the Atlantic waves that have rolled in untouched for 3,000 miles.

The North Coast is a fabulous playground for family holidays. Accomodation is available in many forms; camp sites, holiday cottages, farmhouses, gastronomic B & Bs and hotels. And whether you seek the surfing camaraderie of Bude or the quieter villages of the far north, the gastronomic pleasures and indulgences of Padstow, to the frenetic pace of Newquay, or the more soulful, arty atmosphere of St Agnes. Cornwall now has a wealth of sophisticated hostelries offering superb food and luxury accommodation, And yet, it still has the surf hostel, too. So much choice.

Inland are small farms and hamlets, the villages increase with size as you move south, as they get nearer to the towns of Bodmin, Truro and Falmouth. In the Camborne-Redruth area there is much to interest the industrial archaeologist, and perhaps the most spectacularly located engine house is to be found at Wheal Coates, north of Chapel Porth.

This stretch of Cornwall has long held a special hold on many families who return year after year for their annual holiday. It is not uncommon to see three generations of the same family enjoying the calm waters of Daymer Bay or Trevone until their offspring progress to the surf schools of Polzeath, and the rips of Booby and Constantine Bays.

In recent years extreme sports from surfing to kite-boarding has exploded onto the scene. Surfing is no longer a niche sport. It has become more than a life-style trend. It is now an everyday sport available to all through the many surf and life-saving schools, and because of the access to protective wet suits and learner boards. Our guide will direct you to the best beaches. The locals have a saying in Newquay: "Arrive with a bucket and spade….and leave with a surfboard!" So give it a go and search for the Perfect Wave.

Watergate Bay

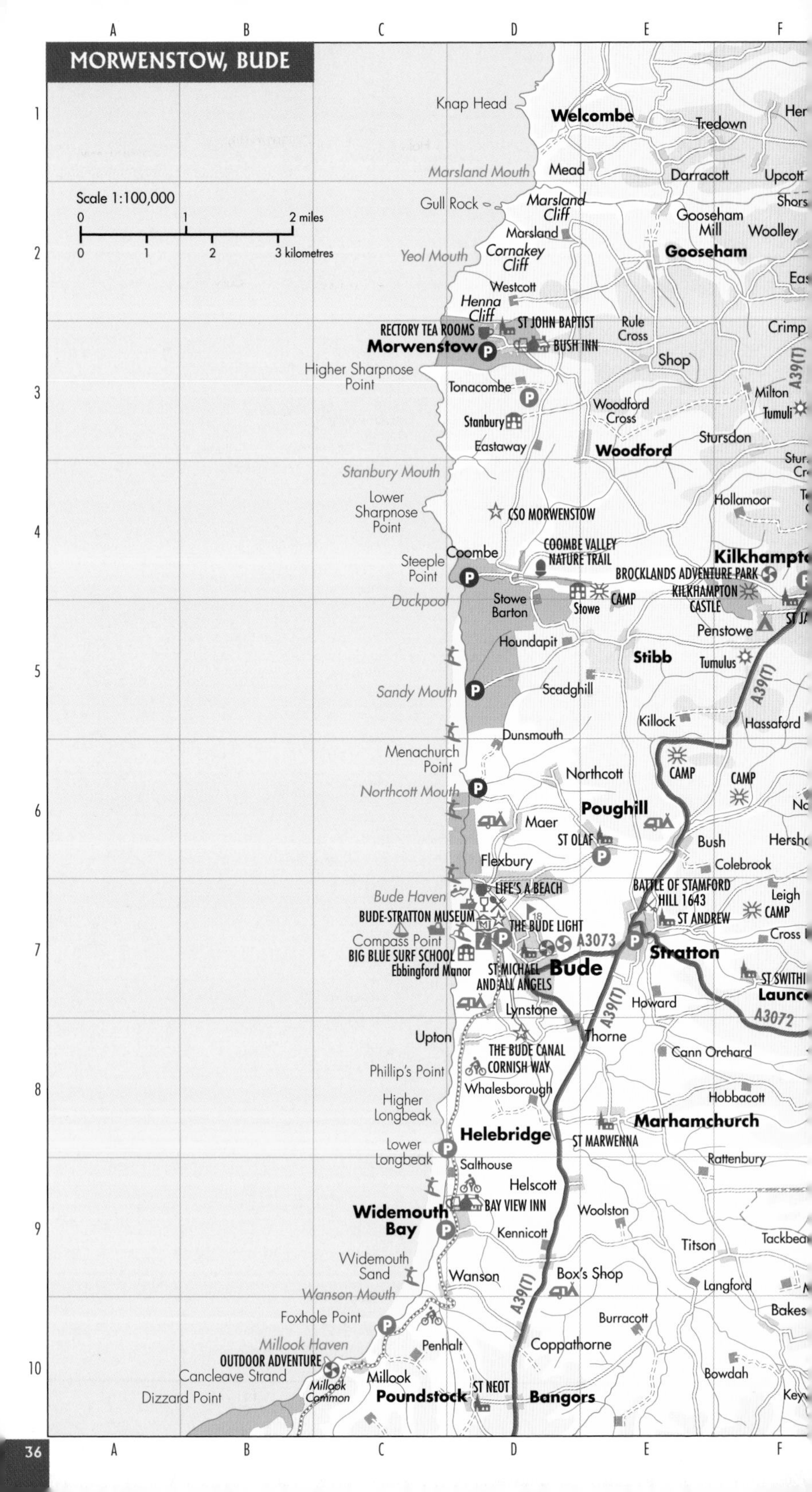
MORWENSTOW, BUDE
Scale 1:100,000
0
1
2 miles
0
1
2
3 kilometres
Knap Head
Welcombe
Tredown
Marsland Mouth
Mead
Darracott
Upcott
Gull Rock
Marsland Cliff
Marsland
Gooseham Mill
Woolley
Yeol Mouth
Cornakey Cliff
Gooseham
Westcott
Henna Cliff
RECTORY TEA ROOMS
ST JOHN BAPTIST
Rule Cross
Crimp
Morwenstow
BUSH INN
Shop
Higher Sharpnose Point
A39(T)
Tonacombe
Milton
Tumuli
Woodford Cross
Stanbury
Stursdon
Eastaway
Woodford
Stanbury Mouth
Lower Sharpnose Point
Hollamoor
CSO MORWENSTOW
Coombe
COOMBE VALLEY NATURE TRAIL
Steeple Point
BROCKLANDS ADVENTURE PARK
Duckpool
Stowe Barton
Stowe
CAMP
KILKHAMPTON CASTLE
Penstowe
Houndapit
Stibb
Tumulus
Sandy Mouth
Scadghill
Killock
Hassaford
Dunsmouth
Menachurch Point
CAMP
CAMP
Northcott
Northcott Mouth
Poughill
Maer
ST OLAF
Bush
Flexbury
Colebrook
LIFE'S A BEACH
BATTLE OF STAMFORD HILL 1643
Leigh
Bude Haven
BUDE-STRATTON MUSEUM
ST ANDREW
CAMP
THE BUDE LIGHT
Compass Point
A3073
Stratton
BIG BLUE SURF SCHOOL
Ebbingford Manor
ST MICHAEL AND ALL ANGELS
Bude
Howard
Lynstone
A3072
Upton
Thorne
THE BUDE CANAL
Cann Orchard
CORNISH WAY
Phillip's Point
Whalesborough
Hobbacott
Higher Longbeak
Marhamchurch
Helebridge
ST MARWENNA
Lower Longbeak
Salthouse
Rattenbury
Helscott
BAY VIEW INN
Widemouth Bay
Woolston
Kennicott
Titson
Widemouth Sand
Wanson
Box's Shop
Wanson Mouth
Langford
Foxhole Point
Burracott
Millook Haven
Penhalt
Coppathorne
OUTDOOR ADVENTURE
Cancleave Strand
Millook
Bowdah
Dizzard Point
Millook Common
Poundstock
ST NEOT
Bangors

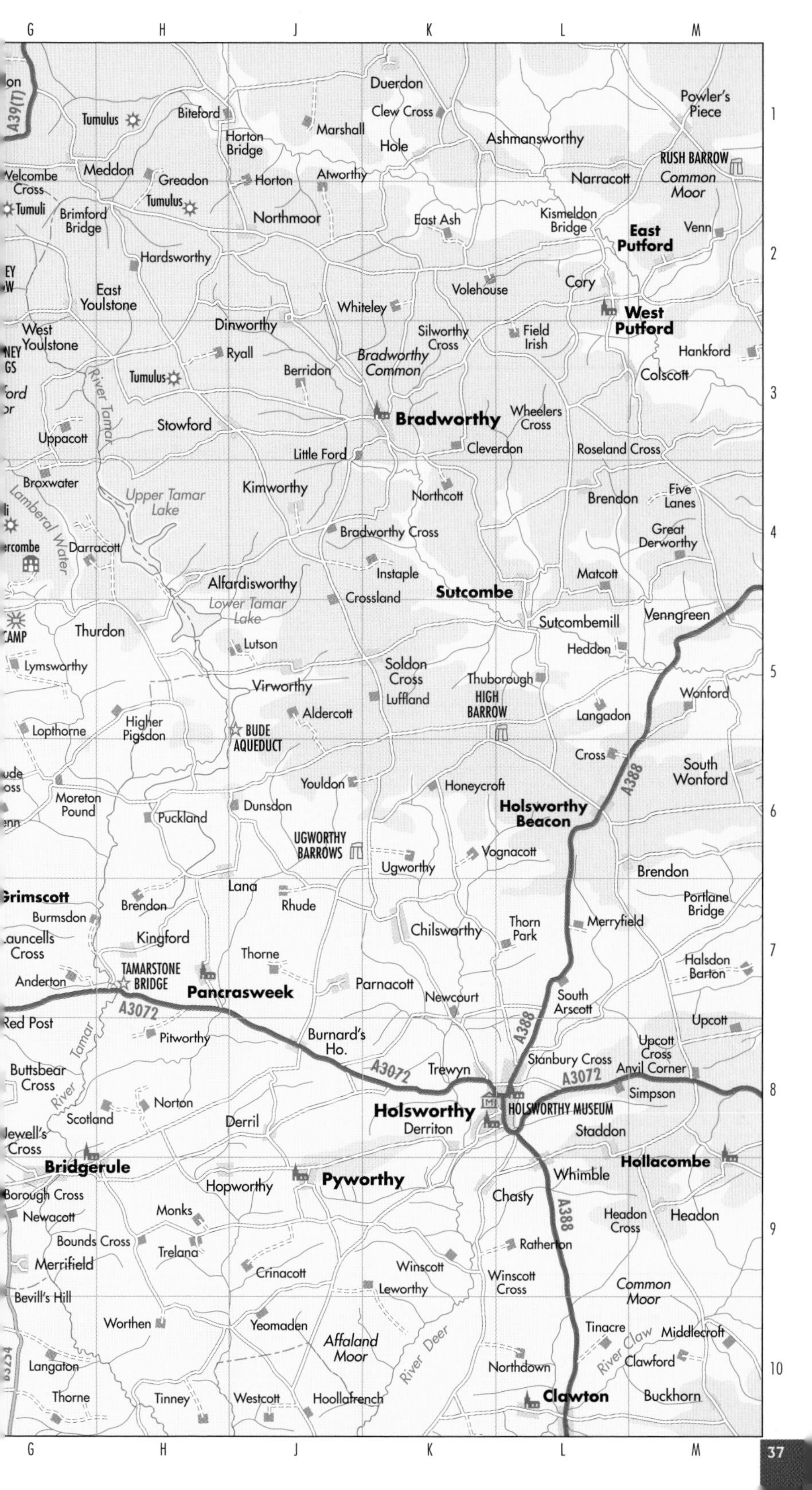

G
H
J
K
L
M
1
2
3
4
5
6
7
8
9
10
A39(T)
Duerdon
Clew Cross
Powler's Piece
Tumulus
Biteford
Marshall
Horton Bridge
Hole
Ashmansworthy
RUSH BARROW
Welcombe Cross
Meddon
Greadon
Horton
Atworthy
Narracott
Common Moor
Tumuli
Tumulus
Brimford Bridge
Northmoor
East Ash
Kismeldon Bridge
East Putford
Venn
Hardsworthy
East Youlstone
Volehouse
Cory
Whiteley
West Putford
West Youlstone
Dinworthy
Silworthy Cross
Field Irish
Hankford
Ryall
Bradworthy Common
Berridon
Colscott
Tumulus
River Tamar
Stowford
Bradworthy
Wheelers Cross
Uppacott
Little Ford
Cleverdon
Roseland Cross
Broxwater
Upper Tamar Lake
Kimworthy
Northcott
Brendon
Five Lanes
Lamberal Water
Bradworthy Cross
Great Derworthy
Darracott
Instaple
Matcott
Alfardisworthy
Crossland
Sutcombe
Lower Tamar Lake
Venngreen
Thurdon
Sutcombemill
Lutson
Heddon
Lymsworthy
Soldon Cross
Virworthy
Thuborough
Luffland
HIGH BARROW
Wonford
Aldercott
Langadon
Lopthorne
Higher Pigsdon
BUDE AQUEDUCT
Cross
South Wonford
A388
Youldon
Honeycroft
Moreton Pound
Dunsdon
Holsworthy Beacon
Puckland
UGWORTHY BARROWS
Vognacott
Ugworthy
Brendon
Grimscott
Lana
Brendon
Rhude
Portlane Bridge
Burmsdon
Merryfield
Launcells Cross
Kingford
Chilsworthy
Thorn Park
Thorne
Halsdon Barton
TAMARSTONE BRIDGE
Anderton
Parnacott
Pancrasweek
Newcourt
South Arscott
A3072
Red Post
Upcott
River Tamar
Pitworthy
Burnard's Ho.
Upcott Cross
Stanbury Cross
A388
Buttsbear Cross
A3072
Trewyn
A3072
Anvil Corner
Simpson
Norton
Holsworthy
HOLSWORTHY MUSEUM
Scotland
Derril
Jewell's Cross
Derriton
Staddon
Bridgerule
Hollacombe
Pyworthy
Whimble
Hopworthy
Chasty
Borough Cross
Monks
Newacott
Headon Cross
Headon
A388
Bounds Cross
Trelana
Ratherton
Merrifield
Winscott
Crinacott
Winscott Cross
Leworthy
Common Moor
Bevill's Hill
Worthen
Yeomaden
Tinacre
Affaland Moor
Middlecroft
River Claw
River Deer
Clawford
Langaton
Northdown
Thorne
Tinney
Westcott
Hoollafrench
Clawton
Buckhorn
G
H
J
K
L
M

Outdoor Adventure ss

BUDE

Seaside resort developed by the Victorians. Long extensive beaches, 3 miles of sand at low tide and popular surfing centre. Coastline has been scene of many shipwrecks - 80 ships wrecked between 1824 - 74. Canal*, carnival and fete - August (third week). 'Blessing of the Sea' - Aug. E/C Th. (D7)

Old Canal. Built in 1819-26 at a length of 43 miles (61km). For 60 years used to transport coal and lime inland, and to export grain and slate. Killed off by other railways. Best sections are at Marhamchurch, Hobbacott Down and Werrington. (D8)

Where to Eat, Drink & Be Merry...

Life's A Beach, Summerleaze Beach. Bistro restaurant offers all types of food from locally caught Bass to burgers and pizzas. A fantastic spot to watch the sunset, and to relax after a day's surf. Open daily in season. (D7)

The Bay View Inn, Marine Drive. Surfer's hangout overlooking the roaring Atlantic. Currently being refurbished with chic, modern bedrooms. Wholesome tasty menu using local farms for hungry surfers. T 01288 361273. (D9)

Places to Visit...

Brocklands Adventure Park. Supakarts, bumper boats and lots more. Fun for all the family. Open daily, 10-5, 6 at peak times. (F4)

Stratton Museum. History of Bude Canal, shipwrecks, lifeboats and railways. Bude 'Heritage Trail'. Open daily Good F-Sept & Th & Su in Oct 11-5. (D7)

Killarney Springs. Family fun park; twin twisters, drop slides, bumper boats, playgrounds, and more. Open daily Apr-Oct 10-6, & W/Es, school hols Nov-East 11-4 (G3)

Combe Valley Nature Trail. Starts at Combe Cottages to follow a green and peaceful wooded valley, rich in oak woods, honeysuckle and birdlife - buzzards, woodpeckers, dippers. Nearby Stowe Barton, home Sir Richard Grenville, County Sheriff of Cornwall in 1577 who was immortalised in Tennyson's poem 'The Revenge'. (D4)

Tamar Lake Wildlife Refuge. Fisherman's paradise, trout and coarse, boats for hire. (H4)

Churches of Interest...

Kilkhampton Church. Norman S. doorway with superb collection of bench ends. Grenville tombs. (F4)

Launcells Church. Fortunate to be the only Cornish church not tampered with by the Victorians. Wall painting and 60 carved bench ends. (E7)

Poughill Church. Bench ends and large wall painting of St Christopher. (E6)

MORWENSTOW

Famous for Richard Stephen Hawker (1803-75; the eccentric and original vicar-poet, and originator of harvest festivals. A compassionate man, he would stalk the wild coast in beaver hat, fisherman's long boots and yellow cloak in search of shipwrecked sailors. Many are buried in his churchyard. And to stir his congregation he would dress as a mermaid. Hawker's Hut, made of driftwood, on edge of cliffs. Rectory Tea Rooms, opposite Bush Inn and churchyard. (D3)

St John The Baptist,
Impressive Norman doorway, wagon roof and wall paintings. In superb lonely location overlooking the Atlantic Ocean. (D3)

STRATTON

A pretty village, now a suburb of Bude with a long and fascinating history. C15 church. Battle of Stamford Hill 1643. (E7)

Xtreme Sports...

Big Blue Surf School, Summerleaze Beach. Learn, improve, excel at one of Europe's top schools with National Team coach Jon Price. Open Apr-Oct. T 01288 331764. (D7)

Outdoor Adventure, Atlantic Court. Activity centre for the ultimate coastal experience; coasteering, surfing, coastal traversing, sea cliff abseils, rock climbing, sea kayaking. Activity Weekends. Accomodation. Tuition. T 01288 362900. (C10)

Coastal Footpath

Marsland Mouth To Millook Haven (Crackington Haven): Approx. 28 miles. A remote and wild coastline; the rocks, razor sharp and contorted, the pathway hard going, yet exhilarating and rewarding. Rest at Morwenstow* and visit the church* and tea room or Inn. Onwards passing Parson Hawker's Hut and two miles on the white satellite dish aerials of the Composite Signals Organisation at Cleave Camp, then into Duckpool* where a path leads up to the Coombe Valley Nature Trail*. At low tide one can follow the sands to Bude, or take the clifftop path. Ascend to Compass Point for extensive views northwards. The path overlooks reefs, buttresses and pinnacles. Easy going to Widemouth Sands*. Through car park, up Penhalt Cliff to Millook Haven with cliffs of contorted slate. Rough ascent to Dizzard Point (500ft), prone to landsliding, onto veined and contorted rock forms of Pencannow Point. Easy descent to the fine sands of Crackington Haven.

Sandy Mouth

Beaches

Welcombe Mouth. Haunt of cruel Coppinger, an C18 smuggler. Pebbles, rocks and sandy beaches at LT. (D1)

Stanbury Mouth. 15 mins walk from P to isolated beach, sand, swift currents, HZ at LT. (C4)

Duckpool. Rocky with strong currents. Footpath leads to Coombe Valley Nature Trail. P. Surfing – LT R breaks off the rocks. (C4)

Sandy Mouth. Expansive beach, rocky at HT, swift currents, HZ at LT, Bass fishing, P/cafe. Surfing - Clean with good beach breaks. Fine, small swell off banks. Beware rip tides. (C5)

Northcott Mouth. Extensive sand, pebbles and rocks. Bathing HZ two hours either side of LT. P. Surfing - Banks at LT create heavy hollow waves backing off at HT except on big swells. Good R hander at N side. Beware rip tides. (D6)

Bude - Crooklets Beach. - Spacious firm sands at LT, bathing HZ at LT. S-B hire, cafe, LG. Surfing - Fine, short breaks for body boarders. With hollow sandbanks waves flow at all stages of tide. At HT Tower Rock produces a good shallow wave. Try Wrangles Rocks to N at LT. (D7)

Millook Haven. Secluded cove, shelves steeply - HZ bathing. (C10)

Bude - Middle Beach. Surfing - Good Ls and Rs with swells up to 6ft. Popular with locals. (D7)

Bude - Summerleaze Beach. Popular surfing beach, roomy firm sands and bathing pool at LT. S-B hire. Access. Surfing - HT sheltered from SW wind. R breaks into harbour. Take-oo can be steep. Beware strong rips. Ls at LT. Hollow fast wave off The Barrels. (D7)

Bude - Upton. Surfing - Good Rs and Ls on the N and S side. Difficult access down cliff. (D8)

Widemouth Sand. Large sandy beach, rock pools, HZ at LT. Tent and S-B hire/WC/P/cafe. Surfing - A popular break for all abilities, at all stages of the tide. Best up to 6ft. (C9)

Aerial View of Bude

Widemouth Bay

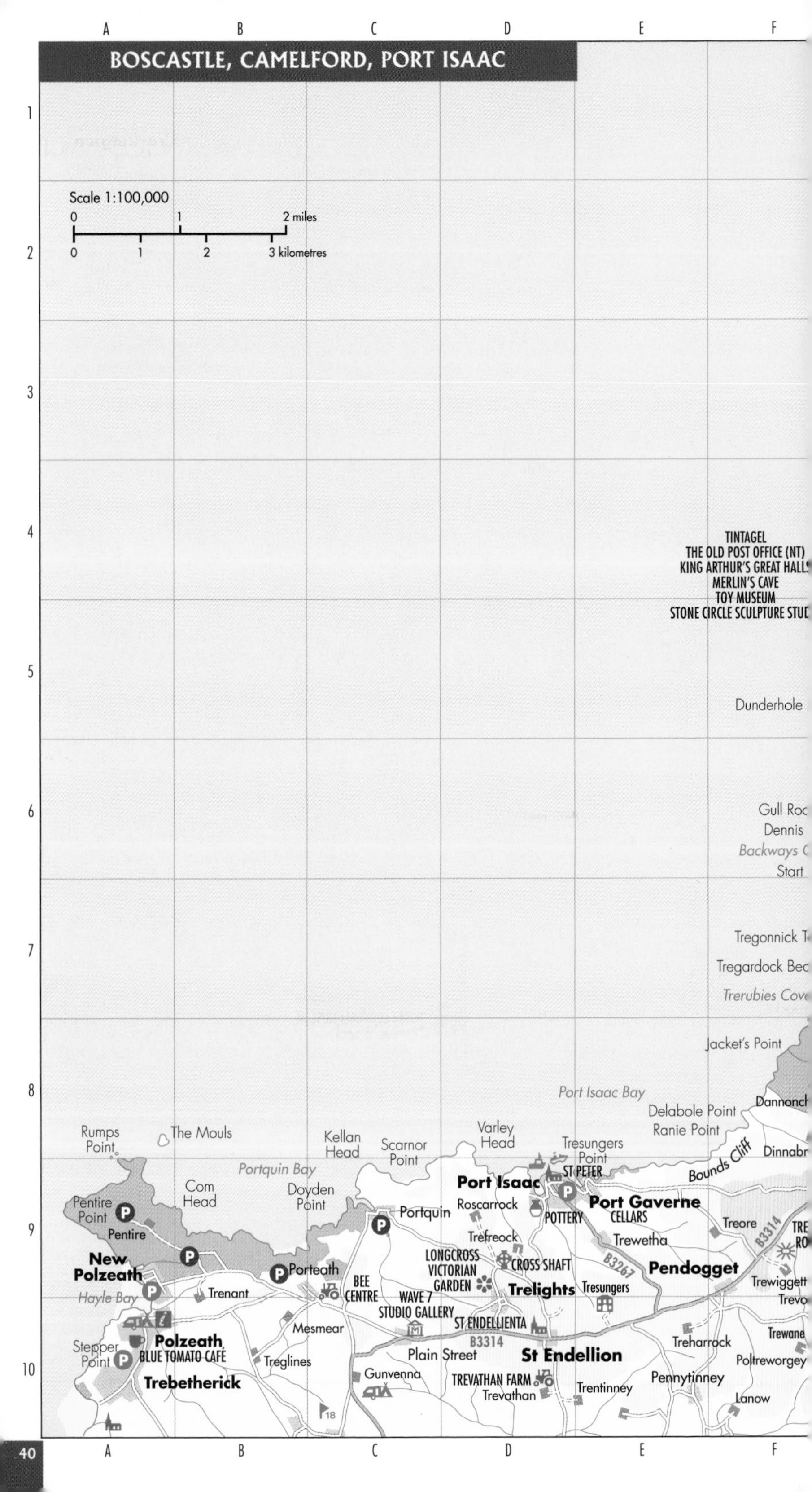
Scale 1:100,000
2 miles
3 kilometres
TINTAGEL
THE OLD POST OFFICE (NT)
MERLIN'S CAVE
TOY MUSEUM
Dunderhole
Dennis
Start
Jacket's Point
Port Isaac Bay
Delabole Point
Ranie Point
Rumps Point
The Mouls
Kellan Head
Scarnor Point
Varley Head
Tresungers Point
Portquin Bay
Bounds Cliff
Com Head
Doyden Point
Port Isaac
ST PETER
Port Gaverne
CELLARS
Pentire Point
Pentire
Portquin
Roscarrock
POTTERY
Treore
Trefreock
Trewetha
New Polzeath
LONGCROSS VICTORIAN GARDEN
CROSS SHAFT
B3267
Pendogget
Porteath
Trelights
Tresungers
Hayle Bay
Trenant
BEE CENTRE
WAVE 7 STUDIO GALLERY
Mesmear
ST ENDELLIENTA
Polzeath
BLUE TOMATO CAFÉ
B3314
Stepper Point
Treglines
Plain Street
St Endellion
Treharrock
Gunvenna
TREVATHAN FARM
Trevathan
Trentinney
Pennytinney
Trebetherick
Lanow

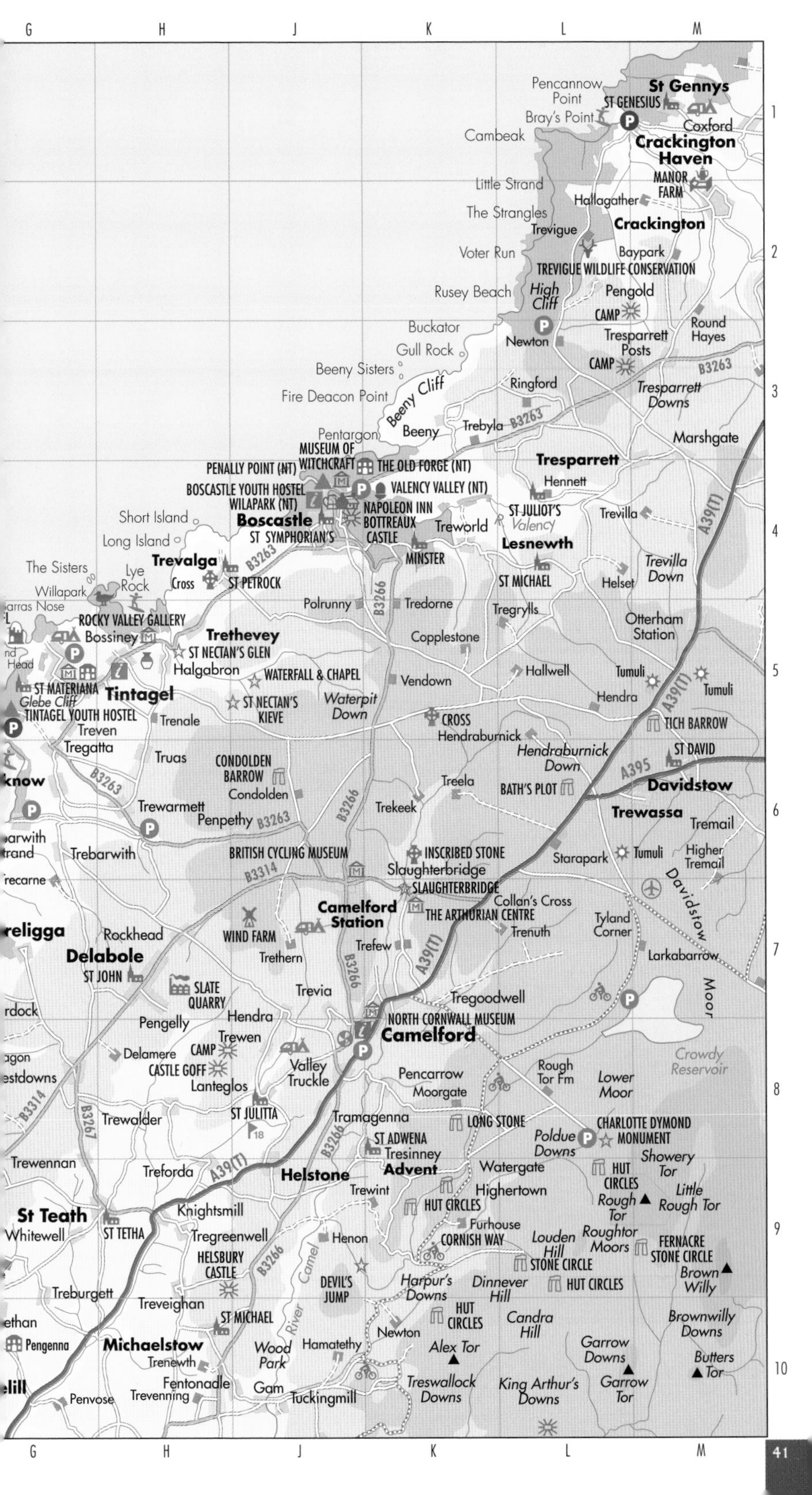

G
H
J
K
L
M
St Gennys
Pencannow Point
ST GENESIUS
Bray's Point
Coxford
Cambeak
Crackington Haven
MANOR FARM
Little Strand
The Strangles
Hallagather
Trevigue
Crackington
Voter Run
Baypark
TREVIGUE WILDLIFE CONSERVATION
Rusey Beach
High Cliff
Pengold
CAMP
Buckator
Newton
Tresparrett Posts
Round Hayes
Gull Rock
Beeny Sisters
CAMP
B3263
Ringford
Beeny Cliff
Tresparrett Downs
Fire Deacon Point
Beeny
Trebyla
B3263
Marshgate
Pentargon
MUSEUM OF WITCHCRAFT
PENALLY POINT (NT)
THE OLD FORGE (NT)
Tresparrett
BOSCASTLE YOUTH HOSTEL
VALENCY VALLEY (NT)
Hennett
WILAPARK (NT)
NAPOLEON INN
ST JULIOT'S
Short Island
Boscastle
BOTTREAUX CASTLE
Treworld
Valency
Trevilla
A39(T)
ST SYMPHORIAN'S
Long Island
Lesnewth
Trevalga
B3263
MINSTER
Trevilla Down
The Sisters
Lye Rock
Cross
ST PETROCK
ST MICHAEL
Helset
Willapark
B3266
Tredorne
Polrunny
Tregrylls
Otterham Station
ROCKY VALLEY GALLERY
Bossiney
Trethevey
Copplestone
ST NECTAN'S GLEN
Halgabron
Hallwell
Tumuli
WATERFALL & CHAPEL
Vendown
Tumuli
ST MATERIANA
Tintagel
Hendra
Glebe Cliff
ST NECTAN'S KIEVE
Waterpit Down
A39(T)
TINTAGEL YOUTH HOSTEL
Trenale
CROSS
TICH BARROW
Treven
Hendraburnick
Tregatta
Hendraburnick Down
ST DAVID
Truas
CONDOLDEN BARROW
A395
Treela
BATH'S PLOT
Davidstow
B3263
Condolden
Trekeek
Trewarmett
B3266
Trewassa
Penpethy
B3263
Tremail
BRITISH CYCLING MUSEUM
INSCRIBED STONE
Higher Tremail
Trebarwith
Starapark
Tumuli
B3314
Slaughterbridge
Davidstow
SLAUGHTERBRIDGE
Collan's Cross
Camelford Station
THE ARTHURIAN CENTRE
Tyland Corner
Rockhead
WIND FARM
Trenuth
Delabole
Trefew
Larkabarrow
Trethern
A39(T)
ST JOHN
B3266
Moor
SLATE QUARRY
Trevia
Tregoodwell
Hendra
NORTH CORNWALL MUSEUM
Pengelly
Camelford
Trewen
CAMP
Delamere
Valley Truckle
Crowdy Reservoir
CASTLE GOFF
Rough Tor Fm
Pencarrow
Lanteglos
Lower Moor
Moorgate
B3314
B3267
Trewalder
ST JULITTA
Tramagenna
LONG STONE
CHARLOTTE DYMOND MONUMENT
ST ADWENA
Poldue Downs
B3266
Tresinney
Showery Tor
Trewennan
Treforda
A39(T)
Helstone
Advent
Watergate
HUT CIRCLES
Trewint
Highertown
Little Rough Tor
Rough Tor
St Teath
Knightsmill
HUT CIRCLES
Furhouse
Whitewell
ST TETHA
Tregreenwell
Henon
CORNISH WAY
Louden Hill
Roughtor Moors
FERNACRE STONE CIRCLE
HELSBURY CASTLE
B3266
STONE CIRCLE
Camel
Brown Willy
DEVIL'S JUMP
Harpur's Downs
Dinnever Hill
HUT CIRCLES
Treburgett
Treveighan
River
HUT CIRCLES
Candra Hill
Brownwilly Downs
ST MICHAEL
Newton
Pengenna
Michaelstow
Hamatethy
Alex Tor
Garrow Downs
Wood Park
Butters Tor
Trenewth
Fentonadle
Gam
Treswallock Downs
King Arthur's Downs
Garrow Tor
Penvose
Trevenning
Tuckingmill
1
2
3
4
5
6
7
8
9
10

Boscastle Harbour

Port Isaac

BOSCASTLE

Pretty village in steep valley leading to sinouos and dramatic harbour, a safe haven on a treacherous coastline, but very difficult to navigate into.

Witchcraft Museum, Valency Valley, NT shop/Visitor Centre. (J4)

The Old Forge (NT). A NT shop and Information Centre housed in an old Blacksmith's forge. Open daily mid Mar to Oct 10-5. (J4)

Museum Of Witchcraft. Long established Museum holds the world's largest collection of genuine witchcraft related artifacts. Open daily East to Halloween, 10.30-6, 11:30-6 on Sun. (J4)

Where to Eat, Drink & Be Merry...

Napoleon,
High St. Full range of beers feeding three beer gardens and two bars; public and officers. Boney's Bistro serves fresh fish and homemade soups and puddings. Children (restaurant) and dogs welcome. B & B. T 01840 250204. (K4)

TINTAGEL

A popular destination associated with Arthurian legend, as inspired by Geoffrey of Monmouth in the C12, and later by Tennyson's 'The Idylls of the King'. Enhanced by the wild and rugged coast, King Arthur's mythological past lives on. Tintagel Castle (EH). Old Post Office (NT); medieval yeoman's house. King Arthur's Great Exhibition Hall. Summer Carnival. (G5)

The Old Post Office, Tintagel jh/nt

King Arthur's Great Hall & Hall Of Chivalry.
A magnificent hall built in memory of King Arthur and his Knights, using 50 types of Cornish stone and 70 stained glass windows. The Arthurian Experience tells the story of Arthur and his Knights. Dogs welcomed. Open daily; summer 10-5, winter 11-dusk. (G5)

Merlins Cave. Crystal mineral, fossil shop and museum. Open daily 10.30-5.30. (G5)

The Old Post Office (NT).
A miniature C14 manor house used in the C19 as a post office. Open daily mid Mar to Oct 11-5.30 (4 in Oct). (G5)

Stone Circle Sculpture Studio, Fore St. Working studio and gallery of Sonjia Tremain whose work reflects archaeology and shamanism. Open daily 10-5. (G5)

Tintagel Castle (EH). An early Celtic settlement 350-800 AD, later developed into an island fortress by the Earls of Cornwall in C12 and C13s. Fragments of the great hall c.1250, the gate and walls survive. The wild and windswept coast married with the romantic legends of King Arthur and encouraged by Geoffrey of Monmouth and Tennyson's Idyll (although doubted by scholars) provide an atmosphere of mystery and wonder. Open as English Heritage times. (G5)

Toy Museum, Fore St. Step back in time through three generations of toys. Over 1,000 exhibits. Collectors shop. Open daily 10-5. (G5)

Special Places to Visit...

The Arthurian Centre.
Site of Arthurian legend and folk lore. Exhibition centre, woodland and river walks, tea room and gift/bookshop. Play area. Open daily. (K7)

Slate Quarry. 1 1/2 mile circumference at depth of 500ft, 375 million years of geological history. Worked continuously since the C16, and possibly by the Romans. Viewing platform and showroom open M-F 8-4.30. (H7)

Rocky Valley Gallery. Displays work inspired by Cornwall's coast and countryside. Rocky Valley is an exquisite place (SSSI) and a footpath leads to cascading waterfalls and unusual rock formations. (H5)

Slaughter Bridge. Possible burial place of King Arthur. A granite slab marks the grave. (K7)

St Nectan's Glen. C5 hermitage of St Nectan. St Nectan's Kieve (60ft) Waterfall and Hermitage Tea Gardens. One of Cornwall's most sacred sites, and a place of beauty and tranquility. Open daily East-Oct. (H5)

Valency Valley (NT). Two-hour walk up dreamlike valley through woodland to St Juliot's Church where Thomas Hardy met his first wife Emma Gifford, the vicar's sister. (K4)

Ancient Cornwall

Tregeare Rounds. 500ft diameter banks and ditches used as cattle enclosure. Strategically unsound. (F9)

CAMELFORD

Attractive main square with some fine buildings. Worth stopping here if you've been held up on the A39. Free parking. Leisure Centre. Fine Museum & Gallery. (K8)

British Cycling Museum, The Old Station. Cycling from 1818 with over 400 machines. Open all year Su-Th 10-5. (J6)

North Cornwall Museum & Gallery, The Clease. Award-winning museum of rural life, 50-100 years ago. Owner a mine of local knowledge. Holds regular exhibitions of contemporary art. TIC. Open Apr-Sept 10-5 M-Sa. T 01840 212954. (K8)

PORT ISAAC

A charming north coast fishing inlet and old port; a steep street runs down to beach and harbour, hazardous when a northerly wind blows. Lobster fishing centre. Trips for mackerel, pleasant inns and parking on beach at LT. Fresh fish for sale. Pottery. Restaurants. St Endellion Music Festival - Aug. (D9)

Port Isaac Pottery. Individual one-off stoneware pots influenced by the sea and Cornish landscape. Seascape paintings by Barbara Hawkins. Open daily East-Oct 10-4. (D9)

The Edge, 6 New Road. Bar and restaurant overlooking the sea. Art displayed. Local fish and meats. Lunches and teas. T 01208 880090. (D9)

PORT QUIN

A hamlet with few cottages on an inlet, pebble beach and C19 folly, Doyden Castle (NT). Invigorating clifftop walks. (C9)

Portgaverne. C19 pilchard fishing centre and exporter of Delabole slate. Remains of large pilchard cellars. (E9)

Churches of Interest

Advent Church. Rare 8 pinnacled tower in lonely moorland setting. (K9)

Trebarwith Strand

Crackington Haven Church. Dedicated to Celtic missionary St Gennys. (M1)

Lanteglos-By-Camelford Church. In picturesque valley, mush restored, C10 Saxon pillars and 4 Celtic crosses. (J8)

Michaelstow Church. Original wagon roof. (H10)

Minster Church. Overlooks wooded valley and sea. (K4)

St Endellion Church. Solitary hill-top position enabled it to avoid the Reformation. Norman font. Famous music festival. (D10)

Tintagel Church. Norman origins in isolated cliff-top position. Sailors' graves. (G5)

Coastal Path

Crackington Haven to Port Isaac: Approx. 32 miles. Hard going up to Cambeak - views from Hartland Point to Trevose Head. Climbing beside further land slipped sections, passing jagged cliffs and The Strangles (beach), scene of many shipwrecks, to High Cliff, at 731ft the highest cliff in Cornwall (although slumping has created a massive sloping undercliff so it lacks the drama of a precipice) and supposedly a favourite courting and riding spot for Thomas Hardy and his first wife Emma Gifford. Then to Beeny Cliff, the only headland carved from Chert, a tough black flint-like rock, and often below, basking seals. Along to Pentaragon Waterfall which falls 100ft down a deep chasm. And, then to Boscastle Harbour* for refreshments, via Penally Point, and the tortuous harbour entrance. The cliff walk to Tintagel along springy turf with spectacular views seaward to jagged rocks is quite superb. Worth a diversion inland to visit Rocky Valley, and St Nectan's Kieve*, a 40 ft waterfall, and ancient hermitage. Return to the coast path; offshore Lye Rock was a renowned a puffin colony; now the cliffs are nesting sites for fulmars, guillemots, razorbills and shags. The landscape is wild and remote, a place of legends, and the romantic setting for the C13 Tintagel Castle* and the mass of older remains on Tintagel Island. On leaving the castle ruins, the path climbs sharply to the cliff top church of St Materiana, guardian of many shipwrecked sailors. Along Glebe Cliff past numerous old slate quarries to Trebarwith Strand*, a lovely beach to freshen up before the switchback path to Port Isaac*.

Beaches & Surfing

Crackington Haven. Popular bathing beach, sands and rocks. HZ at LT. S-B hire/WC/cafes. Surfing - Sheltered from N winds. Holds big swells. Good waves break off at HT. (L1)

The Strangles. Steep descent down 700ft cliffs. Rocks, sand at LT, swift currents; bathing very HZ. (L2)

Rusey Beach. P near Newton Farm, steep descent, sand at LT, very HZ bathing. (L2)

Bossinney Haven. P in village, steep 1/2 mile descent to little coves below huge cliffs. Popular surfing. (G5)

Trebarwith Strand. Popular family beach. S-B hire/WC/P/Cafe. Surfing - Beach submerged at HT. Average breaks with consistent waves. S end good Ls, and is protected from N winds. (G6)

Portgaverne. Sandy beach, pebbles - good bathing, access and cafe. (E9)

Port Quin. Tiny stony beach, rock pools for prawning. P. (C9)

Lundy Bay. 1/4 mile from road P. Smoothe rocks and shelving sand. HZ of incoming tide. Surfing - Quiet, big swells. Strong SW winds blow out breaks. (B9)

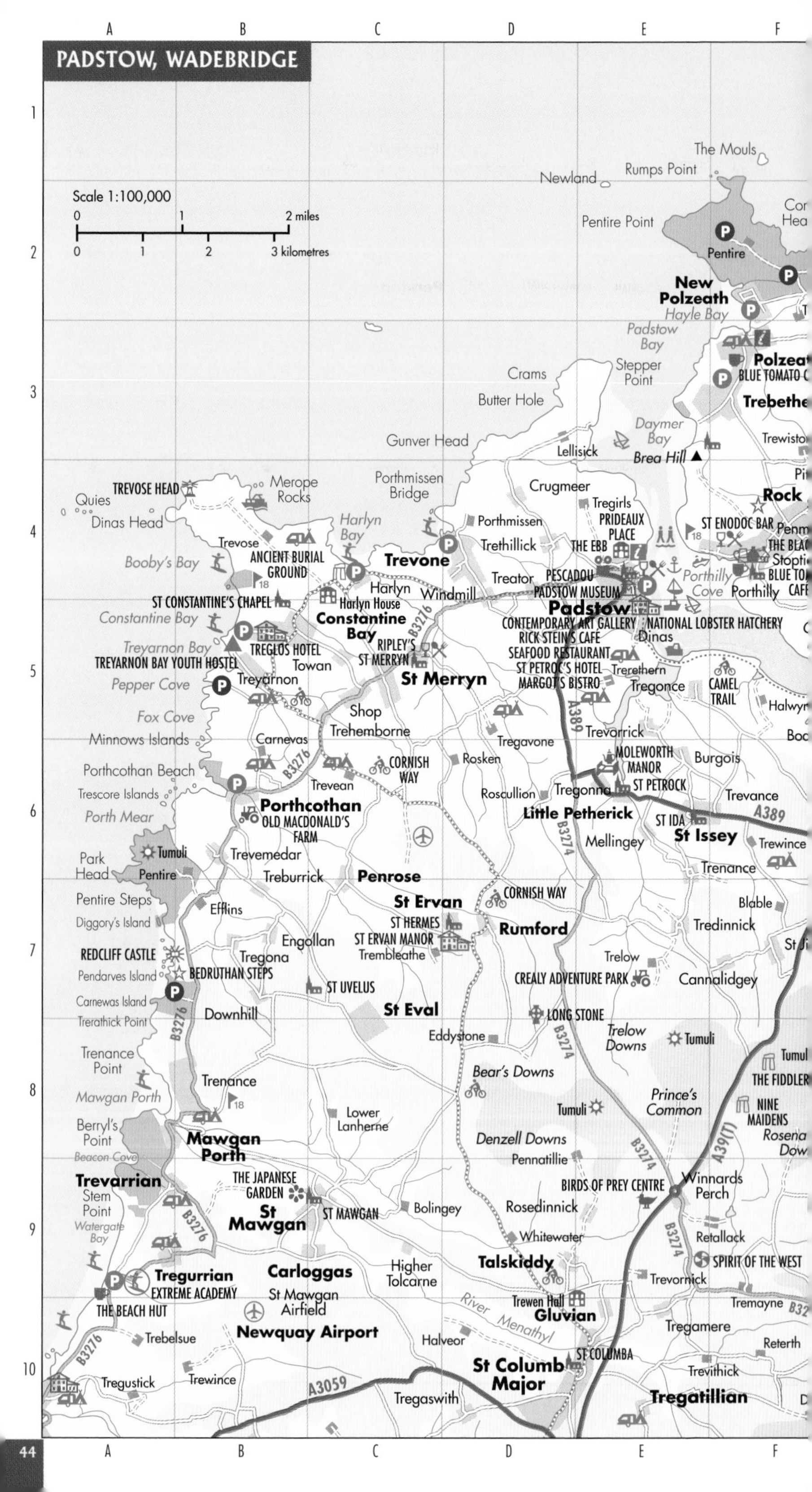

PADSTOW, WADEBRIDGE
Scale 1:100,000
2 miles
3 kilometres
The Mouls
Rumps Point
Newland
Pentire Point
Pentire
New Polzeath
Hayle Bay
Padstow Bay
Stepper Point
Crams
Butter Hole
Daymer Bay
Brea Hill
Gunver Head
Lellisick
Porthmissen Bridge
Crugmeer
Tregirls
TREVOSE HEAD
Merope Rocks
Quies
Dinas Head
Harlyn Bay
Porthmissen
PRIDEAUX PLACE
Trevose
Trethillick
THE EBB
ST ENODOC BAR
Rock
Booby's Bay
ANCIENT BURIAL GROUND
Trevone
Treator
PESCADOU
Porthilly Cove
Porthilly
Harlyn
Windmill
PADSTOW MUSEUM
ST CONSTANTINE'S CHAPEL
Harlyn House
Padstow
Constantine Bay
Constantine Bay
B3276
CONTEMPORARY ART GALLERY
NATIONAL LOBSTER HATCHERY
Treyarnon Bay
TREGLOS HOTEL
RIPLEY'S
RICK STEIN'S CAFE
Dinas
ST MERRYN
SEAFOOD RESTAURANT
TREYARNON BAY YOUTH HOSTEL
Towan
ST PETROC'S HOTEL
Trerethern
Pepper Cove
Treyarnon
St Merryn
MARGOT'S BISTRO
Tregonce
CAMEL TRAIL
Shop
A389
Fox Cove
Trehemborne
Trevorrick
Minnows Islands
Carnevas
Tregavone
CORNISH WAY
MOLEWORTH MANOR
Burgois
Rosken
Porthcothan Beach
Trevean
Roscullion
Tregonna
ST PETROCK
Trevance
Trescore Islands
Porthcothan
Little Petherick
ST IDA
St Issey
A389
Porth Mear
OLD MACDONALD'S FARM
B3274
Mellingey
Trewince
Park Head
Tumuli
Trevemedar
Trenance
Pentire
Treburrick
Penrose
Pentire Steps
St Ervan
CORNISH WAY
Blable
Efflins
Diggory's Island
ST HERMES
Rumford
Tredinnick
Engollan
ST ERVAN MANOR
Trembleathe
REDCLIFF CASTLE
Tregona
Trelow
Pendarves Island
BEDRUTHAN STEPS
CREALY ADVENTURE PARK
Cannalidgey
ST UVELUS
Carnewas Island
St Eval
Downhill
LONG STONE
Trerathick Point
B3276
Trelow Downs
Eddystone
Tumuli
Trenance Point
B3274
Bear's Downs
THE FIDDLERS
Trenance
Prince's Common
Mawgan Porth
Tumuli
NINE MAIDENS
Berryl's Point
Lower Lanherne
Mawgan Porth
Denzell Downs
A39(T)
Beacon Cove
Pennatillie
Trevarrian
THE JAPANESE GARDEN
B3274
Winnards Perch
BIRDS OF PREY CENTRE
Stem Point
St Mawgan
ST MAWGAN
Bolingey
Rosedinnick
B3276
Watergate Bay
Whitewater
Retallack
B3274
SPIRIT OF THE WEST
Talskiddy
Tregurrian
Carloggas
Higher Tolcarne
Trevornick
EXTREME ACADEMY
St Mawgan Airfield
Trewen Hall
Gluvian
Tremayne
River Menathyl
THE BEACH HUT
Newquay Airport
Tregamere
Trebelsue
Halveor
B3276
Reterth
ST COLUMBA
St Columb Major
Trevithick
Tregustick
Trewince
A3059
Tregaswith
Tregatillian

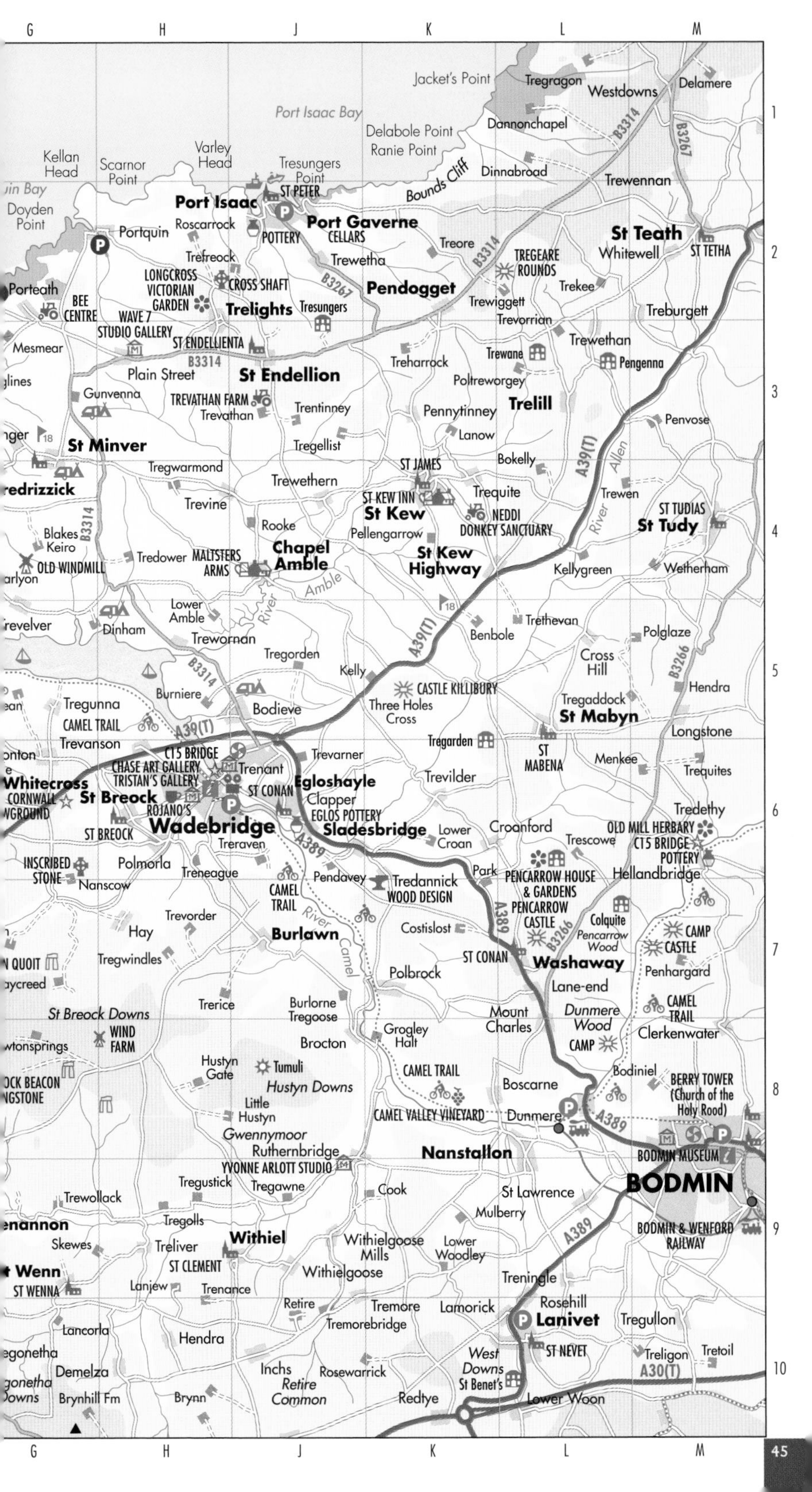

G
H
J
K
L
M
1
2
3
4
5
6
7
8
9
10
Jacket's Point
Tregragon
Westdowns
Delamere
Port Isaac Bay
Dannonchapel
B3314
B3267
Delabole Point
Ranie Point
Kellan Head
Scarnor Point
Varley Head
Tresungers Point
Bounds Cliff
Dinnabroad
Trewennan
Doyden Point
Port Isaac
ST PETER
Portquin
Roscarrock
POTTERY
Port Gaverne
CELLARS
Treore
St Teath
Whitewell
ST TETHA
Trefreock
Trewetha
TREGEARE ROUNDS
Porteath
BEE CENTRE
LONGCROSS VICTORIAN GARDEN
CROSS SHAFT
Pendogget
Trekee
Trelights
Tresungers
Trewiggett
Trevorrian
Treburgett
WAVE 7 STUDIO GALLERY
Mesmear
ST ENDELLIENTA
Trewethan
Trewane
Pengenna
Treharrock
B3314
Plain Street
St Endellion
Poltreworgey
Gunvenna
TREVATHAN FARM
Trevathan
Trentinney
Pennytinney
Trelill
Penvose
Lanow
St Minver
Tregellist
Bokelly
Tregwarmond
ST JAMES
Trewethern
A39(T)
River Allen
Trequite
Trewen
Trevine
ST KEW INN
St Kew
NEDDI DONKEY SANCTUARY
ST TUDIAS
St Tudy
Rooke
Blakes Keiro
Pellengarrow
Chapel Amble
St Kew Highway
OLD WINDMILL
Tredower
MALTSTERS ARMS
Kellygreen
Wetherham
River Amble
Lower Amble
Dinham
Trethevan
Polglaze
Trewornan
Benbole
Tregorden
Cross Hill
B3266
Kelly
Hendra
CASTLE KILLIBURY
Burniere
Tregaddock
Three Holes Cross
Tregunna
Bodieve
St Mabyn
CAMEL TRAIL
Tregarden
Longstone
Trevanson
ST MABENA
CT5 BRIDGE
Trevarner
Menkee
Trequites
CHASE ART GALLERY
TRISTAN'S GALLERY
Trenant
Whitecross
Trevilder
CORNWALL
St Breock
ST CONAN
Egloshayle
Clapper
EGLOS POTTERY
Tredethy
ROJANO'S
Wadebridge
ST BREOCK
Sladesbridge
Lower Croan
Croanford
OLD MILL HERBARY
Trescowe
CT5 BRIDGE POTTERY
Treraven
A389
INSCRIBED STONE
Polmorla
Park
Hellandbridge
Nanscow
Treneague
Pendavey
Tredannick WOOD DESIGN
PENCARROW HOUSE & GARDENS
CAMEL TRAIL
PENCARROW CASTLE
Colquite
Pencarrow Wood
Trevorder
River Camel
Costislost
CAMP
CASTLE
Hay
Burlawn
ST CONAN
Washaway
Tregwindles
Polbrock
Penhargard
Lane-end
Trerice
Burlorne Tregoose
CAMEL TRAIL
St Breock Downs
Dunmere Wood
Mount Charles
WIND FARM
Grogley Halt
Clerkenwater
Brocton
CAMP
Hustyn Gate
Tumuli
CAMEL TRAIL
Hustyn Downs
Boscarne
Bodiniel
BERRY TOWER (Church of the Holy Rood)
Little Hustyn
CAMEL VALLEY VINEYARD
Dunmere
Gwennymoor
Ruthernbridge
BODMIN MUSEUM
YVONNE ARLOTT STUDIO
Nanstallon
BODMIN
Tregustick
Tregawne
Cook
St Lawrence
Trewollack
Mulberry
Tregolls
BODMIN & WENFORD RAILWAY
Skewes
Withiel
Treliver
Withielgoose Mills
Lower Woodley
ST CLEMENT
Withielgoose
ST WENNA
Lanjew
Trenance
Treningle
Retire
Tremore
Lamorick
Rosehill
Lancorla
Tremorebridge
Lanivet
Tregullon
Hendra
ST NEVET
West Downs
Treligon
Tretoil
Demelza
Inchs
Retire Common
Rosewarrick
St Benet's
A30(T)
Brynhill Fm
Brynn
Redtye
Lower Woon

The Seafood Restaurant ss

PADSTOW.

A labyrinth of narrow alleys and picturesque houses, and safe haven on the treacherous north coast. May Day heralds the Padstow Hobby Horse 'Obby Oss' who prances and dances the streets taunting young maidens, celebrating the coming of summer. C16 Raleigh's Court House on South Quay. Prideaux Place*, C15 church. Boat trips. Centre of fine cuisine. (E5)

National Lobster Hatchery, South Quay. The fascinating world of lobsters and their environment. Open daily from 10. (E5)

Padstow Contemporary Art Gallery, 3a Parnell Court. Displays local artists and craftspeoples work; sculpture, ceramics, furniture and paintings. Open Apr-Oct M-Sa 11-4. (E5)

Padstow Museum, Market Place. Maritime and local interest - 'Obby' oss. Open East to Oct M-F 10.30-4.30, Sa 10.30-1. (E4)

Prideaux Place. Home of the Prideaux-Brune family. Filled with treasures, pictures, portraits, porcelain and exquisite furniture. Open Easter week, then 14 May-6 Oct Su-Th 1.30-5. T 01841 532411. (E4)

Where to Eat, Drink & Be Merry in Padstow...

Rick Stein's Cafe, 10 Middle St. Light lunches, coffees, pastries and a reasonably priced three-course dinner each evening from the Master. (E5)

Stein's Seafood Delicatessen, Riverside. Treat yourself to hot takeaway seafood dishes and stir frys. A great destination to head to after a night under canvas, a rip tide surf or a head-butting souwesterly on the coastal footpath. T 01841 532700. (E5)

St Petroc's Hotel & Bistro. Stein's smaller hotel has been renovated to provide a light and airy feel. As you'd expect, there's plenty of seafood, and meat and veggie dishes. T 01841 532700. (E5)

The Seafood Restaurant. Needs no introduction. Rick Stein's restaurant has established an international reputation since opening 30 years ago. The fish comes literally straight off the boats in the harbour (via a judicious by-your-leave in the kitchen) and onto your plate. Essential to book (unless you're Beckham or Madonna). Stein's success has had a positive spin-off for all the other restauranteurs in Cornwall (many who have worked with Stein) and has made Cornwall a destination for fine cuisine. Bravo! T 01841 532700. (E5)

Pescadou, South Quay. Modern, friendly restaurant providing value for money fayre in foodie Padstow. Serves fish dishes, too. T 01841 532359. (E5)

The Ebb. 1a The Strand. Minimalism and artworks in tandem with international cuisines provide tasty fayre. Dinner. T 01841 532565. (E5)

Trevathan Farm. Strawberry farm with shop and restaurant. Fruit in season. Pets corner. Open daily. (J3)

The Great Hall, Prideaux Place ss

St Enodoc Bar & Restaurant ss

WADEBRIDGE

A very busy river port in the C19. Busy market town and venue for the Royal Cornwall Show in June. Magnificent C15 bridge with 17 arches. Superb views across town and river from the New Bridge on the A39. Mid-point for cycling the Camel Trail. Cinema. E/C W. (H6)

Camel Trail. Eleven-mile trail from Bodmin to Padstow; suitable for jogging, walking, cycling and birdwatching. Cycle hire in Padstow and Wadebridge. (H5)

Arts & Crafts in Wadebridge

Chase Art Gallery, The Platt. Two galleries (in town, and by Camel Trail) display original paintings, pottery, sculpture and jewellery. Open M-Sa 9.30-5.30. (H6)

Tristan's Gallery, 49 Molesworth St. Fine Art photographic gallery; Nudes, Landscapes, Seascapes and Still Life. Open M-Sa 10-4. (H6)

Outside Wadebridge...

Eglos Pottery, Egloshayle. Handmade stoneware and porcelain pieces by Penny McBreen with images of fish, lizards and flowers. Studio and showroom open daily. (J6)

Yvonne Arlott Studio. Unique traditional and contemporary artwork created from a mixture of turning and carving techniques. Open daily. T 01208 832315. (H9)

Wave 7 Studio Gallery. Enthusiastic new gallery displaying a fine mix of arts and crafts. Open daily Tu-Su from 10.30. (H3)

Wood Design. Stephen Roberts makes made-to-order custom pieces of contemporary furniture. Showroom open daily from 10. (K7)

Special Places to Eat, Drink & Be Merry...

Bluetomatocafe, Polzeath. Overlooks Hayle Bay in enviable position. Serves up coffees, pastries, al fresco lunches and dinner (booking advised), champagne cocktails. T 01208 862333. Also in Rock. (F3)

Maltsters Arms. Pretty pub overlooking village green. Customised Sharps beers. Log fires. Restaurant serves fresh fish, local ice creams. T 01208 812473. (J4)

Rojano's, Eddystone Rd, Wadebridge. Spacious and light with cool ambience. Pizzas and pasta (takeaway). Also in Padstow. (H6)

Ripley's. Former head chef at Stein's Seafood Restaurant, Paul Ripley has married together the wonders of West Country produce with simple, straightforward cooking. Fine Art lines the walls. Open Tu-Sa Dinner. T 01841 520179. (C5)

St Enodoc Bar & Restaurant. Family-friendly hotel noted for its superb cuisine. T 01208 863394.

St Kew Inn. Hidden away down narrow lanes. Dine in the RH rooms if you can. Large garden. Specials board - try the fish. (F4)

The Black Pig, Rock Road. O Divine Swine; culinary delicasies of near perfection. Great art covers the white walls. Lunch 12.30-2 M Tu F-Su, Dinner 7-9.30 M Tu Th-Su. T 01208 862622. (F4)

St Ervan Manor ss/ds

Ripley's

Porteath Bee Centre. Living honeybee exhibition behind glass. Honey products available on sale and cream teas. Pooh Corner for kids. Shop open daily all year 10.30-4.30. Exhibition East-Oct M-Sa. (G2)

Spirit Of The West. American theme park with cowboy museum, gun fights and 'Silver City' ghost tours. Advemture Soft Air (prebooked only). Open daily East-Sept 10.30-dusk. (E9)

Special Places to Stay...

Molesworth Manor. Former Rectory close to Padstow offers spacious B & B accomodation. Three Living Rooms. Continental breakfast (no fatty fry-ups). No dogs. T 01841 540292. (E6)

St Ervan Manor. New style Gourmet B & B with 5 rooms and award-winning chef, Nathan Outlaw producing fabulous cuisine from local produce. T 01841 54025. (C7)

Treglos Hotel. Has been a family run hotel for forty years and you are assured the high standards expected of a quality hotel. Most of the luxurious rooms have dramatic views. Swimming pool and beauty treatment rooms. Specialised Breaks. T 01841 520727. (B5)

Treglos Hotel ss

Gardens to Visit..

Japanese Garden & Bonsai Nursery. Set in a sheltered valley. Features Water, Stroll and Zen gardens. Woodland garden. Open daily from 10-6. (H2)

Longcross Victorian Garden. 2 1/2 acres; lake, maze-walkway, herbaceous plants, cream teas. Freehouse tavern serving food. Plant sales. Disabled facilities. Open daily 11-dusk. (H2)

Special Family Places to Visit...

Cornish Birds Of Prey Centre. Falcons, hawks and owls. Waterfowl lake. Flights twice daily at 12 & 2.30. Open daily 10-5. (E9)

Crealy Adventure Park. Megaslides, twisters, water slides. Shire horses, farm museum, 120 acres to wander. Restaurant. Open daily East-Oct 10-5. (E7)

Neddi Donkey Sanctuary. Feed and groom the animals. Coffee shop. Bouncy castle. Open daily Apr-Oct 10-5. (K4)

Old Macdonalds Farm. Small farm park, especially for young children. Pet the animals, bottle feed lambs, pony rides, train rides, trampolines, crazy golf, cafe, camping. Open daily East-Sept 10-6. T 01841 540829. www.oldmacdonalds.co.uk (B6)

Churches of Interest

Little Petherick Church. Quaint C14 in wooded valley. (E6)

St Enodoc Church. C13 origins with crooked spire and grave of Sir John Betjamin (Poet). Lies amongst the sand dunes, dug out in 1863. (F3)

St Kew Church. Fine C15 interior with wagon roofing and magnificent glass. (K4)

St Mawgan-In-Pydar Church. Large with C13 nave and Arundell family brasses. (C9)

Coastal Footpath

Port Isaac To Padstow: Approx. 12 miles. Choice of strenuous coastal or gentler inland route as far as Port Quin. For inland route: from Pine Haven follow the path for a half mile, then it turns westwards, passing Roscarrock Farm, south of Reedy Cliff to Port

St Enodoc Church

Quin, a tiny hamlet, mostly owned by the National Trust. On the headland beyond stands Doyden Castle, a Gothic folly built as a pleasure house and drinking den in C19. Below are black fiercesome rocks stained with green. The path west passes rocky-sandy surfing coves of Epphaven and Lundy, and the dramatic collapsed sea cave of Lundy Hole, before heading out to the headlands of The Rumps (with remains of Iron Age cliff castle) and Pentire. Now the path follows the Camel estuary, past Polzeath and Daymer Bay and across the dunes to ferry at Rock for crossing the Camel to Padstow.

Padstow To WaterGate Bay (Newquay): Approx. 16 miles. A coastline dotted with superb sandy beaches and pounded by mighty Atlantic rollers but best appreciated out of season. Splendid views at Stepper Point, then on past caves and sheer cliffs at Butter Hole and Pepper Hole. The path hugs the coastline past camp sites and beaches ideal for a quick dip. Coastline peppered with stacks and islands; and none more spectacular than at Bedruthan Steps* where legend has it that stacks used as stepping stones by the Cornish giant, Bedruthan. Walk the cliff tops in summer, the carpets of wild flowers fill the air with the scent of burnet rose and gorse. Reaching Stem Point it's possible to walk the sands to Newquay at low tide, alternatively the headland path is easy going.

Beaches & Surfing

Hayle Bay, New Polzeath. Wonderfully spacious family beach, S-B hire/P/WC/cafe/access. Surfing - Crowded and popular beach break. Picks up most swell. RH wave off Pentire Point produces big swells. (F2)

Daymer Bay. Sheltered with firm golden sands, dunes and bathing safest at HT. WC/P. (E3)

Porthilly Cove, Rock. Spacious sands, ferry to Padstow, access/WC/cafe. (E4)

Padstow, St Georges Cove. Sheltered inlet, 10 minute walk from town. (E4)

Treyarnon Bay

Padstow, Harbour Cove. Spacious sandy cove 20 minutes walk from town. (E4)

Trevone Bay. Sands, rock pools, Round Hole - collapsed cave. WC/LG/cafe. (C4)

Harlyn Bay. Firm sands sheltered from south westerlies. WC/P/LG/Inn/café. Surfing - Popular beach with strong SW winds and big swells. Can be fast and hollow at all stages of tide. Best with incoming tide. (C4)

Booby's Bay. Spacious sands, swirling currents, HZ bathing, rock pools at LT, access/P/LG. Surfing - Good R reef break from low to mid tide. Strong rips, for the experienced only. (B4)

Constantine Bay. Spacious sands, swirling currents, HZ bathing, rock pools at LT, access/P/LG. Surfing - One of the best swell magnets. In the middle are good Rs and Ls. At S end break L off the reef. (B5)

Treyarnon Bay. Sheltered, popular family beach, bathing is HZ near rocks/access/WC/LG/P. Surfing - Good at mid to HT. Various peaks. LH wave for experienced with breaks off reef at LT. (B5)

Trethias, Pepper Cover & Fox Cove. Access by foot to small inlet with sandy patches. (B5)

Porthcothan. Sandy bay, bathing HZ at LT. P/WC. Surfing - L & R beach breaks. (B6)

Bedruthan Steps. One of Cornwall's most dramatic and spectacular beaches. Firm golden sands, massive rocks, and caves. Steep staircase descends to beach. NT Info Centre/cafe//WC at car park. (A7)

Daymer Bay

Bedruthan Steps

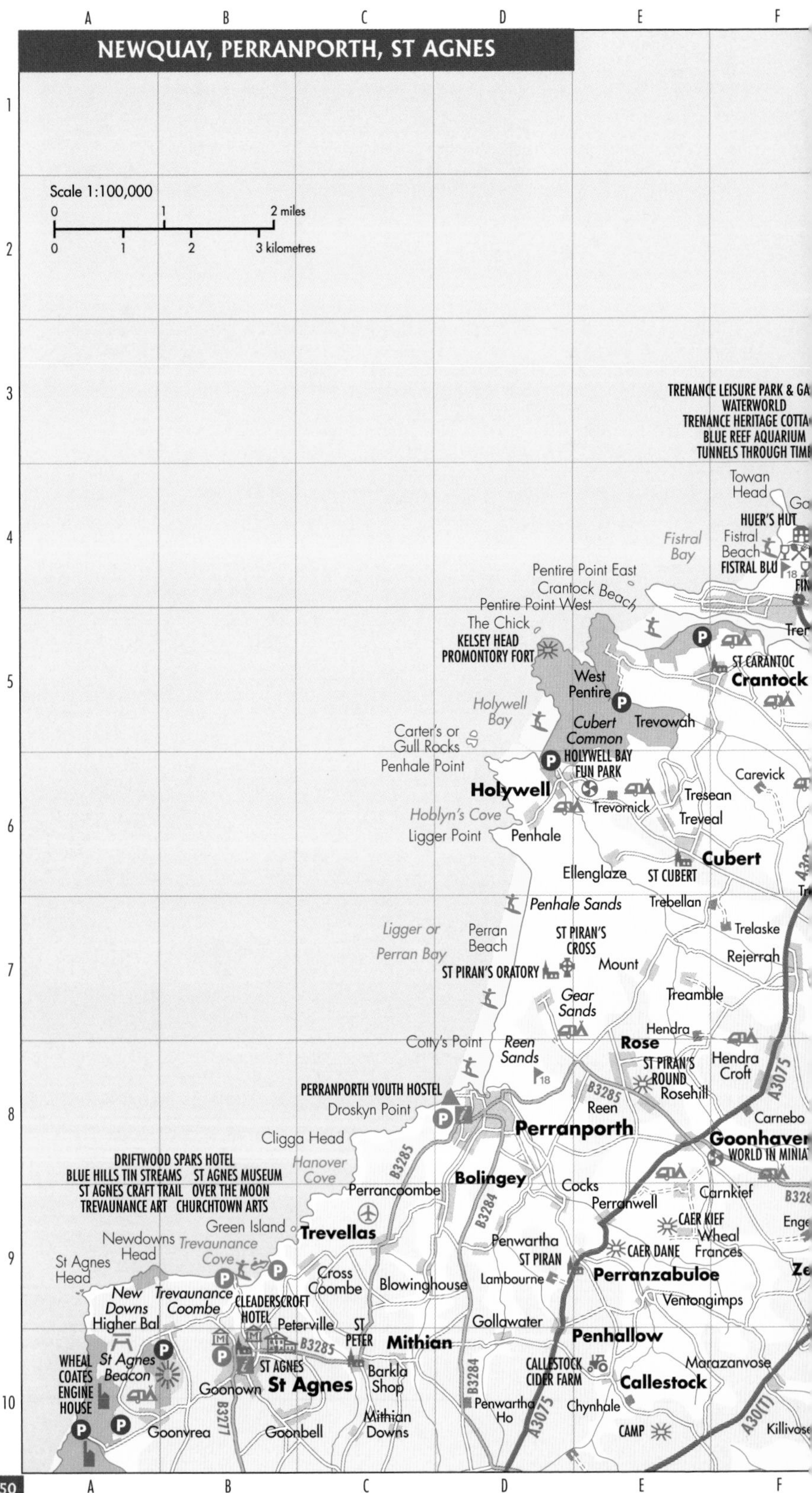
Scale 1:100,000
0 1 2 miles
0 1 2 3 kilometres
TRENANCE LEISURE PARK & GA
WATERWORLD
TRENANCE HERITAGE COTTA
BLUE REEF AQUARIUM
TUNNELS THROUGH TIM
Towan Head
HUER'S HUT
Fistral Bay
Fistral Beach
FISTRAL BLU
Pentire Point East
Crantock Beach
Pentire Point West
The Chick
KELSEY HEAD PROMONTORY FORT
ST CARANTOC
Crantock
West Pentire
Holywell Bay
Cubert Common
Trevowah
Carter's or Gull Rocks
Penhale Point
HOLYWELL BAY FUN PARK
Carevick
Holywell
Trevornick
Tresean
Hoblyn's Cove
Treveal
Ligger Point
Penhale
Cubert
Ellenglaze
ST CUBERT
Penhale Sands
Trebellan
Trelaske
Ligger or Perran Bay
Perran Beach
ST PIRAN'S CROSS
Rejerrah
ST PIRAN'S ORATORY
Mount
Gear Sands
Treamble
Hendra
Cotty's Point
Reen Sands
Rose
ST PIRAN'S ROUND
Hendra Croft
Rosehill
A3075
B3285
Reen
PERRANPORTH YOUTH HOSTEL
Droskyn Point
Perranporth
Carnebo
Goonhaven
WORLD IN MINIA
Cligga Head
DRIFTWOOD SPARS HOTEL
BLUE HILLS TIN STREAMS
ST AGNES MUSEUM
ST AGNES CRAFT TRAIL
OVER THE MOON
TREVAUNANCE ART
CHURCHTOWN ARTS
Hanover Cove
Bolingey
Cocks
Perranwell
Carnkief
Perrancoombe
Green Island
Trevellas
CAER KIEF
Wheal Frances
Newdowns Head
Trevaunance Cove
Penwartha
St Agnes Head
ST PIRAN
CAER DANE
Cross Coombe
Blowinghouse
Lambourne
Perranzabuloe
New Downs
Trevaunance Coombe
CLEADERSCROFT HOTEL
Ventongimps
Higher Bal
Peterville
ST PETER
Gollawater
Mithian
Penhallow
St Agnes Beacon
ST AGNES
Barkla Shop
CALLESTOCK CIDER FARM
Marazanvose
WHEAL COATES ENGINE HOUSE
Goonown
St Agnes
Callestock
B3277
B3284
Penwartha Ho
Chynhale
A30(T)
Mithian Downs
Goonvrea
Goonbell
CAMP
Killivose

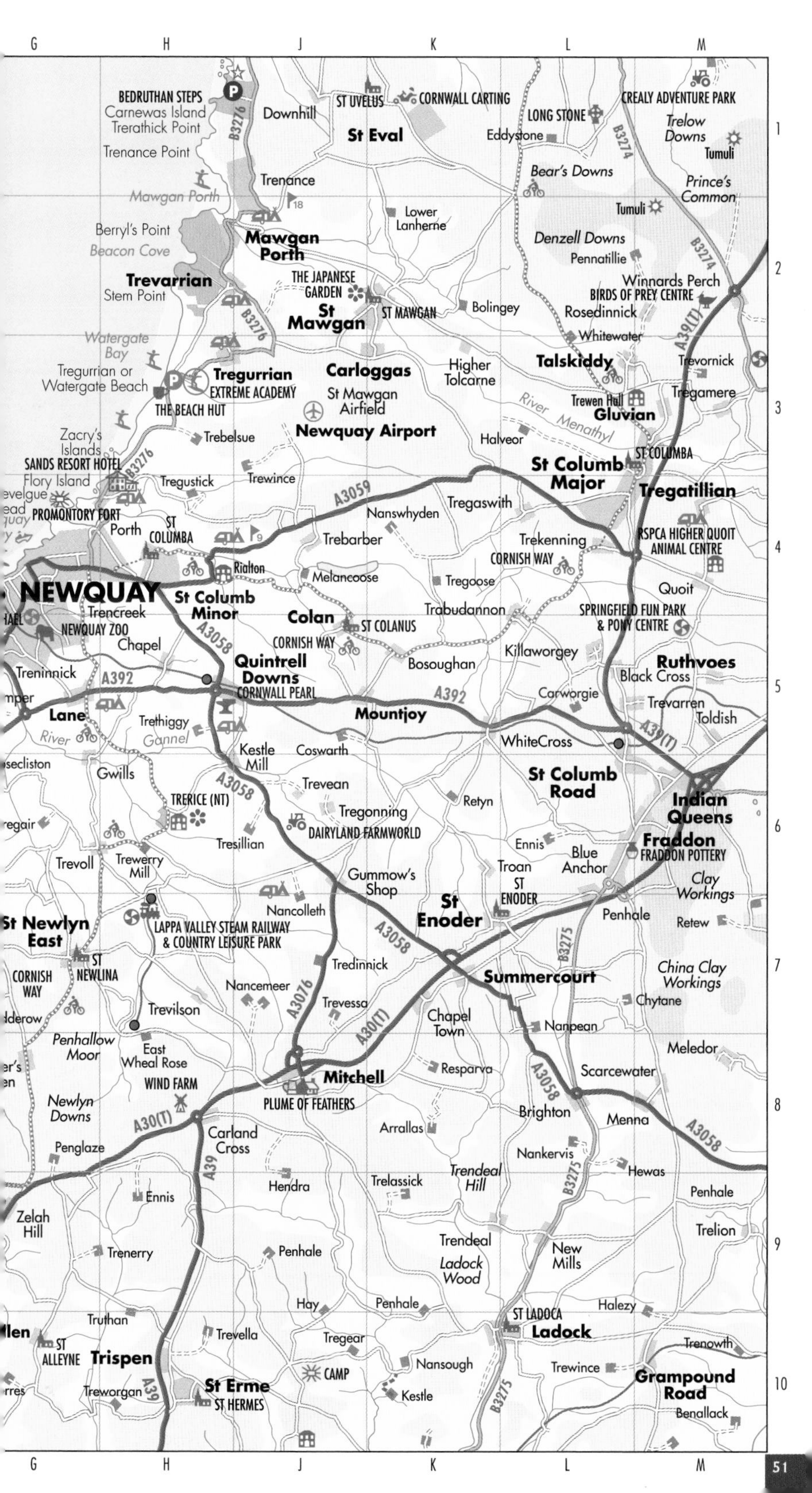

G
H
J
K
L
M
1
2
3
4
5
6
7
8
9
10
BEDRUTHAN STEPS
Carnewas Island
Trerathick Point
Trenance Point
Mawgan Porth
Berryl's Point
Beacon Cove
Trevarrian
Stem Point
Watergate Bay
Tregurrian or Watergate Beach
THE BEACH HUT
Zacry's Islands
SANDS RESORT HOTEL
Flory Island
PROMONTORY FORT
Porth
NEWQUAY
NEWQUAY ZOO
Trencreek
Chapel
Treninnick
Lane
River Gannel
Gwills
Trevoll
St Newlyn East
ST NEWLINA
CORNISH WAY
Penhallow Moor
Newlyn Downs
Penglaze
Zelah Hill
Ennis
Trenerry
Truthan
ST ALLEYNE
Trispen
Treworgan
St Erme
ST HERMES
B3276
Downhill
Trenance
Mawgan Porth
THE JAPANESE GARDEN
St Mawgan
ST MAWGAN
Tregurrian
EXTREME ACADEMY
Trebelsue
Tregustick
Trewince
ST COLUMBA
Rialton
St Columb Minor
A3058
Quintrell Downs
CORNWALL PEARL
A392
Trethiggy
Kestle Mill
TRERICE (NT)
Tresillian
Trewerry Mill
LAPPA VALLEY STEAM RAILWAY & COUNTRY LEISURE PARK
Trevilson
East Wheal Rose
WIND FARM
A30(T)
Carland Cross
A39
Trevella
ST UVELUS
CORNWALL CARTING
St Eval
Lower Lanherne
Carloggas
St Mawgan Airfield
Newquay Airport
A3059
Nanswhyden
Trebarber
Melancoose
Colan
ST COLANUS
CORNISH WAY
Bosoughan
Mountjoy
Coswarth
Trevean
Tregonning
DAIRYLAND FARMWORLD
Gummow's Shop
Nancolleth
Tredinnick
Nancemeer
A3076
Trevessa
Mitchell
PLUME OF FEATHERS
Hendra
Penhale
Hay
Tregear
CAMP
Kestle
Bolingey
Higher Tolcarne
Halveor
Tregaswith
Tregoose
Trabudannon
Retyn
St Enoder
Chapel Town
Resparva
Arrallas
Trelassick
Trendeal Hill
Trendeal
Ladock Wood
Penhale
Nansough
Eddystone
LONG STONE
Bear's Downs
Denzell Downs
Pennatillie
Rosedinnick
Whitewater
Talskiddy
Trewen Hall
Gluvian
River Menathyl
St Columb Major
Trekenning
CORNISH WAY
Killaworgey
Carworgie
WhiteCross
St Columb Road
Ennis
Troan
ST ENODER
Blue Anchor
Summercourt
B3275
Nanpean
Scarcewater
Brighton
Nankervis
New Mills
ST LADOCA
Ladock
Trewince
CREALY ADVENTURE PARK
Trelow Downs
Tumuli
Prince's Common
B3274
Winnards Perch
BIRDS OF PREY CENTRE
A39(T)
Trevornick
Tregamere
ST COLUMBA
Tregatillian
RSPCA HIGHER QUOIT ANIMAL CENTRE
Quoit
SPRINGFIELD FUN PARK & PONY CENTRE
Ruthvoes
Black Cross
Trevarren
Toldish
Indian Queens
Fraddon
FRADDON POTTERY
Clay Workings
Penhale
Retew
China Clay Workings
Chytane
Meledor
Menna
A3058
Hewas
Penhale
Trelion
Halezy
Trenowth
Grampound Road
Benallack

NEWQUAY

Popular seaside resort; the superb beaches give it the edge as Cornwall's (West Country) foremost surfing centre. Has all the facilities of a modern resort; indoor and outdoor pools, cinema, 2 theatres, Zoo*, Sea Life Aquarium*. Fishing/boat trips from Quay. Huer's Hut on headland (Lookout for pilchards), Carnival week - End May/early June. (G4)

Where to Eat, Drink & Be Merry...

Ed's, The Edwardian Hotel, 3-7 Island Crescent. Laid back unpretentious restaurant offering well prepared food for catholic tastes. Great puds. T 01637 874087. (G4)

Finns Restaurant, South Quay Hill. Overlooks the harbour; fish is the speciality (and possibly supplied by local fisherman, just off the boats). Open from 10.30 am. T 01637 874062. (G4)

Fistral Blu, Fistral Beach. In superb position overlooking the beach. Two restaurants (bistro and formal) produce everchanging menus using local produce. T 01637 878782. (F4)

Where to Stay & Relax (with kids)...

Sands Resort Hotel. Family/sports hotel offering modern facilities with many sporting options, spacious suites, health and beauty centre and children's clubs. T 01637 872864. (G3)

Newquay Zoo ss

What to Visit in Newquay...

Blue Reef Aquarium. Overlooking one of England's most popular surfing beaches...houses the creatures which live beneath those crashing waves! Journey through the wonderful underwater worlds from the Cornish coastline to the undersea gardens of the Mediterranean. Café/gift shop. Open daily, 10-5. (F4)

Newquay Fun Factory, 1 St Georges Road. Adventure play centre for children, 2 to 12 years old. Coffee shop. Open daily Jul-Aug 10-9, Sept-Jul 10-6. (G4)

Newquay Zoo. Experience the wildlife amongst the exotic lakeside gardens and see 100s of animals from around the world. Highlights are feeding times and animal encounters. Cafe. Open daily Apr-Sept 9.30-6, Oct-Mar 10-5. T 01637 8733342. (G5)

Trenance Heritage Cottages Museum. Step back and view life in the 1900s. Open Mar-Oct daily 10-6. (G4)

Fistral Blu

Trenance Leisure Park & Gardens. Multi-leisure park with Zoo, Waterworld, mini railway, tennis courts, crazy golf and boating lake, all set in lakeside gardens. Open daily. (G4)

Tunnels Through Time. Life-size figures and scenes capture Cornwall's exciting and legendary past: smugglers, giants, sea creatures, highwaymen, mermaids. Open East-Oct Su-F & BHs 10-dusk. (G4)

Family Fun Places to Visit Outside Newquay....

Callestock Cider Farm. 40 varieties of fruit products made; from scrumpies to chutneys. Open all year M-F 9-5, except xmas to mid-Jan. (E10)

Cornwall Pearl. Exhibition centre/Workshop with gemstore selling a complete range of jewellery. Tea house. Champagne & Oyster Bar. Open daily 9.30-5.30. (J5)

Dairyland Farmworld. Britain's Leading Farm Park; Milking Parlour, Cornish Countrylife Museum, 12,000sq.ft indoor play area, Nature Trail & Playground and the county's friendliest farm animals to pat, feed & pet. Open Apr-Oct 10-5. (J6)

Holywell Bay Fun Park. All action outdoor fun park - go karts, battle and bumper boats, laser day pigeon shooting, cafe. Open daily East-Oct 10-5. (E6)

Lappa Valley Railway & Leisure Park. Steam railway giving a 2 mile return trip along a 15" gauge line to a pleasure area with boating lake, crazy golf, maze, two miniature railways, walks and film show. Cafe and gift shop. Open daily East-Oct & 1/2 term 10.30-5.30. www.lappavalley.co.uk. (H7)

Springfields Fun Park & Pony Centre. Pets corner, bottle feeding, tractor rides and play areas. Cafe. Open daily mid-Apr to Sept 10-6, Oct-Nov 10-4. (M5)

World In Miniature And The Wild West Town Of Tombstone. Miniatures of the Taj Mahal to the Great Sphinx. Children's entertainment centre and cafe. Open daily Mar-Oct from 10. (F8)

Dairyland Farmworld ss

Gardens & Houses to Visit Outside Newquay...

Trerice (NT).
A delightful, small secluded Elizabethan manor house rebuilt in 1571, containing magnificent fireplaces, plaster ceilings, oak and walnut furniture. Small lawn mower museum. Refreshments. Open daily 26 Mar-29 Oct 11-5. (H6)

Trerice nt

CRANTOCK.

Early religious centre and busy port until the Gannel estuary silted up. Village stocks in churchyard, superb beach. (F5)

Churches to Visit....

Crantock Church.
Religious community established in C5, Norman font, C14 chancel and village stocks. (F5)

Cubert Church.
C14 tower, pulpit made of old bench ends. (E6)

St Piran's Oratory.
Ruins of C7 church & burial place of St Piran an early Celtic missionary. Now buried beneath sand for protection.(D7)

Lappa Valley Railway ss

PERRANPORTH.

The glorious 3 miles of sand make this a popular holiday and surfing centre. Nearby St Piran's Round where on occasion plays are performed. Now buried beneath sand dunes, St Piran's Oratory, site reached by a 30 minute walk for dedicated hagiologists. (D8)

Where to Stay & Relax..

Cleaderscroft.
Superb position for touring and walks. 5 mins to beach/coastal path. 4-posters. Family accomod. Style and comfort in historic building. No pets/smokers. Open all year. T 01872 552349. (B10)

Driftwood Spars Hotel.
C17 Inn built of massive granite blocks and timbers, a stones throw from the beach, hosts three bars (real ales), mixed menus, a family room, brewery and a Carvery. Accomodation. Promotes local arts and crafts. T 01872 552428. (B9)

St Piran's Round. An ancient amphitheatre where plays were performed in the C17. (E8)

ST AGNES.

Former mining community. Skyline jagged with disused mine engine houses. Birthplace of John Opie in 1761, Cornwall's famous painter, Fellow of the Royal Academy at 26 and buried in St Paul's Cathedral. Family resort and centre for dramatic coastal walks. Museum. Arts and Crafts Trail. (B10)

Where to Stay & Relax..

Cleaderscroft.
Superb position for touring and walks. 5 mins to beach/coastal path. 4-posters. Family accomod. Style and comfort in historic building. No pets/smokers. Open all year. T 01872 552349. (B10)

Driftwood Spars Hotel.
C17 Inn built of massive granite blocks and timbers, a stones throw from the beach, hosts three bars (real ales), mixed menus, a family room, brewery and a Carvery. Accomodation. Promotes local arts and crafts. T 01872 552428. (B9)

Galleries & Museums to Visit...

Blue Hills Tin Streams.
The skills of the ancient tinner; from rock to metal. Giftware. Open Apr-Oct M-Sa 10.30-5. (B10)

Churchtown Arts,
5 Churchtown. C15 building houses arts and crafts gallery. Workshops and studios to view. Open 9.30-5.30, Su 10-5. (B10)

Over The Moon, 6a Churchtown Square. Display of thirty artists' work; large sculpturals and ceramic pieces. Open M-Sa 9.30-5.30. (B10)

St Agnes Museum. Tin mining to turtles, fishing to folklore. Open daily East to Sept 10.30-5. (B10)

St Agnes Pottery.
Wide range of hand-thrown stoneware, earthenware and porcelain. Open M-Sa 9.30-5. (B10)

Trevaunance Art & Design,
Trevaunance Cove. Eight workshops produce work on their premises; paintings, jewellery, shoe making, needlework. Open daily 10.30-5. (B9)

ST COLUMB MAJOR.

Isolated town with superb C14 church. Hurling competition every Shrove Tuesday and Saturday of following week. Also venue for Cornish wrestling. (L3)

Fraddon Pottery.
Stoneware pots of Celtic design made from local materials. Tuition on hand. Open Tu-Sa 10-4. (M6)

Pub to Visit...

Plume Of Feathers. Simple, wholesome fare. Cream teas. Large garden. Dogs and children welcome. B & B. T 01872 510387. (J8)

WATERGATE BAY

Extreme Academy. It's all beach action; kitesurfing, traction-kiting, buggying and kite-boarding, waveski, mountain boarding, and of course, surfing. Tuition and kit hire. Beach Hut Bistro. Annual events. T 01637 860840. (H3)

The Beach Hut.
Fresh, simply cooked food in a sensational location. What more could you ask for? Fish feature strongly. Daily Specials. Popular with all ages. Open from 10. T 01637 860877. (H3)

Ancient Cornwall

Trevelgue Head.
Defended by 7 lines of banks and ditches. Hut circles suggest Iron Age occupation. (G4)

Learning to Surf, Fistral Beach

Extreme Academy, Watergate Bay ss

Coastal Footpath

Newquay To Trevaunance Cove (St Agnes): Approx. 16 miles. This section is a very busy holiday area with many camp sites and seductive beaches. Cross the Gannel by the tidal bridge or ferry (in summer). Out of season, follow the road to Trevemper, (or cross the Trethellan tidal bridge at low water). Worth a detour to pretty Crantock. Easy going around Penhale Point; alternatively, a route via Holywell Bay, Ellenglaze, Mount and Gear. At Penhale Sands one sees the first sign of Cornish tin mining: desolate engine houses and chimneys on hill tops, silhouettes which appear increasingly frequently as one walks westwards. Climbing out of Perranporth the path is relatively easy-going and follows the cliff edge to Trevaunance Cove.

Beaches & Surfing

Mawgan Porth. Popular family beach, fine bathing and access/S-B hire/LG/WC/café. Surfing - Good beach break Ls into River Menathyl. Beacon Cove less crowded. (H1)

Watergate Bay. - Two miles of glorious sands and access to hotel, surf-canoeing. S-B hire/WC/P/café. Surfing - Good beach break. Popular with Newquay locals. (H3)

The Cribber. Big wave spot for the experienced big wave surfers only. Very dangerous rips. Beware! (F4)

Newquay - Porth Beach.
Flat spacious golden sands. Fine surfing and bathing (avoid river). Blow Hole at Trevelgue Head. P/LG/WC/cafe. (G4)

Newquay - Lusty Glaze.
Sands sheltered by cliffs, access via steps from cliff top, surfing S-B/LG/WC. (F4)

Newquay - Tolcarne Sands.
Suntrap below Narrowcliff Promenade, surfing. (F4)

Newquay - Great Western Beach. Sheltered suntrap, access via path beside Great Western Hotel, surfing S-B hire/LG. (F4)

Newquay - Towan Beach.
Ideal family beach; golden sands, good bathing. Near harbour and town centre. S-B hire/LG/WC. (F4)

Newquay - Fistral Beach.
Surfing - Venue for European Championships. Consistent swell across beach with peaky barrelling Ls and Rs. South Fistral breaks L, better at HT. North and Little Fistral break L and R. North breaks at HT. The LT barrels have made the waves at N end a crowd puller. (F4)

Crantock Beach.
Spacious golden sands sheltered by Pentire Point. Bathers must avoid The Gannel, pedestrian ferry to Newquay. S-B hire/LG/WC/P. Surfing long hollow Rs at S end over the sand bank. Protected from N and NE winds. Good Ls when S end has big swell. (E5)

Porth Joke (Polly Joke).
15 minutes walk from P to a suntrap of yellow sand, nestling between low cliffs. Seals laze opposite on the Chick. (E5)

Holywell Bay.
Popular family beach, dunes, bathing HZ at LT. Access P/WC/LG/cafe. Surfing - Average beach break. Protected at S end. 10 minute walk from P. (D5)

Penhale /Perran Beach, Perranporth. The ideal family beach; a vast 2 mile stretch of sand with dunes behind, bathing HZ at LT and near Chapel Rock. S-B hire WC/LG/cafe at southern end. (D7)

Penhale.
Surfing - Rs peel off at N end. (D7)

Perranporth.
Surfing - Good at mid-tide with long rides. Watch your position with strong tidal flow. Ls break off the headland. (D8)

Trevaunance Cove (St Agnes).
Smallish sandy beach, effervescent blue sea and strong currents on ebbing tide. S-B hire/WC/P/LG/café. Surfing - SAS HQ. Yet water quality still poor. Mid-tide produces powerful surf. SW wind unusually creates waves. Can be crowded. (B9)

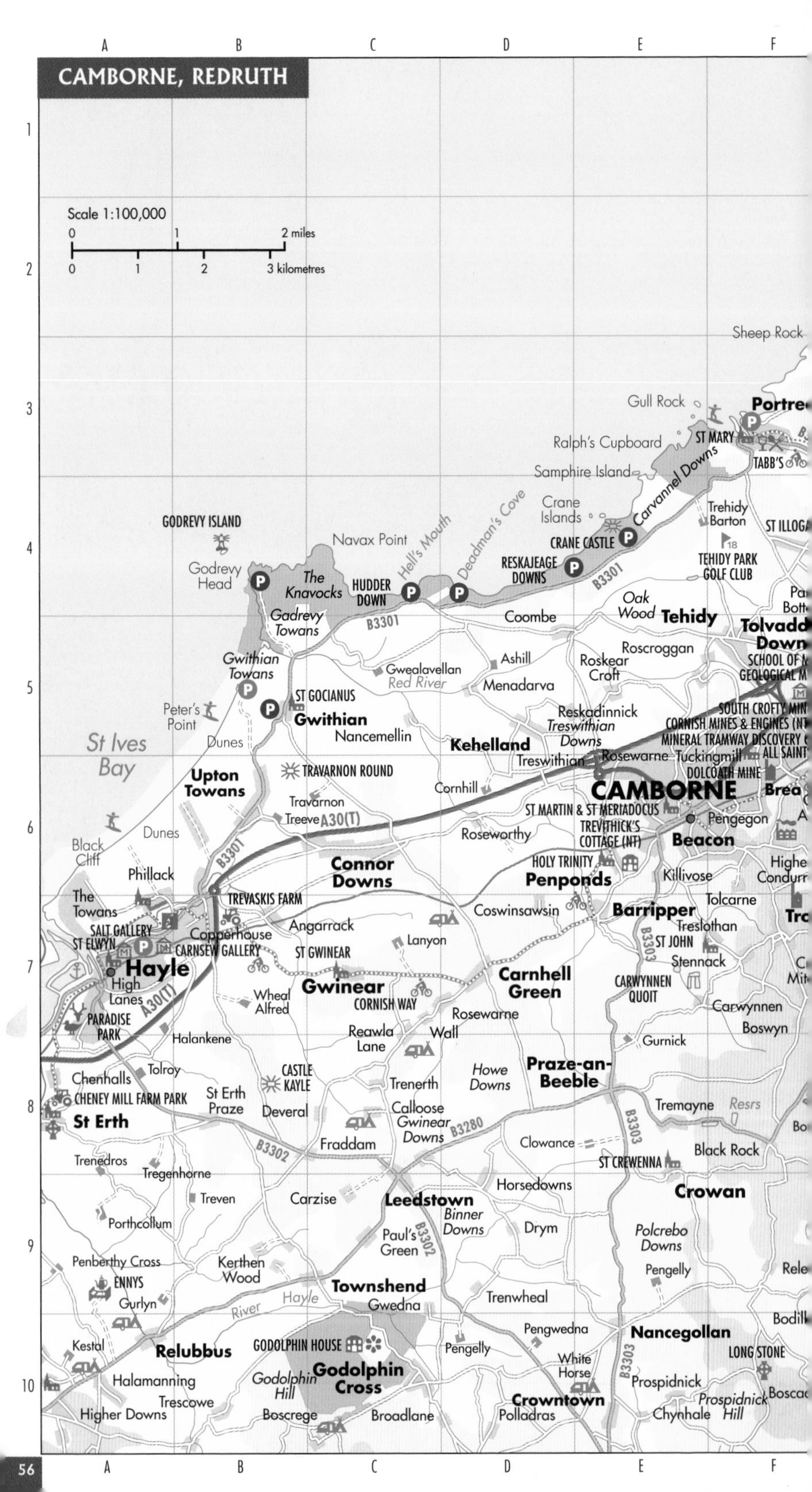

CAMBORNE, REDRUTH
A
B
C
D
E
F
1
2
3
4
5
6
7
8
9
10
Scale 1:100,000
0
1
2 miles
0
1
2
3 kilometres
Sheep Rock
Gull Rock
Portre
Ralph's Cupboard
ST MARY
Carvannel Downs
TABB'S
Samphire Island
Crane Islands
Trehidy Barton
ST ILLOGA
CRANE CASTLE
18
TEHIDY PARK GOLF CLUB
RESKAJEAGE DOWNS
B3301
GODREVY ISLAND
Navax Point
Hell's Mouth
Deadman's Cove
Godrevy Head
The Knavocks
HUDDER DOWN
Gadrevy Towans
B3301
Coombe
Oak Wood
Tehidy
Tolvadd Down
Roscroggan
SCHOOL OF M
GEOLOGICAL M
Gwithian Towans
Gwealavellan
Red River
Ashill
Menadarva
Roskear Croft
Peter's Point
ST GOCIANUS
Gwithian
Nancemellin
Reskadinnick
Treswithian Downs
SOUTH CROFTY MIN
CORNISH MINES & ENGINES (NT
MINERAL TRAMWAY DISCOVERY
ALL SAINT
St Ives Bay
Dunes
Kehelland
Treswithian
Rosewarne
Tuckingmill
DOLCOATH MINE
Upton Towans
TRAVARNON ROUND
Cornhill
CAMBORNE
Brea
Travarnon
Treeve
A30(T)
ST MARTIN & ST MERIADOCUS
Pengegon
Black Cliff
Dunes
Roseworthy
TREVITHICK'S COTTAGE (NT)
Beacon
Phillack
B3301
Connor Downs
HOLY TRINITY
Penponds
Killivose
Higher Condurr
The Towans
TREVASKIS FARM
Coswinsawsin
Barripper
Tolcarne
Tro
SALT GALLERY
Copperhouse
Angarrack
Treslothan
ST ELWYN
CARNSEW GALLERY
ST GWINEAR
Lanyon
B3303
ST JOHN
Stennack
Hayle
High Lanes
A30(T)
Gwinear
Carnhell Green
CARWYNNEN QUOIT
Wheal Alfred
CORNISH WAY
Carwynnen
PARADISE PARK
Rosewarne
Boswyn
Halankene
Reawla Lane
Wall
Gurnick
Tolroy
CASTLE KAYLE
Howe Downs
Praze-an-Beeble
Chenhalls
Trenerth
CHENEY MILL FARM PARK
St Erth Praze
Tremayne
Resrs
St Erth
Deveral
Calloose
Gwinear Downs
B3280
B3303
Fraddam
Clowance
Black Rock
Trenedros
B3302
ST CREWENNA
Tregenhorne
Horsedowns
Crowan
Treven
Carzise
Leedstown
Binner Downs
Porthcollum
Drym
Polcrebo Downs
Paul's Green
B3302
Penberthy Cross
Kerthen Wood
Pengelly
ENNYS
Townshend
Trenwheal
Gurlyn
River Hayle
Gwedna
Bodill
Pengwedna
Nancegollan
Kestal
Relubbus
GODOLPHIN HOUSE
Pengelly
White Horse
LONG STONE
B3303
Halamanning
Godolphin Hill
Godolphin Cross
Prospidnick
Trescowe
Crowntown
Prospidnick Hill
Higher Downs
Boscrege
Broadlane
Polladras
Chynhale
A
B
C
D
E
F

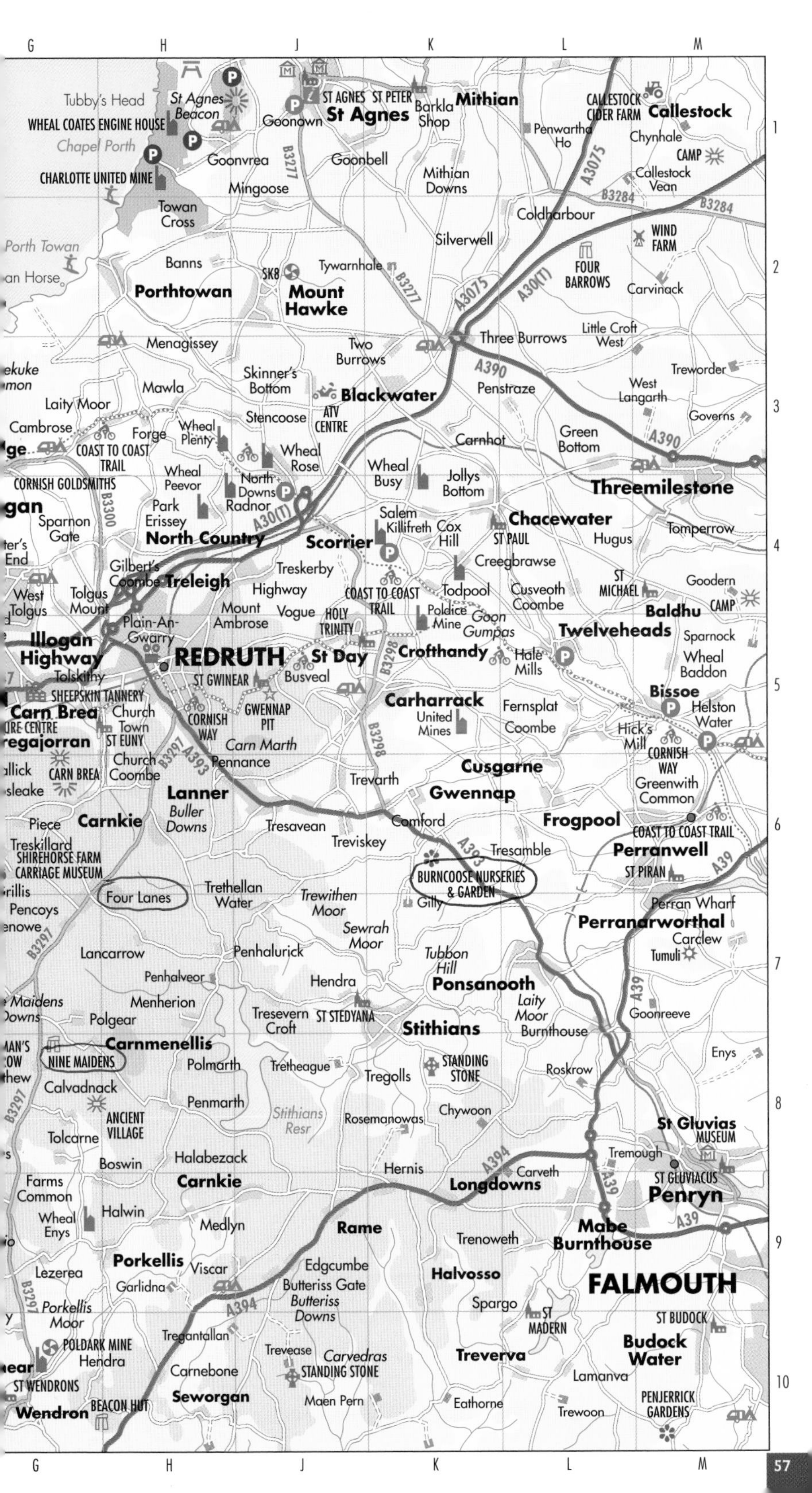
G
H
J
K
L
M
1
2
3
4
5
6
7
8
9
10
Tubby's Head
St Agnes Beacon
WHEAL COATES ENGINE HOUSE
Chapel Porth
CHARLOTTE UNITED MINE
Goonvrea
Mingoose
Towan Cross
Goonown
ST AGNES
ST PETER
St Agnes
Barkla Shop
Mithian
Goonbell
Mithian Downs
Penwartha Ho
CALLESTOCK CIDER FARM
Callestock
Chynhale
CAMP
Callestock Vean
A3075
B3284
B3277
Coldharbour
WIND FARM
Silverwell
FOUR BARROWS
Carvinack
Porth Towan
Banns
Porthtowan
SK8
Tywarnhale
Mount Hawke
A30(T)
Three Burrows
Little Croft West
Menagissey
Two Burrows
A390
Treworder
Skinner's Bottom
Mawla
Penstraze
West Langarth
Laity Moor
Blackwater
Cambrose
Forge
Wheal Plenty
Stencoose
ATV CENTRE
Governs
COAST TO COAST TRAIL
Wheal Rose
Carnhot
Green Bottom
CORNISH GOLDSMITHS
Wheal Peevor
North Downs
Wheal Busy
Jollys Bottom
Threemilestone
B3300
Sparnon Gate
Park Erissey
Radnor
Salem
Killifreth
Cox Hill
Chacewater
ST PAUL
Hugus
Tomperrow
North Country
Scorrier
Gilbert's Coombe
Treleigh
Treskerby
Creegbrawse
Goodern
West Tolgus
Tolgus Mount
Highway
COAST TO COAST TRAIL
Todpool
Cusveoth Coombe
ST MICHAEL
CAMP
Plain-An-Gwarry
Mount Ambrose
Vogue
HOLY TRINITY
Poldice Mine
Goon Gumpas
Baldhu
Illogan Highway
REDRUTH
St Day
Crofthandy
Hale Mills
Twelveheads
Sparnock
Tolskithy
ST GWINEAR
Busveal
B3298
Wheal Baddon
SHEEPSKIN TANNERY
Carn Brea
Church Town
CORNISH WAY
GWENNAP PIT
Carharrack
United Mines
Fernsplat Coombe
Bissoe
Helston Water
ST EUNY
Carn Marth
Hick's Mill
CORNISH WAY
B3297
A393
Church Coombe
CARN BREA
Pennance
Trevarth
Cusgarne
Greenwith Common
Lanner
Gwennap
Buller Downs
Piece
Carnkie
Tresavean
Comford
Frogpool
COAST TO COAST TRAIL
Treskillard
Treviskey
Tresamble
Perranwell
SHIREHORSE FARM CARRIAGE MUSEUM
BURNCOOSE NURSERIES & GARDEN
ST PIRAN
A39
Pencoys
Four Lanes
Trethellan Water
Trewithen Moor
Gilly
Perran Wharf
Perranarworthal
Sewrah Moor
Carclew
Tumuli
Lancarrow
Penhalurick
Tubbon Hill
Penhalveor
Hendra
Ponsanooth
Menherion
Laity Moor
Polgear
Tresevern Croft
ST STEDYANA
Stithians
Goonreeve
Burnthouse
Carnmenellis
NINE MAIDENS
Polmarth
Tretheague
Tregolls
STANDING STONE
Enys
Roskrow
Calvadnack
ANCIENT VILLAGE
Penmarth
Stithians Resr
Rosemanowas
Chywoon
St Gluvias
MUSEUM
Tolcarne
Boswin
Halabezack
Hernis
A394
Carveth
Tremough
Farms Common
Carnkie
Longdowns
ST GLUVIACUS
Penryn
Wheal Enys
Halwin
Medlyn
Rame
Trenoweth
Mabe Burnthouse
Lezerea
Porkellis
Viscar
Edgcumbe
Halvosso
FALMOUTH
Garlidna
Butteriss Gate
Butteriss Downs
Spargo
ST MADERN
ST BUDOCK
Porkellis Moor
POLDARK MINE
Hendra
Tregantallan
Trevease
Carvedras
STANDING STONE
Treverva
Budock Water
Carnebone
Lamanva
ST WENDRONS
BEACON HUT
Sewargan
Maen Pern
Eathorne
Trewoon
PENJERRICK GARDENS
Wendron

Wheal Coates ab/nt

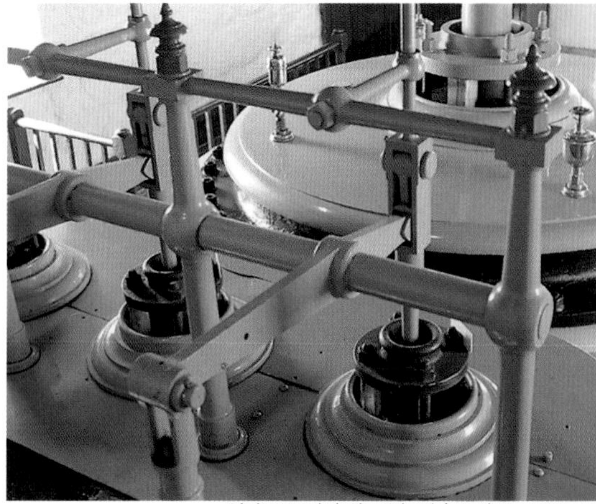
Cylinder Cover and Valve Chest, Taylor's Shaft, Cornish Mines & Engines nt

CAMBORNE & REDRUTH.

Famous mining centre, and birthplace of Richard Trevithick 1771 - 1833. Designer of the high pressure steam pump which revolutionised mining, enabling water to be pumped out at great depths. Tin mining halted in the 1930's due to imports of cheap malaysian tin. Two towns create a long urban sprawl. Camborne School of Mines Museum*, Cornish Engines*. Mineral Tramways*. Cinema. (E6 & H5)

Cornwall's Industrial Heritage – What to See & Visit...

Cornish Mines & Engines (NT).
Cornwall's largest Engine built in 1892 and in pristine condition. These two great beam engines were used for pumping water and winding men and ore up and down from depths of over 550 metres. Site includes the Industrial Discovery Centre at East Pool. Open Su-F, Mid Apr to Oct 11-5. (F5)

Dolcoath Mine.
At 3,500 ft below the surface, Cornwall's deepest mine. Shut down in 1921 following the tin slump after WW1. (F6)

Mineral Tramways Discovery Centre,
Penhallick. Cornwall's industrial past revealed; Portreath Tramroad, 11km and Great Flat Lode trails, 10km. Interpretation Centre. Open all year Tu-Su 10-4, Sa 1-4. (G5)

Poldark Mine. Underground exploration with easy and difficult routes. Suitable for elderly and the fit and fearless. Poldark museum and film. Surface fun for the family. Open East, then all year 10-6. (H10)

School Of Mines Geological Museum & Art Gallery. Pool. World-wide collection of minerals. Exhibition of local artists. Open daily. (F5)

South Crofty Mine, Dudnance Lane, Pool. Former tine and copper mine organise underground trips so wear old clothes and gum boots. Hard hats provided. Open M-Sa. Pre-book on: 01209 715777. (F5)

Trevithick's Cottage (NT).
Richard Trevithick, the Cornish engineer and inventor of the high-pressure steam engine lived here between 1810-1815. A thatched cottage open Apr-Oct W 2-5, donations welcome. (E6)

GWENNAP

A district with an abundance of disused mines, engine houses, and old engine tracks from former copper and tin mines. Gwennap Pit. See below. (J5)

Gwennap Pit.
Ampitheatre caused by mining subsidence. Landscaped in 1803. Excellent acoustics, known as the Methodist 'Cathedral'. Open all year. John Wesley first preached here 1762, and in 1773 to a congregation of 32,000. Annual Methodist Meeting - spring BHM. Visitor Centre open June-Sept M-F 10-4.30, Sa 10-12.30. (J5)

HAYLE

Formerly a small port and industrial centre. The foundries once made all the castings for every Cornish mine, and at nearby Copperhouse there were tin and copper smelting works. The Saltings is a reserve for migratory birds. 3 miles of superb sands. (A7)

Carnsew Gallery, 42-43 Penpol Terrace. Original work by resident artists and craftsmen from Cornwall. A blend of mixed media through ceramics. Open May to mid-Oct M-Sa 10-4.30. (A7)

The Salt Gallery, 57 Fore St. Finest contemporary gallery in Cornwall with monthly exhibitions for paintings and ceramics and separate Installation Space. Open Tu-Sa 10-5.30 or by appoint. T 01736 753356. (A7)

Paradise Park. Wildlife conservation sanctuary with 400 birds and animals in 100 avaries in a 7 acre garden. Australian Aviary. Eagles of Paradise flying displays. Open daily summer 10-5, winter 10-4. (A7)

Shire Horse Farm & Carriage Museum.
Shire and Suffolk Punches. Horse drawn, agricultural and private vehicles. Open Apr-Oct M-F 11-4. T 01209 713606. (G6)

PORTREATH

Harbour built by Francis Bassett to serve local mines. In 1809 the terminus for one of the country's first railway lines. Many interesting industrial remains. (F3)

Special Places to Visit.....

Godolphin House.
Romantic Tudor and Stuart mansion, c.1475. The Godolphin family's courtly ambitions and taste are expressed in the evolving design of the house. Tin mining provided wealth for this family of entrepreneurs, soldiers, poets and officials. C16 and C17 English furniture. Open Apr-Sept Tu Th & F 2-5, BH Ms 11-5. M-F 10-4. (C10)

Mount Hawke - Sk8.
Skateboarding park undercover. Youth Group charity status. Open daily. T 01209 890705. (J2)

Where to Eat, Drink & Be Merry...

Tabb's, Tregea Terrace. Discreet and professional husband and wife team, the Tabb's know how to cater for their guests; seasonal dishes with a twist. Chocoholics beware. This is heaven. Lunch 12-2, Dinner 7-9. T 01209 842488. (F3)

Trevaskis Farm.
PYO fruit. Farm shop. Restaurant. Open daily 10-5. (B7)

Ancient Cornwall

Carwynen Quoit. Fine specimen, three legs and large capstone. (E7)

Carn Brea. Traces of neolithic settlers. Focus of legends and giants. Site of C15 castle. A 90ft Obelisk built in c.1836 in memory of Lord de Dunstanville, At 783ft, a superb viewpoint. (G6)

Coastal Footpath

Trevaunance Cove (St Agnes) To Hayle (& St Ives): Approx 24 (28) miles. From Perranporth to Godrevy Point the coast is quite magnificent. Around St Agnes Head, a profusion of heather, gorse and sea pinks, and much evidence of tin workings with the ruins of many old mine shafts. Rounding the headlands the views are distant and dramatic, bare cliffs and rolling heathland stretching westwards, the sea below all sparkling blues and turquoise. Scramble up St Agnes Beacon (630ft) for spectacular views west down the coast inland to Bodmin Moor, and across the peninsula to Falmouth and St Michaels Mount. From Chapel Porth to Porthtowan the path up over Mulgram Hill past Great Wheal Charlotte. On to Portreath and for much of the way a barbed wire fence on your left marks the perimeter of Nancekuke airfield. From Portreath to Godrevy Point along North Cliffs

The Salt Gallery ss

there's superb cliff scenery and invigorating walking. The lonely stretch from Bassett's Cove to the savage Hell's Mouth has been a graveyard of many ships over the centuries; a place of drama, and melancholy, and fierce crashing seas. The path passes inland to Gwithian then returns seaward to follow the edge of the towans (sand dunes) to Hayle. Thereafter it follows the road round the Hayle estuary and returns to the coast for the last stretch into St Ives.

Beaches & Surfing

Chapel Porth. Spacious sands at LT, but beware of fast-flowing incoming tides along this coast and strong currents, bathing can be HZ. Bass fishing/caves, S-B hire LG/P/WC. Surfing – Submerged at HT. Powerful surf. (H1)

Porthtowan. Surfing – Fine beach break. HT protected from SW winds. Crowded in summer. (G2)

Portreath. Popular family beach with golden sands, fast HZ incoming tides, caves, S-B. hire/LG/P/WC/cafe. Surfing – On beach beginners keep L and surf the beach break. Can be crowded. By harbour N end produces good breaks in a fair swell. (F3)

Godrevy Towans. Sand, rocks and dunes. Enter beside Red River WC/LG. (B4)

Gwithian Towans. Surf, dunes and P/WC/LG/cafe. Surfing – Peaks suitable for novices. At HT cut off by rocks. (B5)

Hayle, The Towans. A vast expanse of firm golden sands ideal for families to spread out Swift currents to be avoided at mouth of estuary, surfing with S-B hire/WC/LG. (A6)

Shire Horse Farm & Carriage Museum ss

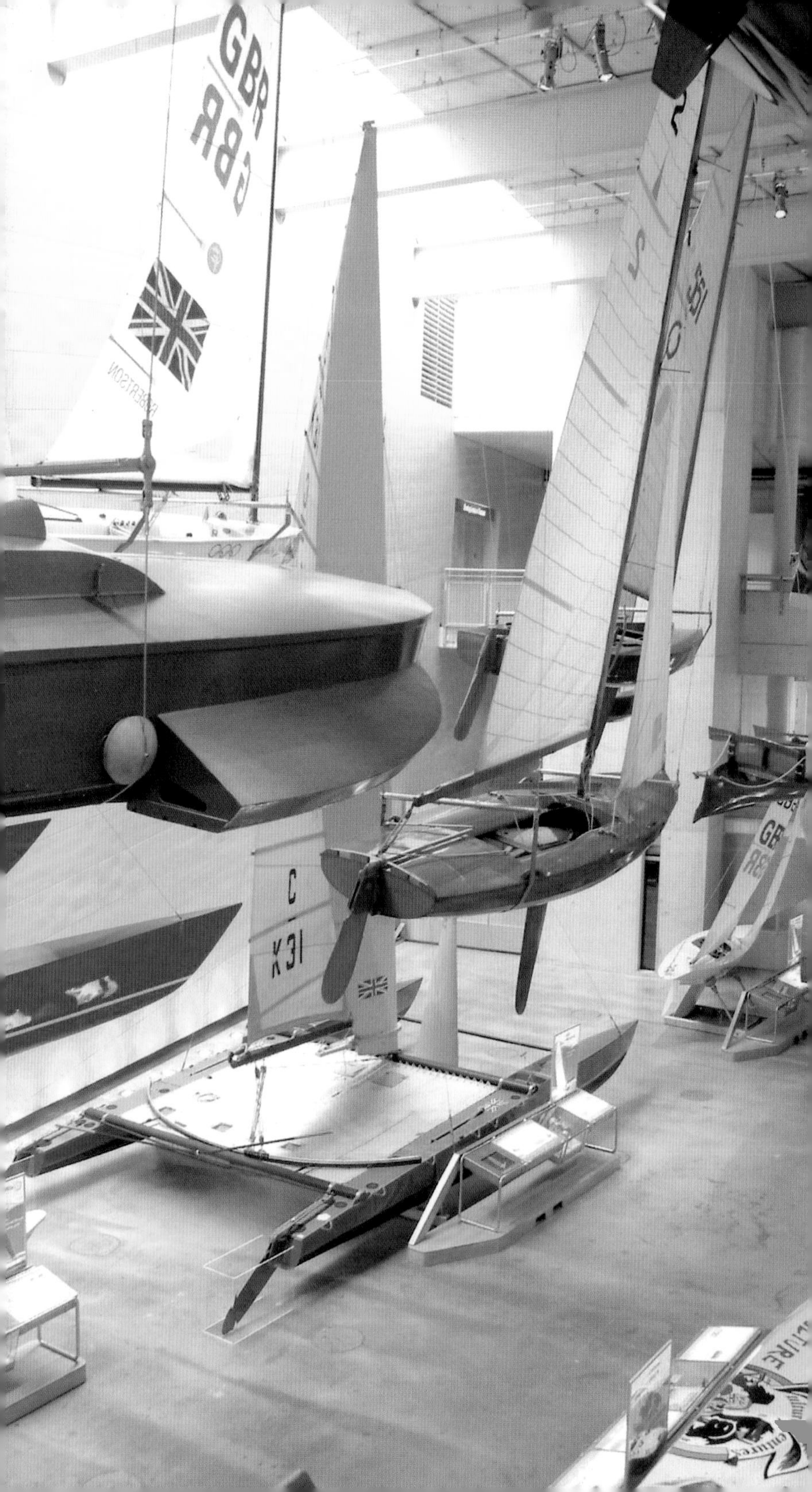
GBR
C
K31

For Chic Hotels, Culture, Glorious Gardens, Harbours, Shopping, Stylish Living, Watersports, Waterside Pubs & Cafes...

This is the affluent heart of Cornwall. The great harbour of Falmouth visited by the Romans and Phoenicians is today a centre of maritime excellence. The magnificent Fal Estuary home to thousands of sailing craft is a playground for water sports. Connected by water, Truro lies twelve miles up river and is Cornwall's only Cathedral city. It's a busy and attractive city with designer shops, flea markets, restaurants and art galleries, and host to a food and drinks festival, on Lemon Quay in late September.

Across the estuary from Falmouth lies the sedate village of St Mawes and the exquisitely beautiful Roseland Peninsula . Not to be missed the church at St Just. The coastal footpath is now tamer and the landscape gentler. It passes some fine chic hotels and pretty harbours on its journey towards St Austell and Charlestown. Hereabouts is Eden, visited by many hundreds of thousands. This project has brought prosperity to this area, and has reminded many (who may have forgotten in their search for Mediterranean or Caribbean sun) of the hidden delights of Cornwall. Fowey has benefited too, and here the gastronome is spoilt for choice, for the many sophisticated eating and drinking holes on offer. It is also a fine place to stay. Not far away are many great gardens to visit; Caerhays Castle, Heligan, Trelissick and more. Spring is the best time, for on display are the camellias, azaleas, magnolias and rhododendrons.

The National Maritime Museum, Falmouth ss

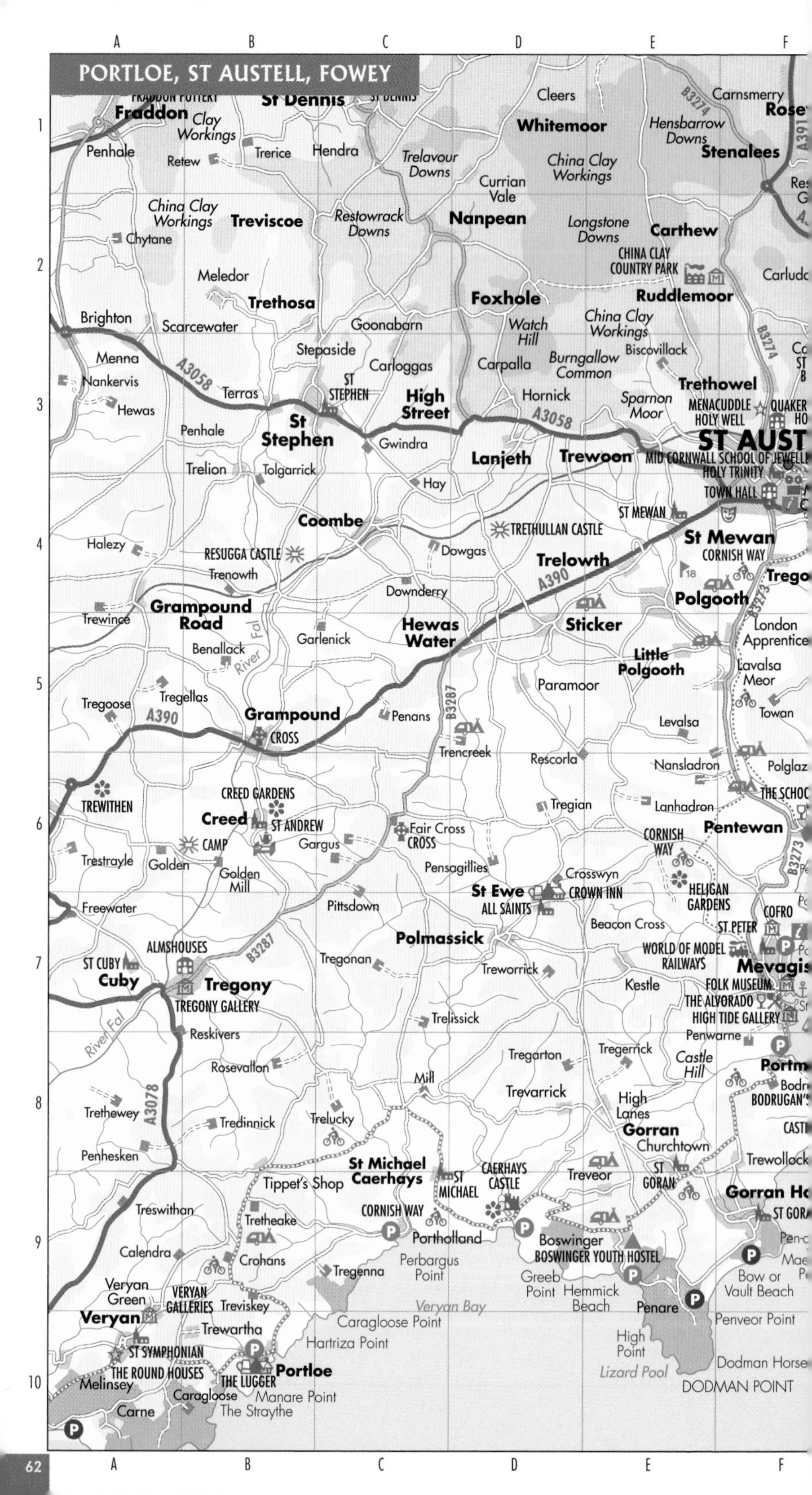
Fraddon
Clay Workings
St Dennis
Cleers
Whitemoor
Carnsmerry
Hensbarrow Downs
Stenalees
Penhale
Retew
Trerice
Hendra
Trelavour Downs
Currian Vale
China Clay Workings
China Clay Workings
Treviscoe
Restowrack Downs
Nanpean
Longstone Downs
Carthew
Chytane
CHINA CLAY COUNTRY PARK
Meledor
Trethosa
Foxhole
Ruddlemoor
Brighton
Scarcewater
Goonabarn
Watch Hill
China Clay Workings
Menna
Stepaside
Carloggas
Carpalla
Burngallow Common
Biscovillack
Nankervis
ST STEPHEN
High Street
Hornick
Trethowel
Terras
Sparnon Moor
MENACUDDLE HOLY WELL
Hewas
St Stephen
A3058
Penhale
Gwindra
Lanjeth
Trewoon
MID CORNWALL SCHOOL OF JEWELLERY
HOLY TRINITY
Trelion
Tolgarrick
Hay
TOWN HALL
Coombe
ST MEWAN
TRETHULLAN CASTLE
St Mewan
CORNISH WAY
Halezy
RESUGGA CASTLE
Dowgas
Trelowth
Trenowth
Polgooth
Downderry
A390
Trewince
Grampound Road
Hewas Water
Sticker
London Apprentice
Garlenick
Benallack
River Fal
Little Polgooth
Lavalsa Meor
Paramoor
Tregellas
Tregoose
A390
Grampound
CROSS
Penans
B3287
Levalsa
Towan
Trencreek
Rescorla
Nansladron
Polglaz
TREWITHEN
CREED GARDENS
THE SCHOOL
Creed
ST ANDREW
Tregian
Lanhadron
Fair Cross
CROSS
Pentewan
CAMP
Gargus
CORNISH WAY
Trestrayle
Golden
Golden Mill
Pensagillies
B3273
Crosswyn
St Ewe
CROWN INN
ALL SAINTS
HELIGAN GARDENS
Freewater
Pittsdown
Beacon Cross
COFRO
ST PETER
Polmassick
ALMSHOUSES
WORLD OF MODEL RAILWAYS
ST CUBY
B3287
Tregonan
Mevagissey
Cuby
Tregony
Treworrick
Kestle
FOLK MUSEUM
TREGONY GALLERY
THE ALVORADO
HIGH TIDE GALLERY
Trelissick
River Fal
Reskivers
Penwarne
Tregarton
Tregerrick
Castle Hill
Rosevallon
Mill
A3078
Trevarrick
Trethewey
High Lanes
BODRUGAN'S
Tredinnick
Trelucky
Gorran Churchtown
Penhesken
St Michael Caerhays
CAERHAYS CASTLE
Trewollock
Tippet's Shop
ST MICHAEL
Treveor
ST GORAN
Treswithan
Tretheake
CORNISH WAY
Portholland
Boswinger
BOSWINGER YOUTH HOSTEL
Calendra
Crohans
Perbargus Point
Tregenna
Bow or Vault Beach
Veryan Green
VERYAN GALLERIES
Treviskey
Greeb Point
Hemmick Beach
Veryan Bay
Penare
Veryan
Caragloose Point
Penveor Point
Trewartha
Hartriza Point
High Point
ST SYMPHONIAN
Dodman Horse
THE ROUND HOUSES
THE LUGGER
Portloe
Lizard Pool
Melinsey
DODMAN POINT
Caragloose
Manare Point
Carne
The Straythe

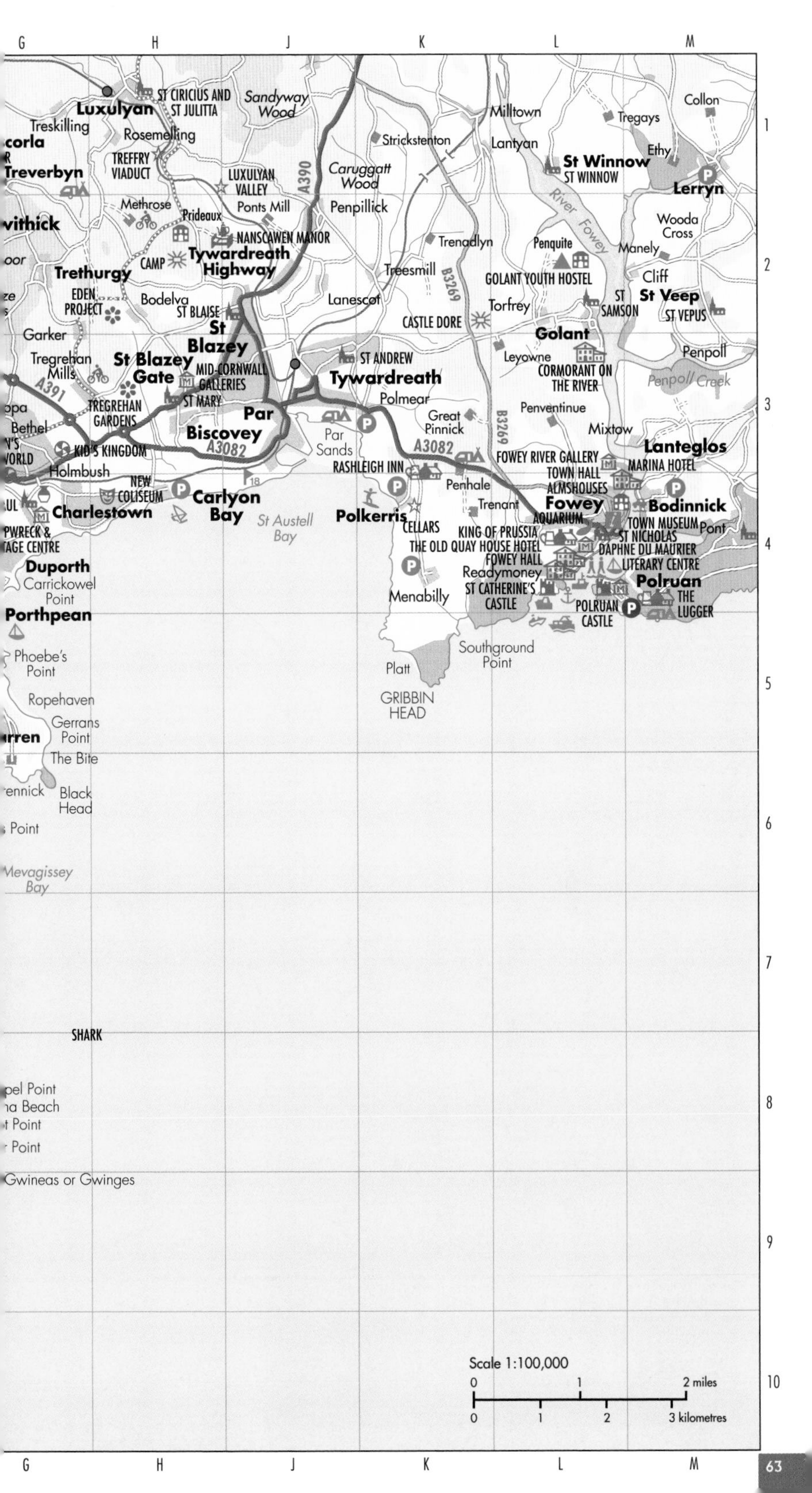

G
H
J
K
L
M
1
2
3
4
5
6
7
8
9
10
Luxulyan
ST CIRICIUS AND ST JULITTA
Sandyway Wood
Treskilling
Rosemelling
Treverbyn
TREFFRY VIADUCT
LUXULYAN VALLEY
A390
Caruggatt Wood
Penpillick
Methrose
Prideaux
Ponts Mill
NANSCAWEN MANOR
Tywardreath Highway
CAMP
Trethurgy
EDEN PROJECT
Bodelva
ST BLAISE
St Blazey
Garker
Tregrehan Mills
St Blazey Gate
MID-CORNWALL GALLERIES
ST MARY
A391
TREGREHAN GARDENS
Bethel
KID'S KINGDOM
Holmbush
Par
Biscovey
A3082
NEW COLISEUM
Carlyon Bay
Charlestown
Duporth
Carrickowel Point
Porthpean
Phoebe's Point
Ropehaven
Gerrans Point
The Bite
Black Head
Mevagissey Bay
SHARK
Gwineas or Gwinges
St Austell Bay
Strickstenton
Trenadlyn
Treesmill
B3269
Lanescot
CASTLE DORE
ST ANDREW
Tywardreath
Polmear
Par Sands
RASHLEIGH INN
Great Pinnick
Polkerris
CELLARS
Menabilly
Platt
GRIBBIN HEAD
Southground Point
Milltown
Lantyan
Tregays
Collon
Ethy
St Winnow
ST WINNOW
Lerryn
River Fowey
Wooda Cross
Penquite
Manely
GOLANT YOUTH HOSTEL
Cliff
Torfrey
ST SAMSON
St Veep
ST VEPUS
Golant
Leyowne
CORMORANT ON THE RIVER
Penpoll
Penpoll Creek
Penventinue
Mixtow
Lanteglos
FOWEY RIVER GALLERY
TOWN HALL
ALMSHOUSES
MARINA HOTEL
Penhale
Trenant
Fowey
AQUARIUM
Bodinnick
TOWN MUSEUM
Pont
ST NICHOLAS
KING OF PRUSSIA
THE OLD QUAY HOUSE HOTEL
DAPHNE DU MAURIER LITERARY CENTRE
FOWEY HALL
Readymoney
Polruan
ST CATHERINE'S CASTLE
POLRUAN CASTLE
THE LUGGER
Scale 1:100,000
0
1
2 miles
0
1
2
3 kilometres

ST AUSTELL

The major town and route centre of this area, which has seen much recent development and prosperity since the opening of first, Heligan Gardens and then, the Eden Project. Brewing centre and formerly an old tin mining village whose prosperity later relied very much on the china clay industry. The hinterland is made up of white mountainous pyramids and man-made lakes, and palm trees. There is a fine C15 perpendicular church, the Holy Trinity and the C18 coaching inn, The White Hart Hotel. A Georgian Quaker meeting house 1829. Brewery Heritage Centre*. Eden Project*.

Bens Playworld. Mega-slides, giant tubes, assault course...fun for kids. Cafe. Open daily 10-7. (G3)

Kids Kingdom, Albert Road. Indoor play centre for family fun. Open daily East-Sept, winter Tu-Su (& M in school hols), 10-6. (G3)

Mid Cornwall School of Jewellery, 19 High Cross St. Holds a wide range of courses. You can even make your own Wedding Ring!. Open by appoint. T 01726 73319. (F3)

St Austell Brewery Visitor Centre. Traditional brewers for 140 years. Guided tours and beer sampling at 11am and 2:30pm. Licensed shop. Open M-F 9.30-4.30. (F2)

Anchorage House,. Nettles Corner. Luxury 5 Star B & B 5 mins from Eden. Awarded "Britains Best B & B" twice. Lap pool, hot tub, huge beds, spa and gym. No children (u 16). T 01726 814071. (G3)

Eden Project ac

Special Places to Visit Outside St Austell....

China Clay Country Park. Mining and Heritage Centre. New exhibitions, open air displays, historic nature trails with spectacular views of modern clay pit. Children's challenge trail, licensed cafe and shop. Open daily Mar-Oct 10-5. T 01726 850362 www.chinaclaycountry.co.uk. (E1)

Eden Project. Major multi-million pound project to turn old china clay pits into vast steel-framed domes (biomes) housing a tropical rain forest and a Mediterranean climate. This project of enormous vision, and ambition, has been an outstanding success, and has drawn visitors in their hundreds of thousands since opening in Spring 2000. Open daily from 10. (H2)

The Background to the China Clay Industry...

William Cookworthy. The Plymouth chemist discovered Kaolin at Tregonning Hill in 1768, a substance to form the basis of England's porcelain industry. Later, extensive finds were discovered around Hensbarrow Downs close to St Austell which became the centre of the industry. Kaolin is a product of changed granite; the rock is extracted from enormous pits, 300ft deep and 1/2 mile across. Only a portion is used, the rest is piled in great white heaps, hundreds of feet high, like towering snow mountains, the 'Cornish Alps' on which vegetation scarcely grows (unless the Alp is part of the Eden Project).

China Clay Country Park ss

CHARLESTOWN.

There's a nostalgic atmosphere about this C18 china clay harbour built by Charles Rashleigh. Home port for famous tall ships of Square Sail Shipyard Company. Shipwreck and Heritage Centre, Diving centre. Pottery. (G3)

Shipwreck And Heritage Centre. The largest shipwreck artefact collection in the UK. Titanic display. Hands-on rescue equipment and lots more. (G3)

Ancient Cornwall

Castle Dore. Prehistoric earthwork with inner ramparts. Deserted in AD 100, occupied in C5. Legendary setting for the love story of Tristan and Iseult. (K2)

MEVAGISSEY

One of Cornwall's most picturesque and unspoilt fishing villages. The fine inner, and more recent outer harbour have been at the centre of the town's history. Shark fishing centre, World of Model Railways, Folk Museum and ferry to Fowey. Nearby, Heligan Gardens. Feast Week - late June. (F6)

Special Places to Visit...

Cofro,
14 Fore St. Affordable works of art by 30 + Cornish artists; jewellery, glass, sculptures, paintings. Open Tu-Su 10.30-4.30. (F6)

High Tide Gallery,
21 Church St. Good mix of Cornish based arts and crafts, and London Art. Open M-Sa 10-4. (F6)

Mevagissey Folk Museum,
East Quay. Exhibits of local origin; fishing, agriculture and domestic life in an old 1745 building where luggers (fishing boats) were built. Open East-Oct 11-6. (F7)

World Of Model Railways,
Meadow St. Over 2,000 models, 50 trains controlled in sequence. Model shop. Open daily Mar-Oct (Nov-Feb W & Su only). (F6)

To Eat & Drink...

The Alvorada, 2 Polkirt Hill. Family-run, Portugese restaurant with a lively atmosphere. Dinner 6.30-12. T 01726 842055. (F7)

The Schoolhouse, West End. Good value cooking in large Victorian schoolroom. Dinner Tu-Sa. T 01726 842474. (F5)

Polkerris. Former pilchard fishing port. Harbour breakwater built by the Rashleighs of Menabilly. Remains of huge pilchard 'palace', possibly Elizabethan. (K3)

POLRUAN

Attractive village with busy boatyard. The main street plunges almost vertically to the small quay on Fowey estuary. Cars not encouraged. Superb views from hill-top car park and walks east to Lantic Bay. Pedestrian ferry to Fowey. (M4)

Mevagissey Harbour

PORTLOE

Little fishing village with a narrow and rocky harbour. The Lugger Inn*. (B9)

The Lugger. C17 smuggler's inn has been turned into a chic, trendy restaurant. Local boats supply the fish. Lunch 12-2, Dinner 7-9. T 01872 501322. (B9)

Bodrugan's Leap. Sir Harry Trelowth of Bodrugan rode his horse over the cliff to be picked up by a passing fishing boat after fleeing the Battle of Bosworth in 1485. (F7)

FOWEY

Narrow streets and brightly coloured houses overlook the superb natural harbour. One of England's busiest towns in the Middle Ages, and home of the 'Fowey Gallants', a bunch of reckless and invincible pirates who raided French and Spanish shipping. Today a busy exporter of China Clay. Museum*, Aquarium*, Fishing trips and passenger ferry to Polruan. Royal Regatta & Carnival week - Aug (2/3 week). (L3)

Special Places to Visit...

Daphne Du Maurier Literary Centre, 5 South St. Explores Foweys literary connections. Houses the TIC. Open daily, all year. T 01726 833616. (L3)

Fowey Aquarium.
Wide collection of marine life. Open daily East-Sept. (L3)

Luxulyan Valley ac

Fowey River Expeditions.
Travel the river upstream by kayak canoe or motorboat. Stopping off at Golant or Lerryn for lunch. Accompanied by staff and safety boat. Runs from May to early Sept. T 01726 833627. (L3)

Fowey River Gallery, 38 Fore St. Cornish contemporary art for serious buyers, and plenty of crafts; ceramics, glass, jewellery. Open M-Sa 10-5 (& summer Su). (L3)

Fowey River. Rises on Bodmin Moor, especially beautiful between Lostwithiel and Doublebois - richly wooded riverbanks. Trout and Sea trout fishing. (L1)

Luxulyan Valley. Wooded ravine overgrown with flowers and fauna. Watered by nearby clay pit. (J1)

Town Museum, Trafalgar Square. Local history and bygones. Open May-Sept M-F 10-5. (L3)

The Old Quay House Hotel ss

Special Places to Stay, Eat & Drink....

Fowey Hall.
Luxurious Victorian house in superb hilltop location. Very much a child-friendly, family hotel with masses of attractions on offer. Dogs welcome. T 01726 833866. (L4)

The Old Quay House Hotel, 28 Fore St. Set in one of the most beautiful estuaries in Cornwall with a resplendent waterside location offering stylish accomodation which is chic, welcoming and relaxed. Award-winning Restaurant (2AA Rosettes and a Remy Award). Open all year. T 01726 833302. (L3)

Marina Hotel & Waterside Restaurant. Former summer residence of the Bishops of Truro. Bedrooms with balconies. Now has a mouth-watering restaurant with chef, Nick Fisher of deserved fame. Fish a delight! T 01726 833315. (L3)

Cormorant On The River.
Small, cosy hotel offering spectacular views over the estuary. Undergoing refurbishment. The King's will look after your every need. T 01726 833426. (L2)

The King of Prussia,
Town Quay. Excellent pub grub; local fish, burgers, with a view to match. Open daily, (L:3)

Galleries to Visit...

Mid Cornwall Galleries. Some of the finest of contemporary British Art and Crafts; paintings, ceramics, silks, glass, jewellery. Changing exhibs. Open M-Sa 10-5. (H2)

Tregony Gallery,
58 Fore St. Friendly little gallery stocking paintings from the Victorian period to today's New Look, plus crafts; ceramics, jewellery etc. Open M-Sa 10-5. (B7)

Gardens to Visit...

Caerhays Castle & Gardens.
60 acres of informal woodland gardens created by J C Williams who sponsored plant hunting expeditions to China. Noted for Camellias, Magnolias and Rhododendrons. Garden open daily mid-Feb to end May, 10-5.00. Castle from mid-Mar 12-4 M-F. T 01872 501310. (D8)

Creed Gardens.
5 acre Georgian Rectory garden. Tree collection, rhododendrons, sunken alpine and walled herbaceous gardens, trickle stream and ponds. Open daily Mar-Sept 10-5.30. (B5)

Heligan Gardens. Explore 200 acres of Cornish countryside, including award-winning productive garden restoration, atmospheric pleasure grounds, sub-tropical 'Jungle', valley and estate land incorporating a pioneering wildlife conservation project. Open daily, all year from 10. T 01726 845100. (E6)

Tregrehan Gardens.
Woodland garden created in the C19 by Carlyon family. Nursery. Camellias. Open mid-Mar to mid-June W-Su & BH Ms 10.30-5. (H2)

Nanscawen Manor House.
Spacious house set in five glorious acres of rhododendrons and camellias. Swimming pool. No children (u12). T 01726 814488. (J1)

Churches of Interest

Fowey Church.
Originally wrecked by pirates, Jacobean pulpit made from a Spanish galleon. Very tall tower. C12 font, Rashleigh monuments. (L3)

Golant church. Beautifully situated C15 with fine wagon roofs and C15 glass. Holy well. (L2)

St Austell Church. C15 tower, C15 carvings of Cornish saints.

Coastal Footpath

Portloe - Fowey:
Approx. 26 miles. Sandy beaches, fishing ports and the many signs of the china clay industry. Past delightful Portholland, lonely coves and remote farmland meeting the

Caerhays Castle & Gardens ss

sea, then steep climb to Dodman Point where there is a granite cross erected in 1896 as mark for fishermen. Offshore are notorious currents, scene of many wrecks.

The path carries on down to Gorran Haven past the long sweep of Vault Beach. Beyond Chapel Point and Bodrugan's Leap*, the path becomes easy going, the landscape has softened.

The harsh cliffs and thunderous roar of the North Coast, Penwith and Lizard are far behind.

Beyond Mevagissey, you are in holiday country as you cross Pentewan Sands, but soon the path is lonely and remote again towards Black Head into St Austell Bay, the coast becomes more built-up as you approach Par Sands, past the t hriving china clay harbour of Par.

Lovely walk through pretty Polkerris, then up to impressive cliffs of Gribbin Head (224ft) and an 84ft landmark, erected by Trinity House in the 1820's. Fine views from the Lizard to Rame Head.

At Polridmouth, sub-tropical flora and on up the path with good views of Fowey Harbour. Passing near the remains of St Catherine's Castle. Follow road into Fowey where there is a regular ferry to Polruan.

Beaches & Surfing

Kiberick Cove. Secluded tricky access, sand exposed at LT. (B10)

Portloe. Good bathing with grey shingle at LT. P/WC/inn. (B9)

East & West Portholland. Shingle with sand at LT. HZ cliffs to sides P/WC. (C8)

Porthluney Beach. Popular sheltered family beach with extended sands. P/WC/kiosk. (D8)

Hemmick Beach. Steep 1 in 5 descent to small sandy beach. (E9)

Bow Or Vault Beach. Steep tricky path down to spacious sands and shingle. (F9)

Gorran Haven. Family resort with fine bathing and spacious sands. P/WC/boats for hire. (F8)

Portmellon. Good bathing off small sandy beach, rocks at both sides. P/WC/inn/cafe. (F7)

Pentewan. Spacious sands, HZ bathing; strong currents, avoid channel. P. Surfing - Sheltered spot. Waves only occur after an enormous swell, rarely in summer. Hollow beach break. (F6)

Porthpean. Popular family beach with safe bathing, rock pools and old fish cellars. P/WC/cafe. (G4)

Charlestown. To west of harbour, sand and pebbles, strong currents. (G3)

Mid Cornwall Galleries

Carlyon Bay. Spacious golden sandy beach with all amenities in adjacent leisure centre. Access to Polgaver Bay, Cornwall's first official naturist beach. Boat hire, water skiing etc P/WC/cafe/bars. No dogs. (H3)

Par Sands. Large extensive sandy bay. Very popular with children, seaside amusements, boating lake, easy access, private harbour, china clay works, effluent on west side. P/WC/cafe/huts. (J3)

Polkerris. Small sandy family beach sheltered by curving harbour wall. Safe bathing, S-B hire/P/WC/cafe/inn. Surfing - Popular. Big swell required. (K3)

Poldridmouth Cove. 15 mins walk fron P sheltered sandy cove. (K4)

Fowey - Readymoney Cove. 20 mins walk from town centre. Small sandy beach at LT, good bathing, sheltered. WC/tea rooms. (L4)

Heligan Gardens ss

FALMOUTH, TRURO, ROSELAND PENINSULA

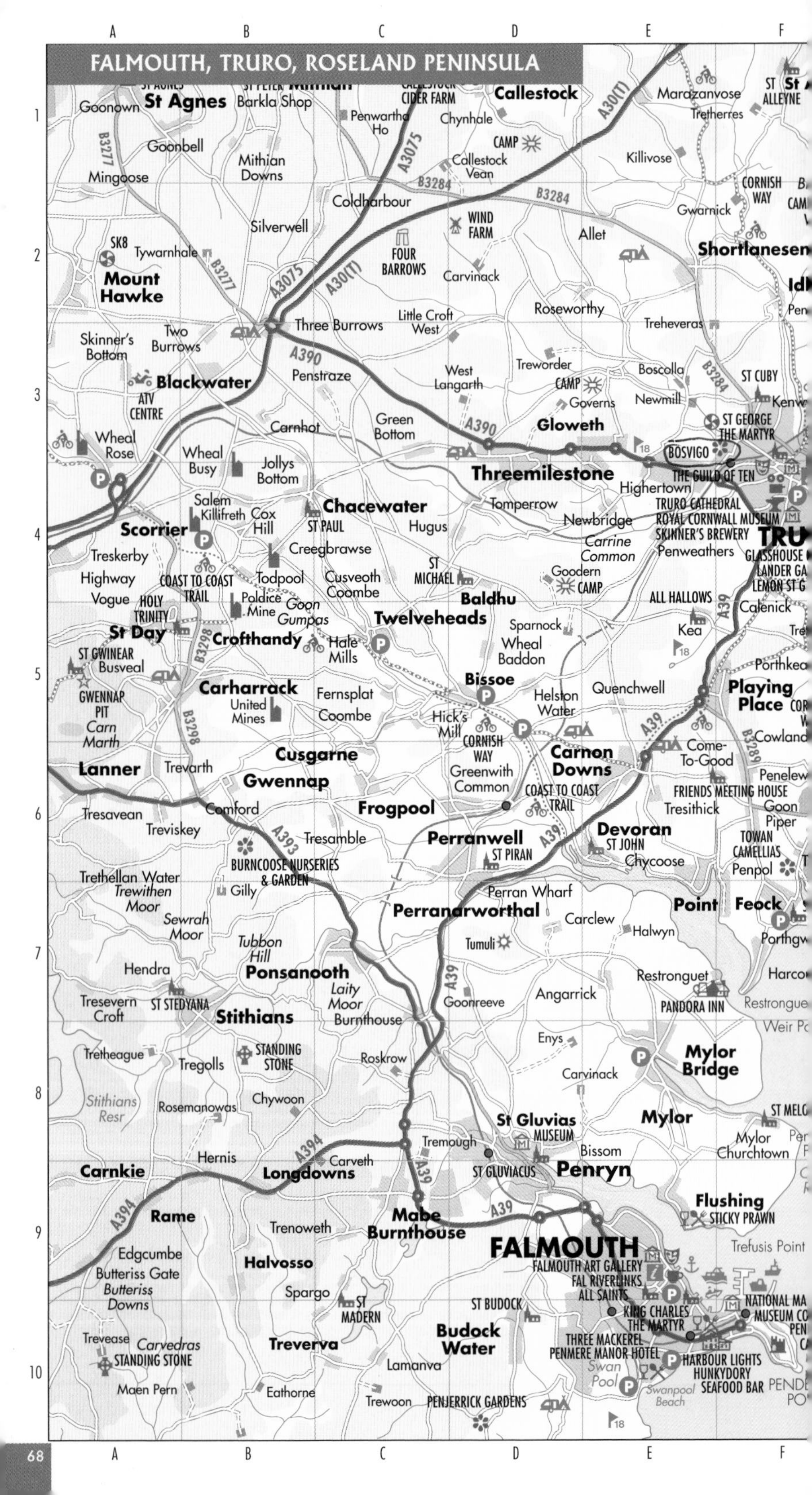

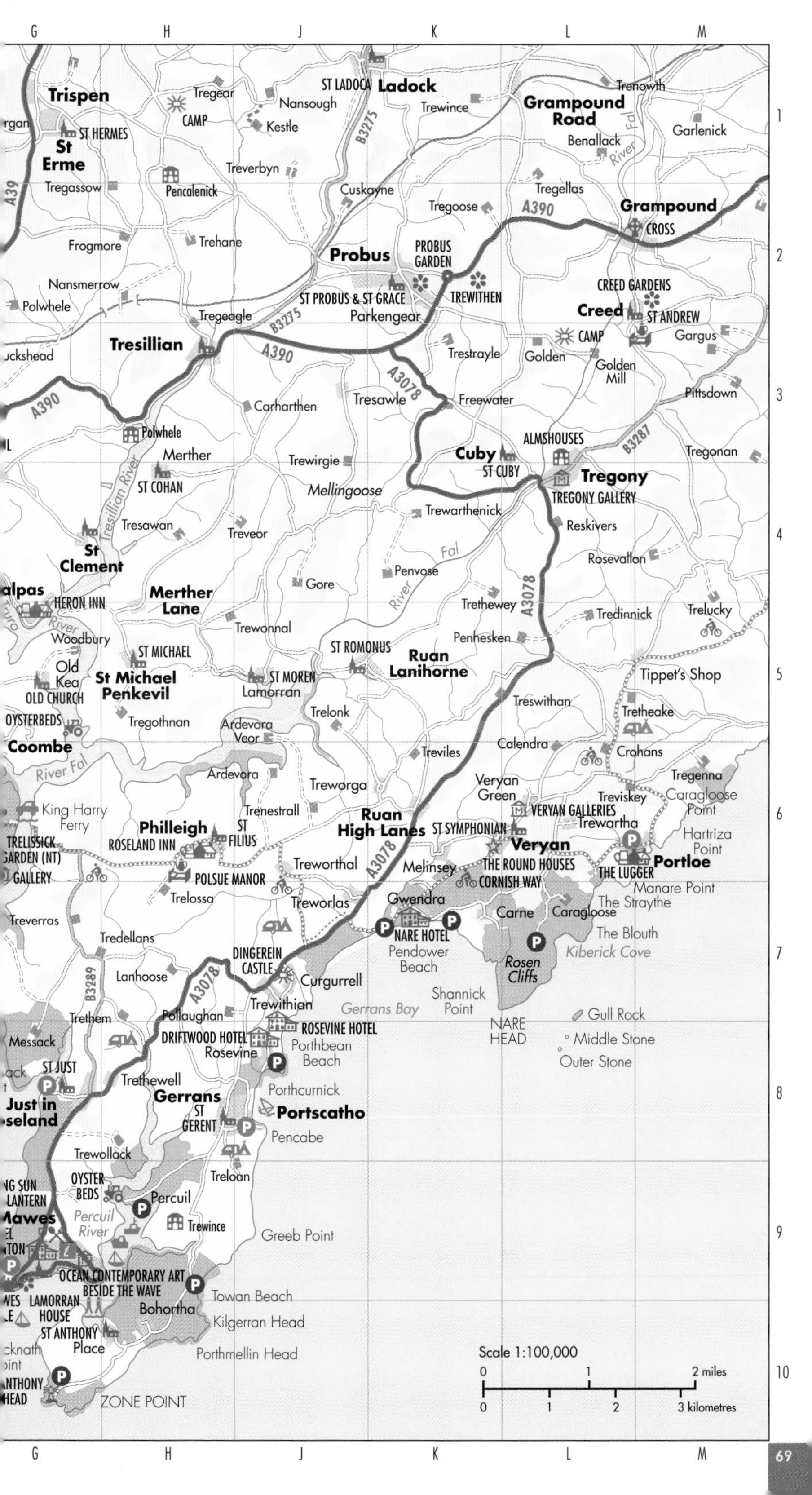
Trispen
St Erme
ST HERMES
Tregear
CAMP
Nansough
Kestle
ST LADOCA
Ladock
Trewince
Grampound Road
Trenowth
Garlenick
Benallack
River Fal
Tregassow
Pencalenick
Treverbyn
Cuskayne
Tregellas
Tregoose
A390
Grampound
CROSS
Frogmore
Trehane
Probus
PROBUS GARDEN
TREWITHEN
CREED GARDENS
Nansmerrow
Polwhele
Tregeagle
B3275
ST PROBUS & ST GRACE
Parkengear
Creed
ST ANDREW
CAMP
Gargus
Tresillian
A390
Trestrayle
Golden
Golden Mill
A3078
Tresawle
Freewater
Pittsdown
Carharthen
Polwhele
Merther
ST COHAN
Trewirgie
Mellingoose
Cuby
ST CUBY
ALMSHOUSES
Tregony
TREGONY GALLERY
B3287
Tregonan
Tresillian River
Tresawan
Treveor
Trewarthenick
Reskivers
St Clement
Fal
River
Penvose
Rosevallon
Gore
Trethewey
A3078
Merther Lane
HERON INN
Tredinnick
Trelucky
Trewonnal
Penhesken
Woodbury
ST MICHAEL
ST ROMONUS
Ruan Lanihorne
Old Kea
OLD CHURCH
St Michael Penkevil
ST MOREN
Lamorran
Tippet's Shop
Treswithan
OYSTERBEDS
Tregothnan
Trelonk
Tretheake
Ardevora Veor
Coombe
Treviles
Calendra
Crohans
River Fal
Ardevora
Treworga
Veryan Green
Tregenna
Caragloose Point
King Harry Ferry
Trenestrall
Ruan High Lanes
Treviskey
VERYAN GALLERIES
Philleigh
ST FILIUS
ST SYMPHONIAN
Trewartha
ROSELAND INN
Veryan
Hartriza Point
TRELISSICK GARDEN (NT)
A3078
GALLERY
Treworthal
Melinsey
THE ROUND HOUSES
THE LUGGER
Portloe
POLSUE MANOR
CORNISH WAY
Manare Point
Trelossa
Treworlas
Gwendra
The Straythe
Treverras
Carne
Caragloose
NARE HOTEL
The Blouth
Tredellans
Pendower Beach
Kiberick Cove
DINGEREIN CASTLE
Rosen Cliffs
B3289
Lanhoose
Curgurrell
Shannick Point
A3078
Trewithian
Gerrans Bay
Trethem
Pollaughan
NARE HEAD
Gull Rock
ROSEVINE HOTEL
Middle Stone
Messack
DRIFTWOOD HOTEL
Rosevine
Porthbean Beach
Outer Stone
ST JUST
Trethewell
Porthcurnick
Gerrans
Just in Roseland
ST GERENT
Portscatho
Pencabe
Trewollack
Treloan
OYSTER BEDS
Percuil
Mawes
Percuil River
Trewince
Greeb Point
OCEAN CONTEMPORARY ART
BESIDE THE WAVE
LAMORRAN HOUSE
Towan Beach
Bohortha
Kilgerran Head
ST ANTHONY
Place
Porthmellin Head
Scale 1:100,000
0
1
2 miles
0
1
2
3 kilometres
ZONE POINT
G
H
J
K
L
M
1
2
3
4
5
6
7
8
9
10

National Maritime Museum ss

FALMOUTH

Overlooks a superb natural harbour. The Phoenicians and Romans came here in search of tin. In the late C16, Sir Walter Raleigh persuaded the Killigrew family to develop the harbour's potential, and for 200 years the centre of the Mail Packet Trade, smuggling and piracy. Popular yachting centre. Pendennis Castle*, Maritime Museum*, Art Gallery*, gardens*, cinema and 3 beaches. Regatta week - mid Aug. E/C W. (D9)

Galleries & Museums to Visit…& Things to Do & See..

Beside The Wave, 10 Arwenack St. Established in 1989 to provide an outlet for Cornwall's leading contemporary artists and craftsmen. Open M-Sa 9.30-5. (C9)

Fal River Links, The Quay. Travel by ferry or take a cruise up river to Trelissick or Truro. Cross to St Mawes. Details: www.falriverlinks.co.uk

Falmouth Art Gallery, The Moor. Maritime pictures and quality temporary exhibitions. Work by J W Waterhouse and Henry Scott Tuke. Open all year M-Sa 9-5.30 (C9)

Falmouth Arts Centre, 24 Church St. 200 seat theatre (cinema) holds music, theatre and dance. Four galleries put on changing exhibs. Open daily. (C9)

National Maritime Museum. With breathtaking views from the 29m tower, one of only three natural underwater viewing locations in the world. Hands-on inter-actives, audio visual immersive experiences, talks, special exhibitions and the opportunity to get out onto the water. This new generation of museum has something for everyone. Open daily. T 01326 313388 www.nmmc.co.uk. (F10)

Ocean Contemporary, 29 Church St. Wide range of paintings and crafts in light, airy gallery. Open M-Sa 10-5.30. (E9)

Where to Eat, Drink & Be Merry…

Hunkdory, 46 Arwenack St. If you get a kick out of Art, the young and beautiful, trendy decor, and sumptuous food (especially fish). This is it. Dinner 6-10. T 01326 212997. (E9)

Seafood Bar, Lower Quay St. Underground bar (Madrid-like) serves up enormous dishes of crustacea and locally caught fish. Followed by fulsome desserts with toppings of clotted cream. Dinner 7-10.30. T 01326 315129. (E9)

Three Mackerel, Swanpool. Location, location cries the Estate Agent, and got it right here. Popular, award-winning restaurant produces imaginative dishes of fish and meats. Lunch 12-2.30, Dinner 6-9.30. T 01326 311886. (E10)

And Sleep…

Penmere Manor Hotel, Mongleath Rd. Georgian country house set in a 5 acre tropical garden. Large beds. Bolitho Restaurant. Fountains Leisure Club. Beauty/Therapy Room. T 01326 211411. (E10)

And Special Inns to Visit…

Heron Inn
In fine situation overlooking the tidal River Fal. Modern, light decor provides a nautical ambience. St Austell's beers. Specials. Children welcome. (G5)

Pandora Inn. C13 thatched pub beside the estuary has a bagatelle of flagstone floors, cosy alcoves and low ceilings. Al fresco pontoon over the river. Owned by the St Austell brewery. Children and dogs welcome. (E7)

Fal Estuary from Trelissick Garden

TRURO.

Cornwall's Cathedral city and administrative centre. Spacious and elegant with some beautiful buildings; Georgian and Regency in Lemon Street, the Assembly Rooms, 1772, Mansion House and Prince's House in Princes Street, and the Cathedral*, 1880-1910. Art Gallery & Museum*. Cinema. (F4)

Truro Cathedral

Galleries & Museums to Visit...

Glass House Gallery, Kenwyn St. Well established gallery showing contemporary art and ceramics on two floors. Extensive Jewellery display. Open M-Sa 10-5.15. (F4)

Lemon Street Gallery, Lemon St. Quality gallery whose aim is to introduce the British Art Scene to Cornwall. Modern and Contemporary art, sculpture and ceramics. Open M-Sa 10.30-5.30. (F4)

Royal Cornwall Museum, River Street. World-famous collection of minerals, archaeology, ceramics, paintings and old master drawings. Open M-Sa 10-5 (except BH's). (F4)

The Guild Of Ten, 19 Old Bridge St. Co-operative of craftsmen and women living in Cornwall. They seek to produce workmanship of the highest quality; knitwear, designer clothing, glass blowing, ceramics etc. Open M-Sa 9.30-5.30. (F4)

The Lander Gallery, Lemon Street Market. Spacious open gallery displays C19 and C20 Cornish masters to contemporary fine art and crafts. Coffee shop. Open M-Sa 9-6. (F4)

The Lander Gallery

Where to Eat, Drink & Be Merry....

Sevens, 77 Lemon St. Light, modern interior with views of food preparation. Ambitious menu with mixed reports. Not cheap. Lunch W-F 12-2.30, Dinner Tu-Sa 6.30-9.30. T 01872 275767. (F4)

Skinner's Brewery, Newham Rd. Visit a working brewery and sample their fine ales. Guided tours & tastings (11 & 2.30), visitor centre and shop. Open M-F. T 01872 271885. (F4)

Nare Hotel ss

PENRYN.

An attractive granite town at the head of Penryn Creek. Picturesque steep main street and handsome restored Georgian houses. Granted Charter in 1236, and much older than its more famous neighbour, Falmouth. In C17, England's busiest port after London. Granite from Penryn's quarries helped to build New Scotland Yard, four London Bridges and the Fastnet Lighthouse. Town Fair - Aug BH W/E. (D9)

Malcolm Sutcliffe Glass Gallery, 2 West St. Blown studio glass made on the premises by Malcolm Sutcliffe, plus jewellery, paintings and cards. Open W-F 11-5, Sa 10-1. T 01326 377020. (D9)

Malcolm Sutcliffe Glass Gallery ss

Penryn Museum. History of ancient town established in the C13; Neolithic, Medieval Glasney College, trade, victualling, piracy, smuggling, copper and tin mining. Open M-F 10-3.30. T 01326 372158. (D9)

Flushing. Tall elegant C18 houses line the waterfront of this former steam packet centre opposite Falmouth. Claims to have the mildest climate in Cornwall. (E9)

Sticky Prawn.
Restaurant in idyllic waterside location with views across to Falmouth. Sea and shellfish dishes. Morning coffee, lunch and dinner.

Rosevine Hotel.
Georgian house set in a lush, thriving garden overlooking the sea. Family-friendly. Old style service.
T 01872 580206. (J8)

The Nare Hotel.
A haven of peace and tranquility with stunning sea views. The Nare enjoys a well-earned reputation for delicious food; seafood a speciality, and a comprehensive wine cellar.
T 01872 50111. (E10)

THE ROSELAND PENINSULA

Where to Eat, Drink, Sleep & be Merry....

Portscatho
Old harbour on the Roseland shore with narrow streets running down to a tiny pier. (J8)
T 01326 373734. (E9)

Driftwood Hotel.
Nothing washed up here except design flair and superb sea views. Family-friendly. No dogs.
T 01872 580644. (H8)

Roseland Inn.
Friendly, crowded pub with log fires and low ceilings. Cornish produce makes up the menu. Daily specials. Booking advised. Dogs and children welcome. T 01872 580254. (H6)

ST MAWES

Attractive, sunny haven popular with yachtsmen, on a tributary of Fal estuary. Castle, boat/fishing trips, Percuil Regatta - Aug. (G9)

Hotel Tresanton.
Chic family-friendly hotel owned by interior designer Olga Polizzi (of the Forte family). Bright and colourful rooms, the odd sculpture here and there, and touch of glamour. Highly acclaimed restaurant noted for seafood.
T 01326 270055. (G9)

Rising Sun.
Quality hotel/Inn provides imaginative cuisine and comfort. Impressive wine list. Pub food. Dogs and children welcome.
B & B. T 01326 270233. (G9)

Green Lantern,
Marine Parade. With fine views over the harbour this little, unpretentious restaurant adds a fusion of flavours to the base raw materials provided locally. Dinner 7-9. T 01326 270878. (G9)

Hotel Tresanton ss

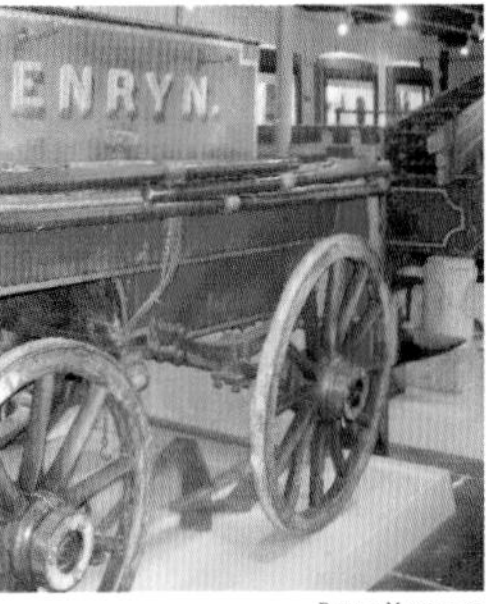

Penryn Museum ss

Churches to Visit..

Creed Church. Lavish windows in S. Aisle. C13 trefoil arch. (L2)

Mylor Church. Celtic cross with Norman doorway and superb setting above the creek. (F8)

Probus Church. C16 Tower, tallest in county, C16 brasses. (K2)

St Clement Church.
C13-14. Above Tresillian River. Well restored in 1868. (G4)

St Just In Roseland Church.
Gorgeous situation overlooking creek with churchyard like a tropical garden. Fascinating tombstones. (G8)

St Michael Penkevil Church.
Late C13-14 in feudal village with C17 & C19 monuments. (H5)

Falmouth - St Charles The Martyr Church.
Classical C17 with oblong tower. (E10)

Special Places to See & Visit....

Carrick Roads.
4 mile long drowned valley fed by 5 tributaries. Boat trips from Falmouth to Truro and St Mawes from Prince of Wales Pier. At Custom House Quay, trips to Helford Passage and Roseland in summer season. Popular with yachtsmen. (F9)

Floe Creek.
Haven for wildfowl and herons. Start of 6 1/2 mile walk around peninsula;- To Towan Beach, coast path to Zone Point, Carricknath Point, St Anthony and back. Shorter 3 1/2 mile walk:- Westwards direct to Porthmellin Head and St Anthony. (H9)

Trelissick Gallery. Set within the National Trust's garden, it is run in partnership with Cornwall Crafts to show off the best of Cornwall's arts and crafts. Open Feb-Dec M-Sa 10.30-5.30. (G6)

Veryan - The Round Houses. Five circular thatched houses built during the days of superstition. Designed with conical roofs, pointed doorways and window arches, so that 'the devil could find no niche in which to hide'. (L6)

Castles, Houses & Gardens to Visit....

Bosvigo.
A plantsman's garden, best seen in summer (June-Aug); series of enclosed and walled gardens with herbaceous borders. Nursery. Open Mar-Sept Th F. 11-6. (E3)

Burncoose Nurseries & Garden. 30 acre woodland garden. Also nursery with 3,000 varieties of trees, shrubs and unusual plants. Light refreshments. Open daily 8.30-5 (Su 11-5). (B6)

Lamorran House Gardens.
4 acre Mediterranean garden overlooking the sea. Water, palms and sub-tropical features. Open Apr-Sept W, F (& first Sa of every month) 10.30-5. (G9)

Penjerrick Gardens. Essentially a spring flowering garden of 16 acres; camellias, azaleas, rhododendrons and tree ferns. Magnificent trees, pond gardens, bamboo. Woodland walk. Open Mar-Sept W, F & Su 1.30-4.30. (D10)

Probus Gardens.
A unique garden demonstrating a wide variety of methods; and 'water-wise gardening' practices. Ideas for planting displays, hanging baskets, greenhouses. Advice centre. Guided tours. Plant Centre. Cafe. Open daily Mar-Dec 9.30-5, Jan-Mar M-F 9.30-4. (K2)

Trelissick Garden (NT).
Extensive park, farmland and woods. Large garden, lovely at all seasons with beautiful views over Fal Estuary and Falmouth Harbour. Woodland Walks beside River Fal. Open daily mid Feb-Nov 10.30-5.30. Shop and Art Gallery as garden, Nov-Feb 11-4. Woodland walk open all year. (G6)

Trewithen Gardens.
30 acre garden renowned for its magnificent collection of camellias, rhododendrons, magnolias and many rare trees and shrubs, surrounded by traditional parkland landscaped in the C18. New sculpture fountain. Gardens open Mar-Sept M-Sa 10-4.30. Su Apr-May only. House open M & Tu Apr-July, & Aug BH M 2-4. T 01726 883647. (K2)

Pendennis Castle (EH).
Built 1544-46 in the age of the cannon and gunpowder as one of a chain of castles Henry VIII erected from 1538 to deter French Invasion. Circular keep with drawbridge, portcullis, spy holes and spiral staircase. Superb viewpoint. To the south-east is the blockhouse built on the rocks. Open as English Heritage times. (F10)

St Mawes Castle (EH).
Built in 1540-43 as link in Henry VIII's chain of coastal defences. A fortress of striking symmetry; trefoil shaped with gun emplacements, drawbridge and heraldic decorations, and set in sub-tropical gardens. Superb viewpoint. Open as English Heritage times. (G9)

Truro Cathedral.
The first English Cathedral to be built since St Paul's. Imposing building designed by John Pearson in the Gothic style in 1880-1910. 3 soaring spires and an unrivalled collection of stained glass. Refectory for light meals 10-4. Open daily 8-6, shop and Chapter House from 10. (F3)

Coastal Footpath

Falmouth To Portloe:
Approx. 10 miles. Two ferry journeys required to continue along the path. The first, a regular ferry to St Mawes all year round, the second in summer only, across Percuil estuary from St Mawes to St Anthony-in-Roseland. At other times, it's usually possible to make arrangements with local boatmen. From At Anthony Head and Zone Point, superb views of Carrick Roads and up the coast to Portscatho. Easy route past Pendower Beach up to Nare Head (331ft), slate cliffs and hedgerows of foxgloves and red campion in summer with lovely descent to Portloe.

Beaches

Falmouth - Swanpool Beach.
Sandy cove, safe bathing, boating adjacent. P/WC/cafe. (E10)

Falmouth - Gyllynvase Beach.
Popular family beach with spacious sands, access P/WC/cafe. (E10). Safe bathing, rockpools and sands. All facilities. (F10)

Towan Beach - Sand dunes, shingle, rock pools and unspoilt. P. (H9)

Porthcurnick Beach - Sandy patches, facilities in Portscatho. P. (J8)

Pendower/Carne Beach.
Lovely sands extend for 1 mile. Fine bathing and rocks. P/WC. (K7)

St Mawes at Dawn

For Contemporary Art, Dramatic Cliffs, Fabulous Beaches, Mediterranean Light, Stone Circles, Sub-Tropical Gardens and Wild Flowers...

A magical and unique atmosphere embraces these two peninsulas as the elements have shaped the landscape and its hardy people.

From the tall cliffs of Land's End, to the great granite boulders of Nanjizal, to the brilliant white sands of Porthcurno, the interior is a patchwork of treeless fields separated by drystone walls. Yet, on the south east corner are the sheltered harbours, Newlyn and Mousehole, and the valleys, Lamorna and Penberth.

Early Man settled here leaving stone circles and ancient burial mounds. The Early Celts came too, and their ancient crosses remain. For a brief period tin and copper mining brought affluence, and the haunted Engine Houses can be seen at Pendeen and Botallack.

In the C19 and C20 the brilliant Mediterranean light beckoned Artists and their followers. The names of Patrick Heron, Barbara Hepworth and Bernard Leach became synonymous with the St Ives movement in the C20. The number of artists increased into the C21, and the towns of Penzance, St Ives and St Just are today thriving centres of Art and craftsmanship.

The Lizard is the most southerly point of Britain, and off Lizard Point, lies the graveyard of many fine ships. This peninsula shares many characteristics with its neighbour Penwith; the warm, equable climate, yet despite the winter gales, is rarely touched by frost or snow. The Lizard is a National Nature Reserve of over 2,000 hectares, and is a wonderland for botanists, geologists, ornithologists, and the amateur nature lover.

It is also a place of many contracts, from the thrashing waves of Porthleven Sands to the peace and calm of the Helford River (a mere six miles to the east) overlooked by the sub-tropical gardens of Trebah and Glendurgan,

Not to be forgotten, the fabulous family beaches (Kynance Cove and Kennack Sands) and little harbours (St Anthony and Helford). Whether you choose to beach it, or muck about in boats, you'll be hard pressed to find a safer or better destination for your summer vacation.

Goonhilly Earth Station ss

THE LIZARD PENINSULA
Boscregge
Millpool
Balwest
CASTLE PENCAIRE
Carleen
"HUEL VOR"
Tregonning Hill
Polladras
Crowntown
KAOLIN DISCOVERED HERE
Trew
Carnmeal Downs
Chynhale
TREVARNO ESTATE GARDENS
Sithney Green
Trannack Downs
Coverack Bridges
Gwavas
Wendron
Crahan
Trevenen
Trevenen Bal
ST GERMOE
Newtown
Tresoweshill
Tresowes Green
Trevena
ST SIDINIUS
Sithney
Lowertown
Germoe
PENGERSICK CASTLE
Ashton
Breage
ST BREACA
Sithney Common
ST MICHAEL
Praa Sands
Rinsey Croft
Penhale Jakes
Antron
FOLK MUSEUM
Helston
Praa Sands
Hendra
Rinsey
Trewithick
CREFTOW GALLERY
MORLEY'S BLUE ANCHOR
Pollard
Rinsey Head
WHEAL TREWAVAS COPPER MINE
Tregew
Praze
Weeth
WHEAL PROSPER COPPER MINE
FLAMBARDS EXPERIENCE
Trewavas Head
Megliggar Rocks
Penrose Hill
R.N.A.S.
Culdrose
ST BARTHOLOMEW
Porthleven
SHIP INN
CRITCHARDS
NET LOFT GALLERY
SMOKE HOUSE
JULIA MILLS GALLERY
Penrose
Nancewidden
Helston Downs
Goonhusband
The Loe
DEGIBNA CHAPEL
Porthleven Sands
Burnuick
Carminowe
Merries
Chyvarloe
Berepper
Gunwalloe
Gunwalloe Fishing Cove
Chyanvounder
Trenoweth
Baulk Head
HALZEPHRON INN
White Cross
Cury
ST CORENTIN
Pedngwinian
Winnianton
ST WINWALOE
Priske
Church Cove
Poldhu Cove
Newton
Poldhu Point
MARCONI MONUMENT
MARCONI CENTRE
ST MELLINUS
Polurrian Cove
MULLION GALLERY
POLURRIAN HOTEL
Mullion
Henscath
Mullion Island
Mullion Cove
STONE CROSS
The Chair
Predannack Wartha
Higher Predannack Downs
Predannack Head
Predannack Wollas
Ogo-dour
Lower Predannack Downs
Pol Cornick
Vellan Head
Soap Rock
Gew-graze
ANCIENT VILLAGE
The Horse
Kynance Cliff
Rill Ledges
Asparagus Island
Kynance Cove
A394
B3303
B3302
B3304
B3297
A3083
A B C D E F
1 2 3 4 5 6 7 8 9 10

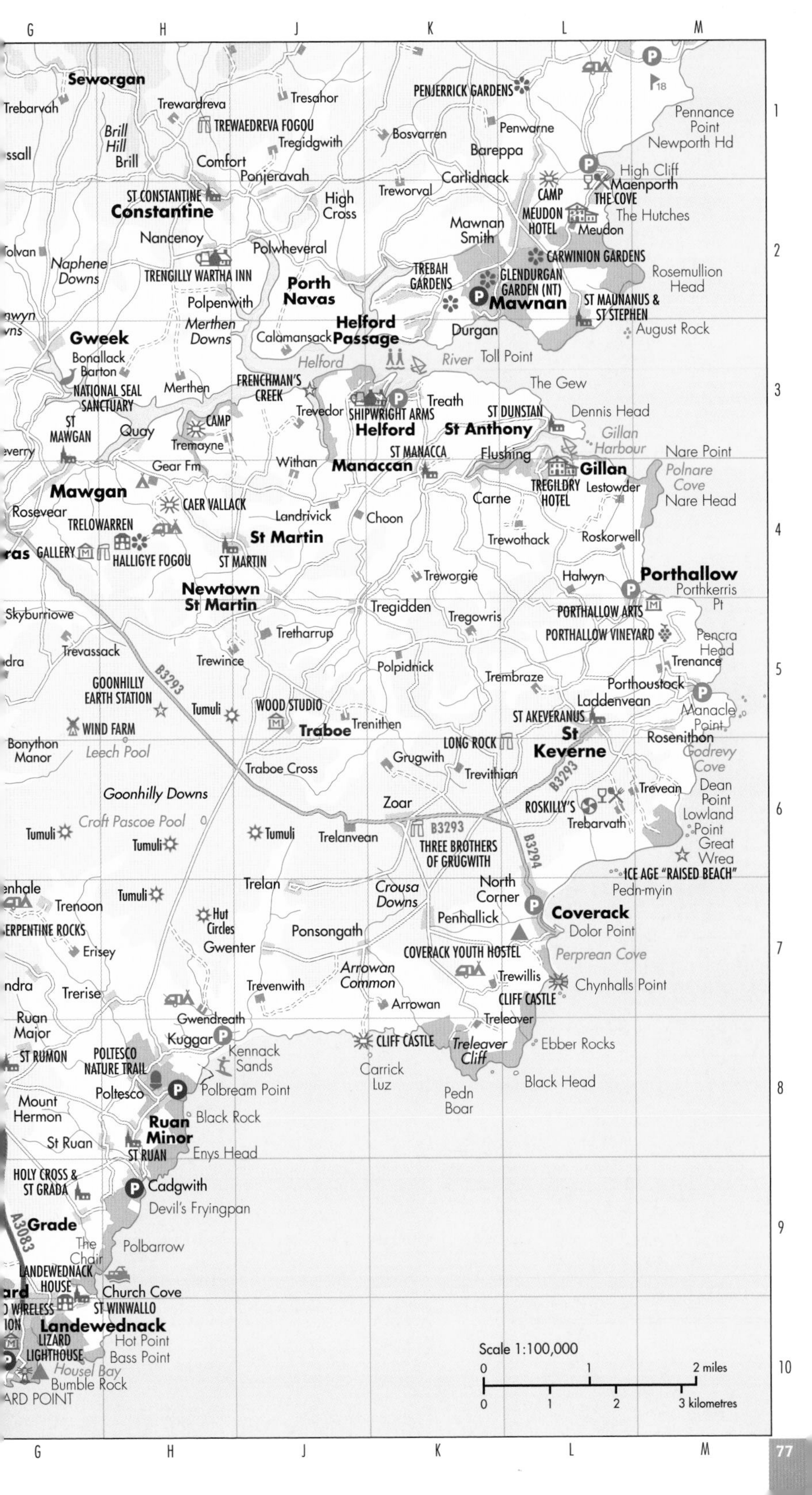
Seworgan
Trebarvah
Trewardreva
TREWAEDREVA FOGOU
Tresahor
PENJERRICK GARDENS
Penwarne
Pennance Point
Newporth Hd
Brill Hill
Brill
Comfort
Tregidgwith
Bosvarren
Bareppa
Ponjeravah
Carlidnack
High Cliff
Maenporth
THE COVE
CAMP
The Hutches
ST CONSTANTINE
Constantine
High Cross
Treworval
Mawnan Smith
MEUDON HOTEL
Meudon
Nancenoy
Polwheveral
CARWINION GARDENS
Naphene Downs
TRENGILLY WARTHA INN
Porth Navas
TREBAH GARDENS
GLENDURGAN GARDEN (NT)
Mawnan
Rosemullion Head
Polpenwith
ST MAUNANUS & ST STEPHEN
Merthen Downs
Helford Passage
Calamansack
Durgan
August Rock
Gweek
Bonallack Barton
Helford
River
Toll Point
NATIONAL SEAL SANCTUARY
Merthen
FRENCHMAN'S CREEK
The Gew
Treath
ST MAWGAN
CAMP
Trevedor
SHIPWRIGHT ARMS
Helford
ST DUNSTAN
St Anthony
Dennis Head
Quay
Tremayne
Gillan Harbour
ST MANACCA
Flushing
Nare Point
Gear Fm
Withan
Manaccan
Gillan
Polnare Cove
Mawgan
TREGILDRY HOTEL
Lestowder
Nare Head
CAER VALLACK
Carne
Rosevear
Landrivick
Choon
TRELOWARREN
Trewothack
Roskorwell
St Martin
GALLERY
HALLIGYE FOGOU
ST MARTIN
Treworgie
Halwyn
Porthallow
Porthkerris Pt
Newtown St Martin
Tregidden
Skyburriowe
Tregowris
PORTHALLOW ARTS
Tretharrup
PORTHALLOW VINEYARD
Pencra Head
Trevassack
Trewince
Trenance
Polpidnick
B3293
Trembraze
GOONHILLY EARTH STATION
Porthoustock
Laddenvean
WOOD STUDIO
Tumuli
Manacle Point
ST AKEVERANUS
WIND FARM
Trenithen
Traboe
St Keverne
LONG ROCK
Rosenithon
Bonython Manor
Leech Pool
Grugwith
Godrevy Cove
Traboe Cross
Trevithian
B3293
Goonhilly Downs
Zoar
Trevean
Dean Point
ROSKILLY'S
Lowland Point
Croft Pascoe Pool
Trebarvath
Tumuli
B3293
Tumuli
Tumuli
Trelanvean
THREE BROTHERS OF GRUGWITH
B3294
Great Wrea
ICE AGE "RAISED BEACH"
Trelan
North Corner
Pedn-myin
Tumuli
Crousa Downs
Trenoon
Coverack
Hut Circles
Penhallick
Dolor Point
Ponsongath
Gwenter
Erisey
COVERACK YOUTH HOSTEL
Perprean Cove
Arrowan Common
Trewillis
Chynhalls Point
Trerise
Trevenwith
CLIFF CASTLE
Arrowan
Ruan Major
Gwendreath
Treleaver
Kuggar
Kennack Sands
CLIFF CASTLE
Treleaver Cliff
Ebber Rocks
ST RUMON
POLTESCO NATURE TRAIL
Carrick Luz
Poltesco
Polbream Point
Black Head
Pedn Boar
Mount Hermon
Black Rock
Ruan Minor
St Ruan
ST RUAN
Enys Head
HOLY CROSS & ST GRADA
Cadgwith
Devil's Fryingpan
A3083
Grade
The Chair
Polbarrow
LANDEWEDNACK HOUSE
Church Cove
ST WINWALLO
Landewednack
LIZARD LIGHTHOUSE
Hot Point
Bass Point
Housel Bay
Bumble Rock
Scale 1:100,000
0
1
2 miles
0
1
2
3 kilometres
G
H
J
K
L
M
1
2
3
4
5
6
7
8
9
10

HELSTON.

Market town famous for the Floral Dance (around 8 May); elegantly dressed couples dance through the streets to welcome the coming of Spring. Sophisticated Georgian houses in Church and Coineagehall Street. Birthplace of Henry Trengrouse, inventor of the rocket lifesaving signals. Boating lake, Folk Museum*, Flambards Experience*. Harvest Fair - Sept (Ist week). (E2)

Where to Go, What to See....

Folk Museum.
Church St. Exhibits of rural life, crafts and industries which flourished in the C19 and C20. Open daily M-Sa 10-1 (-4 holidays), all year. www.kerrier.gov.uk. (E2)

The Blitz Experience, Flambards ss

Flambards Experience.
All weather attraction; Victorian Village and Britain in the Blitz experiences, Space Quest, live entertainment, Science Centre, Wildlife Experience, best thrill rides in Cornwall. Open most days Early Apr to end Oct 10.30-5. T 01326 573404. (E3)

Loe Pool.
The largest natural lake in the West Country inhabited by wildfowl, and surrounded by rhododendrons and wild flowers. In evidence since the C14, the River Cober was blocked by silt and the Loe Bar developed to form a bank of flint shingle. (D3)

Creftow Gallery,
Church St. Artists co-operative. Open M-Sa 10-5. T 01326 572848. (E2)

Fisherman Preparing Their Boats at Dawn, Cadgwith

Where to Eat, Drink & Be Merry...

Morley's.
Tucked away off the main street this little restaurant provides excellent dishes from local produce. A find. T 01326 564433. (E3)

The Blue Anchor,
Coinagehall St. Brewers of Spingo Beer, a strong ale. Beware on leaving, the gutters beside the pavement can be overlooked and a tumble, or mishap, must be avoided. (E2)

CADGWITH.

Thatched cottages of darkly mottled serpentine rock, boats beached on the shingle cove create a picturesque yet workaday scene. Haunt of artists. Superb coastal scenery. Cafe/Inn. Fresh fish for sale. Gallery. (H9)

COVERACK.

Charming, picturesque old fishing village and former smuggling centre. Small protected harbour. Fish (& chip) restaurant in old lifeboat station. (L7)

Glendurgan Garden mw/nt

GWEEK.

Attractive village at head of Helford estuary and former port to Helston and mining areas until C19. Old quays, boatyards and Seal Sanctuary. (G3)

National Seal Sanctuary.
Rescuing, rehabilitating and releasing seal pups from around our coasts, the Sanctuary is also a permanent home for seals and sealions unable to return to the wild. Feeding Talks throughout the day, Nature Trail Walk, Seal Hospital, Nursery, Convalescent and Resident Pools. Cafe and gift shop. Open daily from 9. (G3)

Helford River.
Beautiful tree-lined (holly and oaks) tidal river with romantic creeks (Frenchman's Creek, immortalised by Daphne Du Maurier's novel) and inlets. Picturesque villages of Durgan, Helford (passenger ferry) and St Anthony popular with 'muck abouters' in boats (Sailaway organise dinghy hire T 01326 231357). Oyster farm at Porth Navas. On the north shore, a profusion of wonderful gardens, see below for details. (J3)

National Seal Sanctuary

Gardens to Visit.....

Carwinion Gardens.
Valley garden with camellias, rhododenrons, azaleas, wild flowers and 100 species of bamboo. Incorporating Towan Camelia and Hydrangea Nursery. Open daily 10-5.30. (L2)

Glendurgan Gardens (NT).
Valley garden of great beauty. Fine trees and shrubs, a maze, a giant's stride, a wooded valley of primulas and bluebells runs down to Helford River. Garden open mid Feb to end Oct Tu-Sa & BH M's 10.30-5.30. (L2)

Trebah Gardens. Magical sub-tropical ravine gardens running down to private beach on Helford River, a canvas of everchanging colour from Spring to Autumn. A garden for the plantsman, artist and family, and a paradise for children. Art Gallery holds the Hunting Art Prizes in Spring. Open daily all year 10.30-5 (or dusk if earlier). T 01326 250448. (K2)

Trebah Gardens ss

LIZARD.

The most southerly village in England. Popular walking centre. Gift shops galore, many selling ornaments made from the purplish Serpentine Rock, unique to the Lizard. There are haunting photographs of shipwrecks in the local pubs. At Church Cove, pretty cottages and converted lifeboat station. Walks to Lizard Point and Kynance Cove, both with cafes. (G10)

Lizard Lighthouse. Large and famous building completed in 1752 with alterations in 1903. Stands amidst treacherous coast haunted by many shipwrecks. Open daily East-Oct, weather permitting. (G10)

Landewednack House. Luxurious B & B offering superb food from local produce. Fine wines. Beautiful protected walled garden. Heated pool. T 01326 290877. (G10)

Where to Stay, Eat, Drink & Be Merry…

Polurrian Hotel. Overlooking Polurrian beach with stunning views. Restaurants. Pools. Gym. Tennis. Creche. Games rooms. Terraces. Garden. High Point Restaurant offers good food at sensible prices. Open daily 10-9.30. 01326 240421. (E7)

PORTHLEVEN.

Attractive large harbour with shipbuilding yard, C19 Harbour House and imposing Wesleyan chapel c.1890. The vulnerable harbour faces south west and was built for the mining industry in 1811. A south westerly gale in 1824 washed it away, later to be rebuilt in 1855, with lock gates. (C3)

Galleries to Visit….

Julia Mills Gallery. A beach-hut style gallery incorporating the workshop of glass-designer, Julia Mills. A perfect setting for the sea-inspied work on show. All her work depicts some aspect of the Cornish environment. Open M-F 10-5, Sa 11-5. T 01326 569340. (C3)

Net Loft Gallery, The Harbour. Range of seascapes and landscapes paintings, ceramics, bronzes and jewellery. Open daily Apr-Oct & Xmas. T 01326 564010. (C3)

LIZARD PENINSULA

Special Places to See & Visit….

Goonhilly Downs. High central plateau on Lizard Peninsula. One of the oldest nature conservancy reserves in the country. Thus, of great interest to botanists, geologists and archaeologists. Profusion of wild flowers, the summer air is acute with scent. Buzzards soar up high. Green serpentine rock forms. Croft Pascoe Nature Reserve. (H6)

Goonhilly Satellite Earth Station. Transmitting millions of phone calls, TV pictures & computer data via the famous massive satellite dishes. Tours, exhibits, films, shop, cafe and more. 0800 679 593. (H5)

Grange Fruit Farm. PYO fruit (strawberries). Farm shop. Cream teas and light lunches. Open daily May-Oct. (F4)

Pengersick Castle. Fortified Tudor manor c. 1500 with evidence of apothocarian garden in C14, to be renovated. This place of legend and mystery welcomes visitors by appointment on 01736 762579. (A2)

Poltesco Nature Trail. 3 miles of wooded valley caves and cliffs. (H8)

Porthallow Arts. Gallery and workshop promotes local artists' work, and runs day courses. Open East-Oct M-Th & Sa 10-6, Su 12-4. (M4)

Mullion Harbour bc

MULLION.

Marconi Monument. The first transatlantic morse code messages were transmitted from this spot on 12 December 1901, and picked up by Gugliemo Marconi in St Johns, Newfoundland. (E6)

Mullion Cove. Dramatic cove at foot of tall cliffs, with harbour built in 1895. Lifeboat until 1901. Offshore, a bird sanctuary on Mullion Island. Fishing trips. (E7)

Mullion Church. Late medieval with fascinating bench ends. (F6)

Mullion Gallery, Nansmellyon Rd. Work of over 80 artists living on The Lizard Peninsula; paintings, ceramics, sculptures, wood carvings. Open M-Sa summer, W-Sa winter. T 01326 241170. (E7)

Where to East, Drink & Be Merry….

Critchards, Harbourside. Foodies love this place. Always something new to look forward to. Fish is the speciality, in all its delicate forms. Dinner 6.30-9. T 01326 562407. (C3)

The Smoke House, Harbourside. Great stonebacked pizzas. Spanish and Thai mussels. Superb vegetables. W is Curry Night. Lively and popular with locals. T 01326 563223. (C3)

Ship Inn. In fine situation overlooking the harbour. Wide selection of fish dishes. Childrens meals and family room. Dogs welcome. (C3)

Mullion Gallery ss

Porthallow Vineyard & Cider Farm. Planted in 1897, the location is well suited for producing quality wines, cider and liquers. Self-guided tour. Open East-Sept M-Sa 11-1, 2-5. (M5)

RNAS Culdrose. The largest helicopter base in Europe. Much is underground. Viewing enclosure with café & shop. Open Day August; see local adverts for details. (F3)

Trelowarren Gallery. Original home of the Cornwall Crafts Association, now regularly holds members and touring exhibs. Open daily 10.30-5.30 Mar-Nov. www.cornwallcrafts.co.uk (G4)

Trelowarren. Home of the Vyvyan family since 1427. Acres of woodland and farmland surround the house. Chateau camping, pottery, cornish herbs and woodland walks. House open East-Sept, W's & BHM's 2.30-4.30 (45' tour). (G4)

Wood Studio, Rosuick Farm. Sculptural woodturning by Samvado. The wonder of wood, turned into amazing shapes; bowls, spheres, obelisks. Open most days 11-6. T 01326 231783. (J5)

Julia Mills Gallery ss

Churches to Visit....

Breage Church. C15 granite with C15 wall painting of St Christopher. (C2)

Gunwalloe Church. C14 unusual detached tower, wall paintings and lies in dunes beside the beach. (E6)

Landewednack (Church Cove) Church. Tower and Norman doorway of serpentine stone. (H9)

Mawgan In Meneage Church. C13-C15 wagon roof and brasses in lovely setting. (G3)

St Keverne Church. Spacious interior, C14, with tall spire. Resting place for many drowned sailors. (L5)

Where to Eat, Drink & Be Merry.....

Halzephron Inn. C16 building overlooking Mounts Bay. Cosy, friendly and daily specials provide a rewarding pit-stop from the coast path. Family room. B & B. (E5)

The Cove, Maenporth Beach. Relaxed and well-priced restaurant offers a tasty selection of fish, meat dishes. Tapas. Lunch 12-3, Dinner 6-9.30. T 01326 251136. (L2)

Trelowarren. Al fresco dining within an enchanting C14 estate. Simple lunches, more adventurous dinners. T 01326 221224. (G4)

Roskilly's. Working farm selling farm produce; ice cream, fudge, clotted cream, preserves etc. Fabulous pasties. Art & Crafts gallery. Restaurant. Open daily 10-dusk (W/Es in winter). Footpaths to woods, meadows and ponds. (L6)

Where to Eat, Drink, Be Merry & Sleep....

Meudon Hotel. Family run Country House Hotel with sub-tropical valley gardens leading to private beach. T 01326 250541. (L2)

Tregildry Hotel. Friendly and relaxed with stunning sea views in quiet, remote location. Proud of their "Highly Recommended" restaurant, and rightly so. T 01326 231378. (L4)

Trengilly Wartha Inn. Popular Inn known for expansive wine list, infinite Malts and restaurant. Beer mats cover ancient beams. Children & dogs welcome. B & B. (H2)

Goonhilly Satellite Earth Station ss

Ogo-dour, Predannack

Coastal Footpath

Praa Sands To Lizard:
Approx. 18 miles. Interesting coastal path: craggy cliffs and splendid sandy beaches. Start with a stiffish climb up to Trewavas Head, then a Cliffside walk to Porthleven. Path follows cliff edge to Loe Bar*, Gunwalloe and Church Cove, apparently buried treasure is hidden here. Onto the caves, arches and black rocks of Mullion Cove.

Fine walking on cliff tops around Vellan Head and past breath taking precipices to Pigeon Ogo, a vast amphitheatre of rock. The crowning glory is Kynance Cove, a spectacle of swirling currents (at HT), whooshing blow holes and wild shaped serpentine rocks, great bathing at LT and a great cafe.

Well-trodden path to Britain's most southerly point, Lizard Point. Caves and caverns about Polpeor Cove. East is the Lion's Den, a large collapsed sea-cave, a sudden vast hole in the cliff turf.

Lizard To Falmouth:
Approx. 26 miles. The east side of the peninsula is less rugged, the slopes are gentler, the landscape becomes more hospitable as one travels northward. First you pass pretty Church Cove, and along cliff top to the Devil's Frying Pan, a larger version of the Lion's Den, it's blow hole roars when the easterlies blow. Through thatched Cadgwith to Kennack Sands where the path is easy going, hugging the cliff edge, and almost at sea level from Coverack to Lowland Point, scene of an Ice Age 'Raised Beach'.

Offshore, at low tide 'The Manacles' are visible, a treacherous reef that has caused the death of more than 400 drowned sailors, many buried in St Keverne's churchyard. The 60ft spire of he church serves as a daymark for sailors and fishermen. At Godrevy Cove, the path turns inland to Rosenithon and Porthoustock to avoid quarries, returning to the coast at Porthallow.

A peaceful stretch to Gillan Harbour, possible to wade the creek at low tide, or continue to bridge crossing the head of the creek at Carne. Through tangled woods to Helford village and ferry across Helford estuary, which runs from Easter to end of October, to either Helford Passage or the beach at Durgan. From here the path passes Mawnan Church and along the cliff tops to Swanpool Beach (Falmouth).

Helford River

Trebah Beach ss

Beaches & Surfing

Praa Sands. Mile of firm golden sands. Good family beach but HZ to bathe at LT. P/WC/LG/café. Surfing – Bigger swell than Perranathnoe. Hence a popular beach. N end protected from W winds and may produce a fast R break. E end can create HZ rips in a big swell. (A2)

Porthleven Sands.
4 miles of sands. A steep, shelving beach with undertow. For strong swimmers only. Scene of many shipwrecks. P. Surfing – On W side of harbour channel. A much discussed reef break, produced by a big swell. LT is hollow and dangerous. HT is affected by the Backwash. Strong rips when big. For the experienced only and not for the squeamish! (C4)

Church Cove.
Pebbles and sand sided by low cliffs. Dunes cover St Winwalloe church. NT P/LG/WC/shop. (E6)

Polurrian Cove.
Access via 3/4 mile path from Mullion church to sandy beach edged by high cliffs. Strong tidal currents. Bathing HZ at LT. (E7)

Poldhu Cove. Popular family beach. Bathing HZ one hour either side of LT. P/WC/LG/Café. (E6)

Mullion Cove.
Tiny beach at LT. Beautiful harbour walls. P/WC/café. (E7)

Kynance Cove.
Large P area. 10 minute walk to steps. Good bathing. White sand at LT. Very popular in summer. Wild-shaped serpentine rocks. At HT the roaring noise of the blow holes. (F9)

Kynance Cove

Pentraeth Beach.
Acces down slippery path to beach of grey sand and rocks. (F10)

Polpeor Cove.
Steep walk down to rocky shore; the most southerly point in Britain. Old lifeboat station. P/WC/café. (G10)

Hounsel Bay.
For the agile down steep path to small sandy beach. (G10)

Carleon Cove. Peaceful cove, 10 min walk from Poltesco. (H8)

Kennack Sands.
Popular bucket and spade family beach with rock pools. Fine bathing. S-B hire/P/WC/cafe. Surfing – Good waves only created after big swells. (J8)

Coverack. Tiny beach, shingle at LT. P/cafe. (L7)

Lowland Point. Ice age 'Raised' on which the passenger liner, 'Paris' was shipwrecked in 1899. Access from St Keverne via Trevean or Trebarvath Farms. (M6)

Porthoustock.
Pebbled shelving beach, quarries to either side. P. (M5)

Porthallow. Small pebbled beach, rocks to sides. P/inn. (M4)

Men-Aver Beach. 20 min coastal walk from Gillan. Isolated with sandy patches and rock pools. (M4)

Gillan Harbour. Shingle and sand, rocky promontory. (L3)

Flushing. Isolated shingle beach with sand at LT. (L3)

Helford Village. Sand and shale visible at LT. P/WC. (K3)

Helford Passage.
Small stony beach in front of Ferry Boat Inn. Sand at LT. P. (J3)

Durgan Beach. Small stony beach down steep hill. P. (K3)

Porthallack Beach.
Shingle beach along coastal path from Durgan. (K3)

Parson's Beach.
Steep path to rocky cove. L2)

Bream Cove.
Isolated sandy beach and rock pools popular with skin-divers. (L2)

Maenporth.
Popular family beach with sheltered and spacious sands. Surfing, P/WC/LG/cafe. (L1)

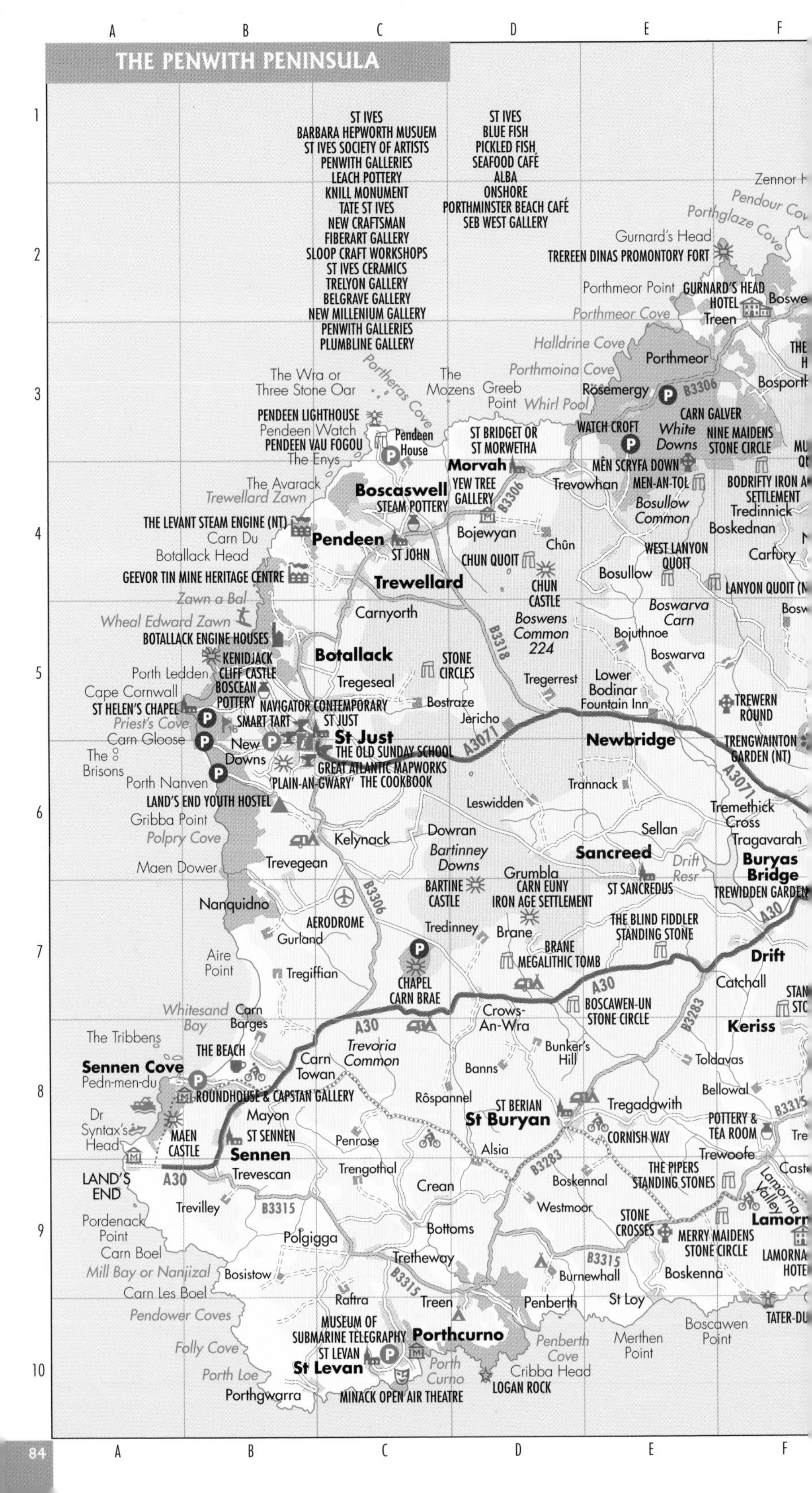
THE PENWITH PENINSULA
ST IVES
BARBARA HEPWORTH MUSUEM
ST IVES SOCIETY OF ARTISTS
PENWITH GALLERIES
LEACH POTTERY
KNILL MONUMENT
TATE ST IVES
NEW CRAFTSMAN
FIBERART GALLERY
SLOOP CRAFT WORKSHOPS
ST IVES CERAMICS
TRELYON GALLERY
BELGRAVE GALLERY
NEW MILLENIUM GALLERY
PENWITH GALLERIES
PLUMBLINE GALLERY
ST IVES
BLUE FISH
PICKLED FISH
SEAFOOD CAFÉ
ALBA
ONSHORE
PORTHMINSTER BEACH CAFÉ
SEB WEST GALLERY
Zennor H
Pendour Cov
Porthglaze Cove
Gurnard's Head
TREREEN DINAS PROMONTORY FORT
Porthmeor Point
GURNARD'S HEAD HOTEL
Boswe
Treen
Porthmeor Cove
Halldrine Cove
Porthmeor
Porthmoina Cove
Rosemergy
B3306
Bosporth
The Wra or Three Stone Oar
Portheras Cove
The Mozens
Greeb Point
Whirl Pool
CARN GALVER
PENDEEN LIGHTHOUSE
Pendeen Watch
PENDEEN VAU FOGOU
The Enys
Pendeen House
ST BRIDGET OR ST MORWETHA
WATCH CROFT
White Downs
NINE MAIDENS STONE CIRCLE
Morvah
MÊN SCRYFA DOWN
The Avarack
Trewellard Zawn
Boscaswell
STEAM POTTERY
YEW TREE GALLERY
Trevowhan
MEN-AN-TOL
BODRIFTY IRON AGE SETTLEMENT
Bosullow Common
Tredinnick
THE LEVANT STEAM ENGINE (NT)
Carn Du
Pendeen
ST JOHN
Bojewyan
Chûn
Boskednan
Botallack Head
CHUN QUOIT
WEST LANYON QUOIT
Carfury
GEEVOR TIN MINE HERITAGE CENTRE
Trewellard
CHUN CASTLE
Bosullow
LANYON QUOIT
Zawn a Bal
Carnyorth
Boswens Common 224
Boswarva Carn
Wheal Edward Zawn
B3318
Bojuthnoe
BOTALLACK ENGINE HOUSES
KENIDJACK CLIFF CASTLE
Botallack
STONE CIRCLES
Boswarva
Porth Ledden
Tregeseal
Tregerrest
Lower Bodinar
Cape Cornwall
BOSCEAN POTTERY
Bostraze
Fountain Inn
TREWERN ROUND
ST HELEN'S CHAPEL
NAVIGATOR CONTEMPORARY
ST JUST
Jericho
Priest's Cove
SMART TART
Carn Gloose
New Downs
St Just
A3071
Newbridge
TRENGWAINTON GARDEN (NT)
The Brisons
THE OLD SUNDAY SCHOOL
GREAT ATLANTIC MAPWORKS
Porth Nanven
'PLAIN-AN-GWARY'
THE COOKBOOK
Trannack
LAND'S END YOUTH HOSTEL
Leswidden
Tremethick Cross
Gribba Point
Sellan
Polpry Cove
Kelynack
Dowran
Tragavarah
Bartinney Downs
Sancreed
Drift Resr
Buryas Bridge
Maen Dower
Trevegean
Grumbla
BARTINE CASTLE
CARN EUNY IRON AGE SETTLEMENT
ST SANCREDUS
TREWIDDEN GARDEN
Nanquidno
B3306
AERODROME
THE BLIND FIDDLER STANDING STONE
A30
Gurland
Tredinney
Brane
BRANE MEGALITHIC TOMB
Drift
Aire Point
Tregiffian
CHAPEL CARN BRAE
Catchall
Whitesand Bay
Carn Barges
Crows-An-Wra
BOSCAWEN-UN STONE CIRCLE
B3283
Keriss
The Tribbens
A30
Trevoria Common
Bunker's Hill
THE BEACH
Carn Towan
Banns
Toldavas
Sennen Cove
Pedn-men-du
Bellowal
ROUNDHOUSE & CAPSTAN GALLERY
Rôspannel
ST BERIAN
Tregadgwith
Dr Syntax's Head
Mayon
St Buryan
POTTERY & TEA ROOM
MAEN CASTLE
ST SENNEN
Penrose
CORNISH WAY
Sennen
Alsia
Trewoofe
LAND'S END
A30
Trevescan
Trengothal
B3283
THE PIPERS STANDING STONES
Lamorna Valley
Crean
Boskennal
Trevilley
B3315
Westmoor
Pordenack Point
Polgigga
Bottoms
STONE CROSSES
MERRY MAIDENS STONE CIRCLE
Lamorn
Carn Boel
Tretheway
B3315
LAMORNA HOTE
Mill Bay or Nanjizal
Bosistow
Burnewhall
Boskenna
Carn Les Boel
B3315
Raftra
Treen
Penberth
St Loy
Pendower Coves
MUSEUM OF SUBMARINE TELEGRAPHY
Porthcurno
Boscawen Point
TATER-DU
Folly Cove
ST LEVAN
Penberth Cove
Merthen Point
Porth Loe
St Levan
Porth Curno
Cribba Head
LOGAN ROCK
Porthgwarra
MINACK OPEN AIR THEATRE

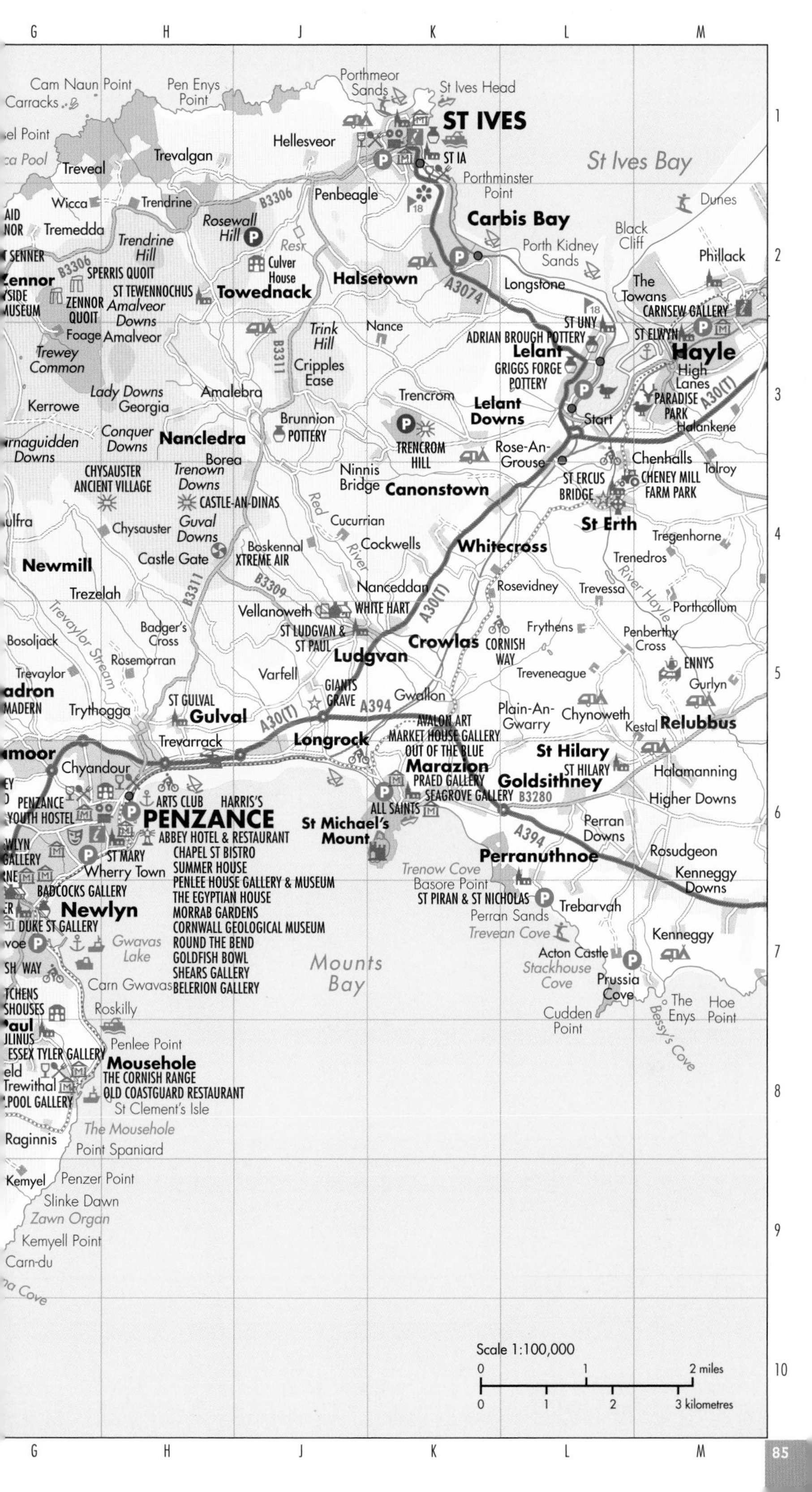
G
H
J
K
L
M
1
2
3
4
5
6
7
8
9
10
Cam Naun Point
Pen Enys Point
Porthmeor Sands
St Ives Head
ST IVES
Hellesveor
ST IA
St Ives Bay
Treveal
Trevalgan
Porthminster Point
Wicca
Trendrine
B3306
Penbeagle
Dunes
Tremedda
Rosewall Hill
Carbis Bay
Black Cliff
Trendrine Hill
Resr
Porth Kidney Sands
Phillack
SENNER
Culver House
SPERRIS QUOIT
Halsetown
ST TEWENNOCHUS
Towednack
A3074
Longstone
The Towans
ZENNOR QUOIT
Amalveor Downs
CARNSEW GALLERY
Foage
Amalveor
Trink Hill
Nance
ST UNY
ST ELWYN
Trewey Common
B3311
ADRIAN BROUGH POTTERY
Lelant
Hayle
Cripples Ease
GRIGGS FORGE POTTERY
High Lanes
Lady Downs
Georgia
Amalebra
Trencrom
Lelant Downs
PARADISE PARK
Kerrowe
Brunnion POTTERY
Start
A30(T)
Halankene
Conquer Downs
TRENCROM HILL
Rose-An-Grouse
Nancledra
Borea
Chenhalls
Talroy
CHYSAUSTER ANCIENT VILLAGE
Trenowin Downs
Ninnis Bridge
Canonstown
ST ERCUS BRIDGE
CHENEY MILL FARM PARK
CASTLE-AN-DINAS
Red River
Cucurrian
St Erth
Chysauster
Guval Downs
Tregenhorne
Whitecross
Cockwells
Boskennal XTREME AIR
Castle Gate
Newmill
Trenedros
B3309
Trezelah
Nanceddan
Rosevidney
Trevessa
River Hayle
Porthcollum
Vellanoweth
WHITE HART
Trevaylor Stream
Badger's Cross
ST LUDGVAN & ST PAUL
Frythens
Penberthy Cross
Bosoljack
Crowlas
CORNISH WAY
Ludgvan
Rosemorran
ENNYS
Trevaylor
Varfell
Treveneague
Gurlyn
GIANTS GRAVE
Gwallon
A394
ST GULVAL
Trythogga
Gulval
Plain-An-Gwarry
Chynoweth
Kestal
Relubbus
AVALON ART
Longrock
MARKET HOUSE GALLERY
Trevarrack
OUT OF THE BLUE
St Hilary
Chyandour
Marazion
ST HILARY
Halamanning
PRAED GALLERY
Goldsithney
SEAGROVE GALLERY
B3280
Higher Downs
ARTS CLUB
HARRIS'S
ALL SAINTS
PENZANCE
St Michael's Mount
Perran Downs
ABBEY HOTEL & RESTAURANT
ST MARY
CHAPEL ST BISTRO
Rosudgeon
Perranuthnoe
Wherry Town
SUMMER HOUSE
Trenow Cove
Kenneggy Downs
PENLEE HOUSE GALLERY & MUSEUM
Basore Point
BADCOCKS GALLERY
THE EGYPTIAN HOUSE
ST PIRAN & ST NICHOLAS
Newlyn
MORRAB GARDENS
Trebarvah
Perran Sands
DUKE ST GALLERY
CORNWALL GEOLOGICAL MUSEUM
Trevean Cove
Kenneggy
Gwavas Lake
ROUND THE BEND
Acton Castle
GOLDFISH BOWL
Mounts Bay
Stackhouse Cove
SHEARS GALLERY
Prussia Cove
Carn Gwavas
BELERION GALLERY
The Enys
Hoe Point
Roskilly
Cudden Point
Bessy's Cove
Penlee Point
ESSEX TYLER GALLERY
Mousehole
THE CORNISH RANGE
Trewithal
OLD COASTGUARD RESTAURANT
St Clement's Isle
The Mousehole
Raginnis
Point Spaniard
Kemyel
Penzer Point
Slinke Dawn
Zawn Organ
Kemyell Point
Carn-du
Scale 1:100,000
0
1
2 miles
0
1
2
3 kilometres

Penlee House Gallery ss

PENZANCE

A lively and busy town tempered by a gentle climate; sub-tropical flowers grow in the Morrab Gardens and at nearby Trengwainton*. Town trail takes you to:- Chapel Street and the Egyptian House*, exquisite shops and restaurants; Market Jew Street dominated by the Ionic columns of Market House, and the Statue of Sir Humphrey Davy, inventor of the miners' Davy lamp. Floating Harbour, Ship & Helicoptor ferries to Isles of Scilly, shark and deep sea fishing trips, swimming pools (in & outdoor), Penlee House Museum*, West Cornwall Spring Show - late March. (H6)

Madron Church.
Mother Church of Penzance, wagon roof. C17 brass. (G5)

Trengwainton ab/nt

Galleries to Visit...

Belerion Gallery, Bread St. Eclectic mix offering a fresh look at the Cornish art scene; pottery, sculpture and paintings.
Open Tu-Sa from 10.30. (H6)

Penlee House Gallery & Museum, Morrab Road. An elegant gallery and museum set within a Victorian house and park. Changing exhibitions mainly feature famous 'Newlyn School' artists (1880-1930). There is an excellent cafe and well-stocked shop. Open daily M-Sa East-Sept 10-5, Oct-East 10.30-4.30. T 01736 363625. (H6)

Shears Gallery, 56 Chapel St. The Early Newlyn and St Ives schools are featured here. Open M-Sa 10-5.

The Goldfish Bowl,
56 Chapel St. New look at figurative art with paintings, ceramics and sculpture. Open M-Sa 10-5. (H6)

Where to Eat, Drink & Be Merry....

Harris's,
46 New St. Well organised establishment with a loyal clientelle provides good food. Interesting French House Wines. Lunch 12-2, Dinner 7-10. M-Sa. T 01736 364408. (H5)

Summer House,
Cornwall Terrace. Enthusiasm for life; Art, design and delectable food with a Mediterranean edge gives this hostelry their uniqueness. 5 double-rooms. T 01736 363744. (H5)

The Abbey Restaurant ss

Chapel St Bistro.
Set in the basement of the Penzance Arts Club surrounded by sculptures and artworks, the atmosphere is congenial, the food is of local produce, and excellent. Dinner 6.30-9.30. Tu-Th & Sa.
T 01736 332555. (H5)

The Abbey Restaurant,
Abbey St. Ben Tunnicliffe is the Business. Award-winning cuisine combining classical and modern techniques to great effect. Proudly uses local suppliers. Dinner times vary from 7-9.30, Lunch F-Su 12-1.30. T 01736 330680.
www.theabbeyonline.com (H5)

Where to stay....

The Abbey Hotel, Abbey St. A sweet gem hidden behind closed walls. Walled garden and courtyard. Luxuriously decorated rooms. T 01736 330680. (H5)

Penzance Arts Club, Chapel St. A touch of Bohemia in colourful surroundings (decor and conversation). Restaurant. Poetry readings, jazz nights. Art on view. T 01736 363761. (H5)

Historic Houses & Gardens to visit

Trengwainton Gardens (NT). Large shrub garden with a vast collection of rhododendrons. Colourful in spring/early summer. Views over Mounts Bay. Open mid Feb-29 Oct Su-Th 10-5. (F6)

Tresco Abbey Gardens, Scilly Isles. A sub-tropical garden with palms, proteas, South African succulents. Garden open daily all year round, 10-4. Shop open Feb-Nov. Day trip by Helicopters from Penzance Mar-Oct.

Miscellaneous

Xtreme Air Co, Castle Gate. Learn to Speedsail, Blo-kart, FlyBoard, Speedkite..action-packed adventures. And more. Tuition on hand. B & B. T 01736 332648. (H4)

ST IVES.

A labyrinth of narrow streets, whitewashed cottages, brightly coloured boats and sandy beaches provide St Ives with a Mediterranean ambience. A favourite haunt of artists in the C19 and C20's. Its charm remains unaltered by the thousands who flock here. Barbara Hepworth Museum*, Leach Pottery*, Tate St Ives*. Music & Arts Festival - Sept. (K1)

Fiberart Gallery

St Ives

Arts, Crafts & Galleries to Visit in St Ives... A Selection

Barbara Hepworth Museum & Sculpture Garden, Barnoon Hill. The house, studio, sculpture garden and workshop of the late sculptoress. 40 sculptures, paintings and photographs. Open all year Tu-Su 10-4.30 and daily Mar- Oct 10-5.30. (K1)

Belgrave Gallery, 22 Fore St. Specialises in the Modern Movement which centred around St Ives, 1940 - 1960s plus contemporary local artists. Open M-Sa 10-1, 2-6. (K1)

Fiberart Gallery, 5 Street-an-Pol. Showcase for artists using fibrous materials. Displaying wall hangings, sculptural forms, wearable pieces and interior design. Open Mar-Oct M-Sa 10.30-5. (K1)

Leach Pottery, Upper Stennack. Founded by Bernard Leach in 1920 (d.1979). Pottery by Janet Leach, Trevor Corser and Joanna Wason. Open daily; summer M-Sa, winter M-F, 10-5. (K1)

New Craftsman, 24 Fore St. Craft shop and gallery featuring paintings, ceramics, jewellery, glass, metalwork and more. Open M-Sa 10-5. T 01736 795652. (K1)

New Millennium Gallery, Street-an-Pol. Leading gallery with contemporary paintings and ceramics in three-storey building. Open Mar-Oct M-Sa 10.30-4.30. T 01736 793121. (K1)

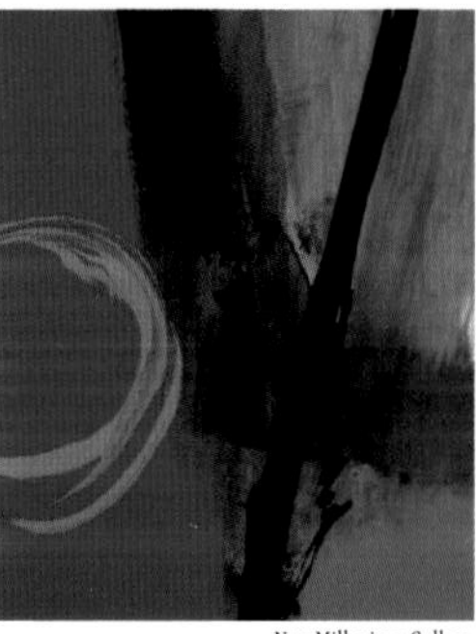

New Millenium Gallery

Penwith Galleries, Back Rd West. Continuous exhibitions of paintings, sculpture and ceramics. Open Tu-Sa 10-1, 2.30-5. (K1)

Plumbline Gallery, 2 Barnoon Hill. Specialises in glass forms and ceramics of exceptional individuality. Open daily. (K1)

St Ives Ceramics, Lower Fish St. Collections of high quality ceramics. Work by John Bedding, Clive Bowen, Bernard Leach and Japanese artists from Mashiko. Open daily 10-5 except Su Jan-Feb. (K1)

St Ives Society Of Artists, Norway Square. Founded in 1927, the Society is a well-established artists group and holds regular exhibitions. Open mid-Mar to Nov M-Sa 10-4.30. (K1)

Tate St Ives, Porthmeor Beach. Displays of contemporary work in a variety of media. Open all year Tu-Su 10.30-5.30 and M in July/Aug. (K1)

The Sloop Craft Workshops, Fish St. Twelve crafts people work here; from patchworks to driftwood furniture. Open daily 10-5. (K1)

Trelyon Gallery, Fore St. Work of over thirty contemporary leading British jewellers. Open daily 10-5 (-10 summer). (K1)

Seb West Studio, Slipway. Born in St Ives Seb paints relief landscapes, abstracts of the Cornish sea and countryside. Open most days. (K1)

LAMORNA.

A pretty village along a wooded valley ending in a small harbour. A favourite of artists and craftsmen. Summer craft exhibitions. Cafe at cove. (F9)

Lamorna Cove Hotel. Wonderful situation overlooking the Cove. The Artist's Palette restaurant has large windows providing sea views. Fish dishes; red mullet, turbot and scallops...rich, yummy puddings. T 01736 731411. (F9)

Red Gurnards, J H Turner & Co., Fish Merchants, Newlyn

MARAZION

Reputed to be the oldest town in Cornwall. Lies opposite St Michaels Mount*, where ancient harbour used to trade in tin from galleries. (K6)

Galleries in Marazion

Avalon Art, West End. Well established gallery with a bright mix of naive and abstract paintings; landscapes and seascapes. Open daily 10.30-5.30. (K6)

Market House Gallery, The Square. Large gallery with a wide range of paintings, ceramics and glass. Open daily. (K6)

Michael Praed Gallery, Market Place. Contemporary art by Michael Praed and large display of ceramics and sculpture. Open as advertised. (K6)

Where to Eat, Drink & Be Merry in St Ives

Alba, Wharf Road. Great views over the harbour from this old Lifeboat Station through wide glass windows. Modern European cuisine. T 01736 797222. (K1)

Blue Fish, Norway Lane. Spanish style fish restaurant overlooks the rooftops and harbour. Choose your meal from the Blue Fish tank. Lunch and Dinner. T 01736 794204. (K1)

Pickled Fish, 3 Chapel St. An other addition to St Ives gastronomies. And it sure holds its own. Classic decor. Expert food. BYO wine. T 01736 795100. (K1)

Seafood Cafe, 45 Fore St. Choose your meal from the counter; fish, meat or fowl, and a sauce to suit you. Super fresh food, and pleasant place to relax. T 01736 794004. (K1)

Porthminster Beach Cafe. A great blend of café and serious restaurant overlooking magical white sands. Child friendly. Open daily Mar to mid-Oct from 10. Lunch 12-4. Dinner 6-10. T 01736 795352. (K1)

Onshore, The Wharf. Great pizzas. It's the position that counts overlooking the harbour. T 01736 796000. (K1)

Adrian Brough Pottery

LAND'S END

The natural landscape plus 6 attractions including The Return to the Last Labyrinth, Air Sea Rescue and End-to-End Story. Craft Studios. Open all year 10-dusk. T 0870 4580099. (A9)

LELANT

Adrian Brough Pottery, 5 Tyringham Place. Beautifully decorated pots of marine life using ceramic styles from Portugal and Korea. Open M-F 9-5, W/Es by appointment. (L3)

Grigg's Forge Pottery. Handmade domestic stoneware and earthenware. Open daily. (L3)

Cheney Mill Farm Park. 12 acres to roam and see farm and wild animals. Adventure Park. Birds of Prey. Picnics. Battery Bikes. Open daily East-Oct 10-5. (M4)

Out Of The Blue, The Square. Full mix of crafts; driftwood, copper, stained glass, jewellery and paintings by resident Cornishmen. Open daily. (K6)

Seagrove Gallery, The Square. Wide range of textiles, jewellery, paintings, pottery and paintings. Courtyard for al fresco coffee and cakes. Open daily summer, winter Th-M. (K6)

MORVAH

Yew Tree Gallery. Spacious gallery in grounds of Keigwin Farmhouse, with sculpture gardens. Exhibitions of contemporary fine & applied art by well-known artists within and beyond Cornwall. Open May-Nov Tu-Sa 10.30-5.30 T 01736 786425. (D7)

St Michael's Mount rr/nt

Blue Drawing Room, St Michael's Mount nt

Aerial View, St Michaels' Mount bc

ST MICHAEL'S MOUNT (NT)

A legendary place of romance and pilgrimage and a child's dream of a fairy castle. Originally the site of a Benedictine chapel established by Edward the Confessor.

In the C14, the spectacular castle was added. Later to be used as a nunnery and military fortress before the St Aubryn family purchased it in 1659, living here ever since. Church dates from 1275. Exquisite Blue Drawing Room with Chippendale furniture. Pictures by Gainsborough and the Cornish Artist, John Opie. Harbour, railway. Open 26 Mar-29 Oct M-F & Su 10.30-5.30, last admission 4.45. Guided tours Nov-Mar if weather and tides permit. Mar-May Tu for pre-arranged educational visits.

Church opens on Sunday at 10.30 for 11am Service. Restaurant and shop open daily Apr-Oct. Special family ticket available.

Please Note: access on foot over the causeway at low tide, or during summer months only, by ferry at high tide (return ferry tickets should not be taken). Make sure the Mount is open before crossing on the ferry! (J6)

Mousehole

Galleries in Newlyn

Badcocks Gallery, The Strand. Changing exhibs every three weeks Mar-Nov. Leading Cornish artists, sculptors, jewellers and craftsmen. Open M-F 10.30-5.30, Sa 11-5.30. (G7)

Duke Street Gallery & Coffee Shop. Combines painting and ceramics with sculpture, photography and crafts by local artists. Open daily. (G7)

Newlyn Art Gallery, New Road. Leading contempory art venue with changing exhibitions of painting, sculpture, drawing and photographty. Gallery shop and coffee point. Open daily M-Sa & BHs 10-5. (G7)

MOUSEHOLE

Pronounced 'Mowzle'. The least spoilt of Cornish fishing villages. Stone cottages huddle around the harbour facing east, sheltered from the prevailing winds. Originally called Port Enys, it was sacked and burnt by Spanish invaders in 1595. Famed for Christmas Lights and Tom Bawcock's Eve, and children's story, The Mousehole. (G8)

Galleries in Mousehole

Essex Tyler Gallery, 3 Brook St. Ornamemtal Raku pottery based on old Japanese methods. Also paintings and jewellery. Open daily Mar-Dec 10-6. (G8)

Millpool Gallery, Mill Lane. Claims to be refreshingly different with off-beat, idiosyncratic and naive art from the West Country. Open daily East-Oct 11-5. (G8)

Where to Eat, Drink & Be Merry...

Old Coastguard Restaurant, The Parade. Panoramic views from light and airy restaurant. Fish (from Newlyn Market) a speciality. Steak and Vegetarian menus, too. Accomodation. Lunch and dinner. T 01736 731222. (G8)

The Cornish Range, 6 Chapel St. Established specialist fish restaurant exploits the local Newlyn market. Dinner only. T 01736 731488. (G8)

Seagrove Gallery, Marazion

NEWLYN

Home of Cornwall's largest fishing fleet and busiest fish market. Cannery for pilchards and mackerel. The medieval quay is a delight. Like St Ives a favourite haunt for artists - Edwardian painters formed the 'Newlyn School' artists colony, much of their work on show in Penlee House in Penzance. Newlyn Art Gallery continues tradition of pioneering artists. Like neighbouring Mousehole, much of old Newlyn was destroyed by Spanish Raiders in 1595. Art galleries. Fresh fish and shell fish merchants aplenty. (G7)

Where to Eat, Drink & Be Merry...

Tolcarne Inn, Tolcarne Place. C18 oak beamed pub is the traditional venue after many "Newlyn Opening". Exhibits local artists and photographers. Jazz on Su. Home-cooked meals and "Specials". Open daily. (G7)

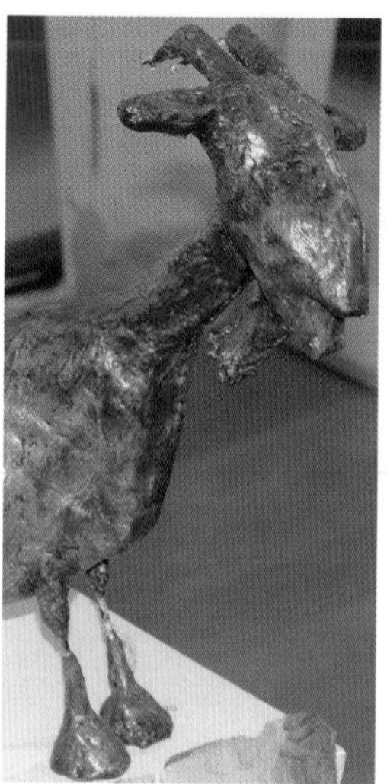
Duke Street Gallery

PORTHGWARRA

Typical isolated "smugglers cove" protected by rocks and gorse-covered downs. (B10)

Porthcurno Beach nt

PORTHCURNO

Small village leads down to one of the great beaches of Cornwall (or anywhere) with its effervescent, turquoise sea and white sands. Best viewed from the western side of the coastal footpath, or the Minack Theatre. Hotels, a plenty. (C10)

Logan's rock.
A huge naturally balanced rock weighing 66 tons. It was dislodged in early C19 by a young naval officer, a nephew of Oliver Goldsmith and such was the outcry, that he was forced to return it almost bankrupting himself. (D10)

Minack Open Air Theatre.
Open Air Theatre cut out of cliff side. Season of plays, musicals, operas in unique 750 seat theatre. Season; End of May to mid-Sept. Exhibition Centre tells the story of Rowena Cade who built the theatre, open all year Apr-Sept 9.30-5.30, Oct-Mar 10-4 (closed 24/25 Dec). T 01736 810181. (C10)

Porthcurno Museum. Secret wartime communication centre built in tunnels. Cable ships and cable laying. Open East-Oct Su-F & BH Sa 10-5, & winter M 10-4. (C10)

ST JUST IN PENWITH

A handsome little town, formerly a hectic mining centre. Imposing Doric facaded Methodist church. The area is rich in prehistoric antiquities. Arts and Crafts centre (with many galleries, and home to many artists). By Bank Square, the ampitheatre 'Plain-an-Gwary', where medieval Cornish miracle plays were perfomed. Water sports festival, Priest's Cove - July. (C5)

What To See, Where To Go... In and Around St Just

Botallack Engine Houses.
Remains of famous tin mine operational from 1720-1914 which employed 500 people. Tunnels and galleries were projected beneath the sea. The roaring Atlantic clearly audible above the miners' heads. In 1893 the roof collapsed drowning 29 men, 500 feet down and never recovered. NB Please keep to paths. (B5)

Geevor Tin Mine. Mining history centre set in magnificent coastal scenery. Underground tours, museum, cafe and shop. Open every day except Sa. Last admission 4pm in summer; 3pm in winter. T 01736 788662. (B7)

Levant Mine & Beam Engine (NT), The oldest steam-powered engine in Cornwall, restored after sixty years. Open all year F 10-5 (winter not steaming) plus East & Spring BH's, Su June-Sept, W mid Apr to Oct 11-5. (B7)

Land's End Aerodrome, St Just. Pleasure Flights and Trial Flying Lessons over the stunning Cornish coastline. Scheduled services to the Isles of Scilly. Small cafe. Free parking for Pleasure Flights. Open daily 9-6. T 01736 785227 www.landsendairport.co.uk (C7)

Pendeen Lighthouse. Built in 1900 to protect vessels from Wra Rocks. Visible for 20 miles. Open daily Apr-Oct, 10-1 hour before sunset Su-Sa. Closed in fog. (C3)

Steam Pottery. Distinctive work by Patrick Lester, also featuring work of other ceramicists. Open daily 10-5. (C7)

Minack Open Air Theatre ss

Botallack Engine Houses

Geevor Tin Mine ss

Smart Tart, Blackbird Barn, Bank Square. Karen Arthur makes functional, quirky bags in colourful, hand dyed fabrics. Open Tu-Sa 10-5, (Summer Su 2-5). (B5)

Stone Age Studio, 8 South Place. Sculptures inspired by the Penwith landscape in Fantastic Realism and Floral Cubism. Open most days from 1pm. Call first: 01736 787872. (B5)

The Cookbook, 4 Cape Cornwall St. Home-made soup, cakes, coffee and cream teas. Supports local artists and writers. Open Tu-Su 10-5. (C6)

The Old Sunday School, Cape Cornwall St. C18 chapel home and studio of D Meehan and N Pickard; landscape paintings and wacky post punk jewellery. Open Tu-Su. (B5)

Land's End Aerodrome ss

Art & Galleries in St Just… a Selection

Boscean Pottery, Boswedden Rd. Apprenticed to the Leach Pottery, Scott Marshall uses ash glazes on his 'oven-to-table' ware. Ceramics on sale. Open daily from 10. (B5)

Great Atlantic Mapworks, West Place. Specialises in work of West Cornwall artists. Open M-Sa 10-5, Su 2-5. (B5)

Nancherrow Studio, 34 Nancherrow Terrace. Two floors of local landscape paintings and sculptures in bronze and stainless steel. Ceramics. Open 10-5. (B5)

Navigator Contemporary Art, 41 Fore St. Wide range of paintings, sculpture and crafts; simplistic, vivid imaginations at work. Shows New artists. Open Tu-Sa 11-5, Su 2-5. (B5)

Where to Eat, Drink & Be Merry

Gurnard's Head Hotel. A welcome refuge if you've battled against a sou'westerly head wind on the coast path. Rich, wholesome fayre will appease a mighty appetite. Family room. Dogs in bar only. B & B. T 01736 796928. (F2)

SENNEN COVE

Most westerly village in England, with popular surfing beach. The Lifeboat Station was established in 1853, the stone pier in 1905. Whitewashed cottages and the Round House Gallery line the front. Fishing trips. (A8)

Round House & Capstan Gallery. Built in 1876. Houses a huge, man-powered capstan and work from Cornwall's finest artists and craftspeople. Open daily from 10 in summer, winter varies; T 01736 871859. (B8)

The Beach Restaurant. A view to die for. Décor of wood and glass with black slate floors. Freshly prepared local produce. Breakfast until 11.30. and light lunches. Supper 7-10. T 01736 871191. (B8)

ZENNOR

Small village noted for the legendary 'Mermaid of Zennor', carved into an old bench end in the C15 church. A blow-hole roars below Zennor Head. Wayside Folk Museum*. (F2)

Wayside Folk Museum. Oldest privately owned museum in Cornwall. Over 5,000 items in 16 rooms. Cornish crafts, bookshop and riverside garden. Open Apr-Oct Su-F (Sa School & BHs). (F2)

Lanyon Quoit wh/nt

Ancient Cornwall

Boscawen-Un Stone Circle (Nine Maiden). Bronze Age circle of 19 stones. Sometimes site of Cornish Gorsedd. (D7)

Carn Euny Ancient Village. Iron Age village discovered in C19. Well preserved 65ft long fogue. (D7)

Castle An Dinas. Good viewpoint with 3 circular defensive walls. 2 barrows. 1920 excavations unearthed arms and water supply. (H4)

Round House & Capstan Gallery

Chun Castle. Impressive fort with two concentric stone ramparts at 300ft diameter. (D7)

Chun Quoit. Mushroom shaped neolithic tomb with massive capstone, 8ft square. (D7)

Chysauster Ancient Village (EH). The best preserved Iron Age village in Cornwall. 8 circular houses. Occupied during Roman Conquest. Access via 1/2 mile long path from road. (H4)

Gurnards Head. Cut off by ramparts and ditches. Circular stone huts. (F2)

Maen Cliff. Iron Age fort with ramparts and ditches. (A8)

Trencrom Hill (NT). Well preserved fort with stone walls. (K3)

Treryn Dinas. Well fortified with five lines of ramparts and ditches. Overlooks fluorescent sea. Site of Logan Rock. (D10)

The Giants House. 13 ft long chamber within barrow 26ft in diameter. (F3)

Lanyon Quoit (NT). Stone Age dolmen; 3 upright and capstone re-erected c.1824. (F7)

Men-An-Tol. A large circular slab with a hole pierced through centre set between 2 upright slabs. Famous for its legendary magical healing powers - children were passed through to cure them of rickets. (A7)

Merry Maidens Stone Circle. 19 stones form the perfect circle; legend has it - girls turned to stone for dancing on a Sunday. (E9)

Nine Maidens Stone Circle. 2 circles of standing stones, 50ft and 60ft in diameter. (F3)

Pendeen Vau Fogou. Lengthy passage, stonefaced and roofed with lintels. In yard of Pendeen Manor Farm. (C3)

Plain-An-Gwarry. Circular embankment (cattle pen) where old Cornish miracle plays were performed. (B6)

Zennor Quoit. One of England's largest dolmens; double-chambered tomb with massive slab. Pieces of Neolithic pottery discovered here. (G2)

Logan Rock (Treryn Dinas)

Mine Shafts, Botallack

Coastal Footpath

St Ives To Land's End:
Approx. 22 miles. Considered by some to be the finest stretch of all: wild, rugged and besieged relentlessly by the elements. The path is lonely and remote, up and down and at times, very hard going following the cliff edge and cliff top. Seals laze on the Carracks. A blow hole roars below Zennor Head. It's worth a detour to Zennor for refreshments and to meet the mermaid in the church. On to Gurnard's Head (good pub), sphinx-like with great views, and then you are entering the heart of tin mining country, so beware of unprotected mine shafts. The cliffs between St Ives and Pendeen sometimes glitter with minerals. Hereabouts, paths criss-cross in all directions and there's much to interest the industrial archaeologist, especially at Geevor, Levant and Botallack. Following the cliff tops, Cape Cornwall appears, marked by a lonely stack, remains of mine abandoned in 1870's. The cliff drops to Aire Point, and ahead the thunderous breakers, and dedicated surfers of Whitesand Bay. And now, the well worn path to Land's End.

Land's End To Hoe Point:
Approx. 27 miles. Another superb stretch of coastline; precipitous cliffs, great blocks of granite, sandy coves and minute valleys with sub-tropical vegetation. Spectacular rock formations to Gwennap Head, equally as wild a headland as Land's End. Here are great gnarled granite boulders, cracked and sculpted by the elements; a popular place for climbers, and below a haunt for seals. There are two paths: the first follows every cranny and contour, the second cuts off along the headlands for a wonderfully invigorating walk. Down into tiny Porthgwarra, and on up to St Levan's Well above the little cove of Porthchapel. Then along to Porthcurno passing the famous open-air Minack Theatre*; beyond an improbably turquoise sea and the outline of Logan's Rock*. On around the dramatic granite columns of Treen Cliff and then Cribba Head, to the tiny fishing cove of Penberth. Along clifftops to Lamorna Cove, a favourite spot for artists. The path continues along the clifftop until Mousehole*. The path resumes east of Penzance at Eastern Green where it crosses the railway line to follow the line of the beach to Marazion, with spectacular views of St Michael's Mount just offshore. Then inland to Perranuthnoe. The going is fairly easy to Hoe Point (Praa Sands).

Penzance Harbour